CW00828607

SOLID BRASS

SOLID BRASS

Written and Illustrated
By
Bob Wick

Best Publishing Company

Edited by Andy Nordhoff
Layout by Kristin Gureck

Copyright © 2001 by Best Publishing Company

All Rights Reserved

No part of this book may be reproduced, stored in a retrieval system, or transmitted in any form or by any means; electronic, mechanical, photocopying, microfilming, recording, or otherwise; without written permission from the publisher, except by a reviewer who may quote brief passages in a review with appropriate credit.

ISBN: 0-941332-93-4
Library of Congress Catalog Number: 00-109191
Composed and printed in the United States of America

Best Publishing Company
website: www.bestpub.com
2355 North Steves Boulevard
P.O. Box 30100
Flagstaff, AZ 86003-0100 USA
Tele: 520.527.1055

DEDICATION

To Theresa, my wife and best friend,
and to our daughters
Kinsey and Kyler, our best chapters.

ACKNOWLEDGEMENTS

After many years of recall and writing, yellow pads and #2 pencils, and a satchel full of scribble and line drawings I lugged from job to job around the world, this book has finally become reality. For her many hours at the computer and sheer determination to bring this project to publication, I thank my wife, Theresa. She has deciphered my chicken scratch page by page, jogged my memory, helped me tighten and polish my work, and push me forward to completion. My appreciation can't fully be expressed in just a few lines, as we've shared many years reaching this goal.

Of course, my goal could not have been reached if not for Best Publishing Company's Jim Joiner and Andy Nordhoff, not only for accepting my manuscript with enthusiasm, but also eliminating the misconceptions I had heard about the author/publisher relationship. Their encouragement and valuable suggestions allowed my voice to come through in these preceding pages.

I am truly grateful to my old friends and comrades for the various photos they dug up and trusted I'd return. Many thanks to Owen Boyle, Phil Cook, Jack Michael Fonner, Elton "Herb" Harris, Jiggs Jackson, Kevin Lengyel, Evie Treen, and Bob Worthington. Many of these photos are as rare as the heavy gear deep-sea diver is today.

This book would mean less to me if I left out anyone who, in my 45 year diving career, either gave me a leg up or some inspiration to point me in a direction. I have to thank my high school teacher Bill Brown, who, among other things, built my first scuba gear in his garage. Thanks to 1st Class Flemming, who went to the captain of my first ship to demand my UDT training orders by released. (Unbeknownst to me, the captain had put a hold on those orders.) And to the damage control sailor, Roberts, who told me many stories about UDT and thought I'd get more diving time in the teams than I would in my four-year enlistment after diving school. And to all the guys in UDT; it was challenging getting there, but I came away from UDT with lasting motivation and experiences to draw from for the rest of my life. Hoo Yah! to Class 17 and all the great people in the diving business that helped me along the way.

Most important to this book, I thank all the people in these stories, some who are gone now but will always be part of the colorful history of the diving business. I am proud to have known you, worked with you, and been a part of your lives.

Bob Wick

CONTENTS

ONE

Underwater Demolition Team Training

H. O. Cunningham—there was something real different about this man. All the other instructors constantly reminded us that we were low-lifes and how weak and unsuitable we were ("Hummingbirds" was their favorite description of us). Each day they tried to make you forget the idea of becoming one of them, but not H. O., he never said much. When he worked with us during pool sessions, he never said more than necessary. His mannerisms were so much different than the others, we couldn't help wondering why he was in the UDT training unit.

As we walked into the classroom we read, written on the blackboard, the subject of the day's discussion—sentry stalking. After everyone was seated, in walked H. O. Cunningham. "Good afternoon Gentlemen, today you will learn sentry stalking weapons and how they are used." He proceeded to tell us about, and demonstrate, the use of the knife, crossbow, piano wire, and others, including his favorite, the six-pound hatchet. Sentry stalking, simply stated, is sneaking in and taking out the sentries that are between you and your objective. So, shortly after my eighteenth birthday, H. O. Cunningham, with his quiet, father-like image, taught us how to split the enemy in half with a six-pound hatchet. This seems a good place to start. "It was a cold and stormy night" has already been used and UDT was where it started for me and my decision to dive for a living.

Commander "Red Dog" Fane was still in command. He is the author of *The Naked Warriors* and the man who gets the credit for keeping the

1

Solid Brass

Frogs together after WWII by proving they had a place in a peacetime Navy. This does seem a long time ago, figuring that since then, the Frogs were turned into SEALS and UDT was officially decommissioned. Since the close of the Vietnam conflict, the ever-changing world situation and operational tasking have prompted the expansion of the SEAL Team in numbers, size, and capabilities. To effectively respond to this evolutionary process, Underwater Demolition Teams have been redesignated as SEAL (Sea-Air-Land) Teams. The newly designated SEAL Teams acquired the SEAL mission and retained the amphibious support mission inherited from their UDT forefathers.

I showed up with my orders at the Amphibious Base in Coronado, California, where Teams 11, 12, and the training unit lived. There was only one other group of Frogs—Team 21 on the East Coast. A total of less than three-hundred in the world. After Hell Week started, I understood the reason. Out of seventy-six starters, we graduated twenty-four.

Hell Week was mentally, as well as physically demanding; the object was to get you to quit. They made it clear to you everyday, just how simple it was to get out. Walk to the office, pick up orders (which were pre-arranged), and before anyone got back to the barracks, you would be gone. We did find out how important sleep was. For the entire week, we got seven and a half hours; not per night, for the whole week. By the third day, we were so physically drained, it was an effort to do five push-ups, even if you could do fifty before the week started.

I remember laboring, doing push-ups in a circle on the grinder, looking toward the center at Paul McNally with tears in my eyes, frustrated and mad, while he was as fresh as a daisy, yelling about what hummingbirds we were. At that moment, you knew in your own mind that you could justify killing this man. Later after training, he was to become a very dear friend.

Our training class was divided into boat crews, seven men to an inflatable rubber boat, called an IBS. One way the instructors kept us competing was to give points to the boat that wins a race, either swimming, log PT, boat races, and so on. The boat with the most points at the end of Hell Week got to sleep in the last morning, while the other crews did business as usual. By the third day, the sleep-in became one hell of

Solid Brass

an incentive. By the fourth day, you would consider prostitution to get a few more points.

We had treasure hunts to further wear us down, in which we had to do a lot of thinking. With our severely fatigued brains, processing information was a tormenting event. The hunts took us all over Coronado. The instructors would give us a clue, we would follow it, and if we were right, there would be another instructor waiting there to give another clue. If we were wrong, we may have traveled five miles for not. This sounds like a kid's game, but when you haven't slept for four days, trying to think while soaking wet and cold, and sand grinding your crotch away, it became a "big guy's" game.

We never went anywhere without our very awkward kapok life jacket and our paddle. These also went to the chow hall and the john with us. We never went to the john by ourselves. Someone would stand while the other sat, so no one would fall asleep and miss muster. Any wonder we became so close.

During one of our treasure hunts, held on the coldest night of the year, Bob Worthington and I were standing, facing each other, thinking very hard about a particularly bad clue. Our chins were resting on our paddles. I heard, off in the distance, someone calling our names. Our heads had come together and we were still standing, sound asleep. The voices had woken us up.

Another of the instructors' favorites was having us go into the pool wearing our kapok jackets. Each boat crew would line up in the water and each person would wrap his legs around the person in front, in a sitting position. Then using only our hands as paddles, race to the other end of the Olympic size pool. The jackets helped float the whole mess. Each pull of our arms would thrust our bodies forward and cause our boots to dig into each other in an area normally set aside for careful scratching. If we were really lucky, they would make us race in the mud pits.

Unfortunately for us, Hollywood decided to immortalize us and send in a crew to film our Hell Week. It was for a TV adventure show called *High Road to Adventure*. We would just get through doing some ball-busting drill and they would ask the instructors if we could do it again. Needless to say, the instructors *loved* it.

3

Solid Brass

Hell Week was taking its toll. The class was getting smaller and smaller. Some whole boat crews folded. We had spent some time in the back bay, where the mud was thick, gooey, and smelled like decay and tidal death. They had us doing all kinds of point-gaining games in this stuff. When we came out of the mud, we were a hundred pounds heavier than when we went in. It would be hours before we were able to wash it off. One guy we called Sunshine (due to the horrible sunburn he got at the beach a few days before training started) could not handle the mud. He said coming back one day, if we went to the mud again he would quit.

A typical race for points in the mud; the guy behind you has his heels dug into your crotch and the entire team moves like a centipede (only slower). *Official U.S. Navy photograph*

Solid Brass

Sunshine came from a well-to-do yachting family from the East Coast. Everyone in his family knew he was going to become a Navy Frogman, so we hated to hear him talk like this. Sure enough, that night we got the word that we would be going to the mud the next morning. It was one of those rare moments when we had an hour in our bunks, we didn't even bother to take off our wet clothes. We were told we would be able to sleep for three hours, but after about one hour, instructor Tiz came in beating on anything that would make noise. After we got outside, it was still dark but we could see that ol' Sunshine was missing. A few of us ran back in and found him still in his bunk. We pulled at him, all of us together couldn't break the death grip he had on his bunk rails. We were dragging his bunk across the barracks when Tiz came back in, told us to leave him and get back outside to muster or we'd all be gone. That was the last we would see of Sunshine.

One of the downsides of the point system was, if you lost any part of your gear, particularly your hat or paddle coming through the surf, your team lost a bunch of points. One night, after taking a hell of a pounding coming through a terribly big surf, the boats dumped and we were scattered all over the beach. Marty was missing. We finally spotted him coming up between breakers. He looked hurt, so we ran out to help him in. Now standing, with his back to us in the darkness, he finally spoke in a mournful tone, usually saved for the loss of a loved one, "I lost my hat."

Another bad dump happened that same night. Again, all of the rafts got turned upside down and Davis got pounded real bad, and held under by a large wave. He came up under an overturned raft where he couldn't see. We were treading water next to the raft and could hear him saying "Oh my God, I'm gone!" He went on seeking forgiveness for being less than a good Christian. We turned the raft over before he could reveal anything more incriminating.

Other than the games I've mentioned, we ran several miles every day, swam several miles every day, and did more exercise in a circle (so we could hate Paul McNally more every day). There were also the obstacle courses that were made uglier every day. The rest we got during Hell Week was just enough to pop our blisters and rub our sore muscles.

Solid Brass

We would take time to talk positively to each other but also find ways to cheat. Sometimes that included some kind of a shortcut, like using a car during a treasure hunt.

When they ran us down the beach, we were in all our clothes, life-jackets, and boondocker boots. They would run us through the surf, back up to the beach, and have us roll in the sand again and again. So we

An illustration of Sunshine's least favorite activity.
Official U.S. Navy photograph

did this training with bleeding crotches, blistered feet, and burnt and cracked skin.

There were things happening to our minds. First time realizations for young men, things that may happen later in life, but presented themselves during this intense period of our lives: finding out how self-discipline works, figuring out how much more we could ask from our bodies than

Some obvious agony under a log. *Official U.S. Navy photograph*

we ever thought possible, finding out how determined a person you are, and understanding camaraderie at its highest level.

These lessons were reinforced by running part of a fifteen mile run with our feet on fire; losing the first layer of skin to sand in our boots; having our clothes soaked from sea water and sweat; our muscles so sore in places that up to now, we didn't even know had muscles. I remember thinking that I had to make it. I couldn't fail. I couldn't let my friends at home down. I couldn't fail those that helped me get this far. This was help you gave yourself. In the first place, no one at home knew I was trying to become a Frog, they knew I joined the Navy to become a diver, not a Frog. I came to grips with myself, maybe for the first time, to this extent.

They always kept us on edge, no sprints, all long distance stuff. When we finally got to lay our heads down, even if they told us we'd be getting a couple of hours sleep, our subconscious knew they were lying. When they came in forty-five minutes later, we'd wake up ready to go. I saw this most vividly at the end of Hell Week. Our boat won the sleep-in, and that night when we went to bed, I told myself I'd wake up, when the other boat crews left, to enjoy the feeling of not having to get up myself. When they all left in the morning, I heard nothing. My subconscious knew I didn't have to get up.

It's easy to recall the strong feelings we had for each other, the uncontrollable laughs we had from being so tired, the songs we sang to keep up moral, and the sadness we felt after one of the guys dropped out after so long. I can still picture us walking the beach for the last time, during Hell Week, Marty with a paddle under each arm, like crutches. He could hardly walk, his crotch was so raw. There wasn't a spot on his feet that didn't have a blister. We were all hurting, but he was a basket case. Ironically, Marty went on to stay in the SEALS past his 50th birthday.

These are the memories I have used to my advantage throughout my life. Hell Week, it turned out, was just one hurdle. The rest of training was just as intense, but you got more sleep. No "atta-boys" for getting through, just a reminder to get lots of rest on Sunday because on Monday we would start the really serious training.

Solid Brass

In the next few months, we were to meet more H. O.s, one particularly easy going, very quiet type, Whitey, not too tall or stocky, had pure white hair and a twinkle in his eye. He also held a fifth degree black belt and taught hand-to-hand combat. We also had Tex Madesett. There has been a lot of print about this man. He was an old plank owner who made it to Normandy and all the World War II places that the Frogs made an impact. He was truly an explosives expert, coming from the mines of Arizona before the Navy. Another plank owner was Tiz Morrison. Tiz taught a little bit of everything. He was a big barrel-chested man, who, while chewing your ass out about something, had a glow about him that made you think he might be chuckling inside. He was also a very decorated Frog, who also had a lot of press through the years. Tiz was one of the first to let on that we might actually graduate.

From left, Bear Tracks, Whitey, and the Author in the UDT Team 12 dive locker. *B. Wick photo*

Solid Brass

The last month of training was spent on San Clemente Island. We did lose two more men there, an officer as well as an enlisted man. But this last month, the instructors seemed to warm up to us some (but even if you looked for it, it still wasn't real obvious).

Our class was before the tobacco scare. All the bad news about tobacco didn't exist—not chewing tobacco, anyway. Somehow the habit got started and at night, when we were all grouped together in our rafts offshore, we'd pass the pouch. If you were the swimmer scout that night, you would swim in and lie in one spot for hours while figuring out the sentry's (instructor's) routine, before taking him out. To kill time, you'd dig a hole in the sand to spit in, cover it up, make a little grave, and maybe find a small piece of driftwood to make a cross.

One day at San Clemente, Tiz came up and asked for a chew because he had run out. When I explained to him that we had also run out, he let me know what poor planning that was and walked off. A few days later, when I came into our tent from a swim, there was a case of tobacco on my bunk. He must have gotten it on the other side of the island, at Wilson Cove, or maybe not—there was no note. Maybe the Tooth Fairy brought it....

The man who headed up the training unit was Commander Chandler. God put him on earth to scare the shit out of young Frog trainees. He was very, very good at it. The only man I have ever been totally afraid of. Anyone who says, "We all put our pants on the same way, one leg at a time," or "All men are created equal," didn't know (or never met) the Commander. This guy was nine feet tall and could make lightening strike at will. But worst of all, he could have you out of there and back in the fleet in ten seconds flat.

Once in class, I was engrossed in the subject matter when someone brought in a note that read, "Bob Wick, you are wanted in Commander Chandler's office." For a young man, this was just about more than life had prepared me for. My life was passing in front of my eyes, I wished it were tomorrow. As I walked into his office, I knew I'd do Hell Week again if only I could avoid this. The door now closed behind me, he looked up and stated matter-of-factly, " You are failing your math. You seem to be getting A's on all your tests but math.

Solid Brass

This is very distressing to me, because I have to assume that you are just not trying. Why haven't you been studying?"

He kept at this for, what seemed, a long period of time. The only good thing was that my knees stayed with me and all the blood rushing to my head didn't do any permanent damage. "I have been," I heard my voice say through the volleyball-size lump in my throat. "I've been to BOQ every night to study with Mr. Miles and Mr. Green. Before I leave at night it is all clear, then I'll have problems in class later. But they are working with me seven nights a week." I don't know where all of this came from, but at my pause for air he said, "I know you have, go back to your class." That had happened several times before to other people for other reasons. Another test on how one works under pressure, I suppose.

When Commander Chandler held a class, no matter what the subject matter, he didn't use notes or aids, he drew from memory. I'm sure, from watching him, he had total recall.

Back at San Clemente, close to our last week there, we had a goat barbecue, a ball game, and even a beer. Some of the instructors had shot a few wild goats on the island. The game was going to be trainees vs instructors. I was the pitcher. When the Commander came up at bat, as might be predicted, I got as wild as the goats. Everyone was yelling, "Calm down, just put one over. Just let him get a hit!"

No sir boy, I wasn't about to just give him a pitch. I wound up, put as much behind the ball as I could, and hit him—dead center! I couldn't believe what just happened, my hardest pitch all day nailed the commander. I have a gray area here; I don't know how I ever got out of that one. Maybe I didn't, he never did invite me over to meet the family.

Another incident that dealt with the Commander was also at the island. Everyone took turns being the night watch. Although the trainees use Coleman lanterns and stoves, the instructors had a little generator for a light plant that was shut down at night. I was told to get this going at 0500 for the Commander's morning shave. Just before start-up, I found it was out of gas and there was none in the gas can. I found a piece of hose, not the nice little hose you can use to siphon, but a big one-inch ID. I went to the nearest truck and put it in the tank. I couldn't just take a little pull from this hose, I had to pull from the lungs. When the gas came, that's right where it stopped, in my lungs. I couldn't get my breath, any air I pulled wouldn't mix with the gas fumes. I gasped for air, saw stars, including the whole Milky Way, just before I caught my first breath. By then, Mr. White happened along, probably to see why the generator plant wasn't running. He helped me back to where my tent-mates could help revive me. Things of all color and description started coming out of my head. Mr. White wanted to send me to Wilson Cove to the medic. I assured him I'd be all right, but I was more concerned about the Commander's shave. Later that day, I was offered a chance to get out of our deepest skin dive, but I declined and made the dive. For all I knew, this could have been another character test.

I saw a good-sized halibut one day while we were blowing obstacles. I used my knife to get him. I stuck my knife belt through his gills to hold him to the explosive bags until we were finished. This was going to beat the hell out of the sea rations we'd been eating. The next day, while the plans of the day were being read, a closing note was, "The Commander said there will be no unauthorized fishing today." Just one lousy pitch and a late morning shave.

The training camp at Clemente was great, with large tents back up the hill a little from the beach. Our outdoor johns were a little higher on the hill, with a commanding view of Santa Catalina. We must have used a thousand dollars worth of special made shape charge explosives to break ground for this john. That price wasn't too bad when you consider we made a two-holer.

The cactus was certainly one of our enemies. At night some seemed to jump ten feet to get you. One night, Balzarini and I were the swimmer scouts to take out the sentry and make sure everything was clear, then signal the rubber boats to come in. This particular night was an officer-trainee night. They had to take the information given them, figure out from the charts where the enemy beach was, and take us there. With their boats, the instructors towed our rafts anywhere we wanted to go, then let us off when our leaders chose the beach. The calculations were off and they missed by a mile (actually they missed by several miles). The two officer-trainees in our crew were Pollock and Green. We inherited Balzarini, my swim partner, after his boat crew all quit. Everybody in our boat crew was half-crazy. We had a hell of an enjoyable time going through training. This particular night though, Balz and

Building sandcastles the UDT way. *Official U.S. Navy photograph*

Solid Brass

I had swam several hours and hadn't hit the beach. When we did, it was the wrong beach. It was a great wall of rock with just a small lip to walk on. Any place that looked like we might climb was full of the worst kind of cactus. We knew there wasn't going to be an instructor waiting here. Getting back into the water was almost as bad as all the cactus spines we had in us. The kelp just grabbed at us and kept us at a snail's pace. Our teeth were chattering so bad, we knew where each other was without looking.

The Author at the U.S. Navy Diving School in San Diego in 1957.

Solid Brass

Someday we'd be using wet suits, but not until we made the team. We should have been listed in the "Who's Who of Channel Swimming" that night.

After many tons of explosives, blowing hundreds of underwater obstacles, being cold to the bone for weeks, good food (goat meat and halibut), we left our island retreat, with the can on the hill with the commanding view, and went home to graduate. But even after graduating, it's

The Author aboard the *Shamrock* in the Cook Inlet in 1999.

not over yet. Just in case someone slipped through with a personality flaw (which was incurable) or the guys on the team wanted you out, you could still be blackballed. We were on a six-month probation. If you were to go to town to display your new bad-ass status in the local pubs, that too could be your ticket back to the fleet.

I drew Team 12, which is of course, the greatest in the world. I didn't have my bags totally unpacked when it was my time for beach watch. That amounted to taking a jeep down to the Hotel Del Coronado rocks and back to the quonset we had on the Strand. My partner that night was a first-class gunner's mate who had just gotten back from town, and was drunk on his ass. He didn't think so and took his rightful place at the wheel. I thought, well what the hell, we're just driving on the beach. He was telling some great "welcome to the team" stories and as we got close to the hotel, we picked up speed, which enabled us to climb the biggest rock in Coronado. My first thought was, "Why me God? I'm still on probation." Perhaps that explains why I was the only one concerned about the oil coming out of the pan. Actually the water was coming out of the radiator faster because the oil hadn't had a chance to warm up yet. We went to the parking garage at the hotel and borrowed pry bars, a jack, and so on. We worked until first light and got her off. Some borrowed oil and water got us back before muster.

TWO

The Teams (Hoo Yah!)

We lived in a barracks on the Amphib Base, but that was just a place to sleep. Everything else was across the highway on the beach, the Silver Strand (years after I left, everything was moved over there). At the barracks, the showers and johns were out the backdoor and across an open grass area that was visible from one of the roads running through the base. One evening, Frank Perry and some others were making a trip to New Mexico for a few days, but I elected to stay behind. The night they were going to leave, we all went to the Manhattan Room for pizza. I don't know what everyone else had, but Frank and I had Italian sausage. They dropped me at the barracks before heading out. Sometime during that night, I sat straight up in my bunk—I had a call to the john like I've only known in Mexico. By the time I'd made it across the grass and got set on the throne, I was violently ill. I'd never had food poisoning before, but after that night I could never make that claim again.

By daylight I was still running back and forth. At first, I worried about some lady driving by, when I was streaking, but soon I just didn't care. Sometimes I didn't make the whole crossing before unloading. It was the weekend and no one was in the barracks but me. And it was sad to think they'd come back Monday to find I'd shit myself to death.

By the time the sun was out and bright over head, I had no problem stopping balls-ass naked right in the middle of the grass and letting go. I had very little control over the situation—from either end. Soon, by the second day there was nothing left but pure water. I knew I needed to

Solid Brass

drink more fluids. I also knew I'd better be within stepping distance to the john before I drank. There were people in the hospital that weren't as sick as I was.

Some days later, when Frank got back from the trip, he told a better story than mine. He had to look ahead, down the highway, for a tree, billboard, whatever. When he yelled, they'd stop and he'd lower his pants with a roll of toilet paper streaming behind, running for some privacy, on some freeway all the way to New Mexico. He had it as bad as me, but didn't have the nice grassy area behind the barracks to do it. One thing I've enjoyed in very few people, was the ability to tell a story about themselves that might be less than flattering.

One of the older inhabitants of our barracks was a man named Amarillo. He had a brother that had invented a pair of floating water-skis that were pulled by an outboard. Two people could ride them. You held on to a bar, which would steer when pulled from side to side. You stood up with one person holding the bar and the second person holding on to your waist. He asked me if I'd like to run the skis while his brother did a promo of his product. We went to a prearranged spot in San Diego Bay to meet his brother. When we drove up, he was standing on one side of the skis and on the other side was one beautiful girl. "This is your ski-ing partner, Sheryl. She was just voted 'Miss San Diego.'" What a nice thing to do, was my thought at the moment. After she took off her coat as we prepared to shove off, there was no doubt who the star of the show would be.

We filmed for several hours. Me steering, her holding on, her steer-ing, me holding on. Finally, he had the film he wanted, and with his blessing we toured the bay with the gas left. It was a sunny, warm day and as we went by the various docks and yachts, we drew quite a crowd. It could have been because they'd never seen a rig like that before, but I doubt it.

Another barrack's inhabitant was one of my running mates and very close friend and sparing partner, Pete McNair from Alabama. People that didn't know us would think we couldn't stand each other's guts, the way we verbally fought all the time. It didn't matter where we were or what we were doing, we always had time to rag on each other. One example was the "who bought last" thing we did at the ice cream machine on the Strand. "I bought last!" "The hell you did!" and on and on, until we finally made a chit that stated "I bought last." We treated that chit the same way we did our money. One day without Mac and only one dime, I got an ice cream. No sooner did I take a bite when, bigger than hell, here came Mac around the quonset at a dead run. I took off running, gobbling as fast as I could, but he was gaining because of my late start. When I could see it was hopeless, I stopped, took my last bite, threw the rest in the sand and stomped it. This, no doubt, illustrates the killer instinct we had gained in our Frog training.

Mac made one of life's "little" decisions while in the teams. He decided to get circumcised. Of course, we visited him every break in the day while he was in the hospital. We brought him all the Playboy-type magazines we could find, made sure he saw our favorites, and explained each picture in detail. They gave him a little aerosol can which he could use if he had a good dream and started to rise to the occasion. He could give his new stitches a little blast of instant freeze and it would all go away. After he came back to the barracks, I'd wake up in the middle of the night laughing as I heard the "hiss" from his little can. "Shut up, you son of a bitch!" was followed by belly laughs that broke the stillness of the night.

A few of the bachelor old-timers had homes in Coronado where we enjoyed spending our free time. One weekend afternoon, we were sitting around Guinea's house, doing a little wine tasting. We had "tasted" several gallons when the phone rang. It was Mac's little girlfriend. Mac waved an "I'm not here" gesture and pointed for me to take the phone which was quickly handed off to me. This little girl was about five feet tall and crazy about my rebel friend. He treated her like so much crap. He and I talked in great lengths about his rotten ways when it came to this girl. Simply put, she was in love and he wasn't.

"Hi, this is Bob, Mac's not here for some reason today," a look of thanks from Mac, "but it's just as well," I said, "I'd like to talk to you anyway. Why don't you give up on that asshole?" Mac spun around in his chair, madder than hell; not at me, but at himself for being dumb enough to let me have the phone. It hadn't been that long since I said I was going to tell her all the crap he did behind her back and why didn't he stay with the fast track ladies and let her find someone who'd bring flowers. "Well, he is my friend, but so are you," I went on, "you're too good for him," on and on. When I finally hung up, he ran across the room and jumped right in the middle of me. I was laughing so hard I had no defense. We later took a walk together, but not to talk—we needed to buy more wine.

Mac did get the last dig. While we were in the Philippines, I spent a lot of time living with some people in a fishing village and banana plantation on the far side of Luzon, an area called Dingalen Bay. In the process, I ended up with a beautiful, hand-forged machete (forged from a Jeep spring left from the war). I had this knife at the barracks in my gear box lucky bag, along with some unusual diving masks I'd collected. I would be at sea when he got his discharge, so we had our good-byes before I set sail. When I got back, Mac had taken my treasures and left a note in their place. "I didn't have any souvenirs to take home and I knew you'd have time to get more, so I took yours. Love ya, Mac." Well, if he had known what that machete meant to me, my dirty, rotten friend wouldn't have taken it.

Dingalen Bay was a special place. We were preparing to participate in a mock war game offshore in a few weeks. This was the largest gathering of ships since WWII. It was the Seventh Fleet, some ships soon to go home and some just getting there. UDT was here before the rest of the fleet, to take surf observation, to be ready for the landing. We were to take turns sleeping on the beach sending back reports. I was so taken by this place, I never wanted to leave. The older guys that found no romance sleeping under a coconut tree were glad I felt this way and let me take their watch. Every so many days they'd bring me a sack full of food and go back to the ship. There was a long white sandy beach, lined with coco palms and fishermen's outriggers pulled up above the high waterline. Behind this was a large banana plantation and the stilt houses lived in by the people who worked the plantation. Also in this beach area was a trading post-type store. I used to have breakfast in the store after I got to know the owners. They would put out a giant pizza pan-looking plate, full of fried rice and over-easy's topped with little spicy sausages.

Solid Brass

There was no refrigeration, so everything was fresh. Pigs and chickens running everywhere. All I wore at any time, were shorts and coral shoes or no shoes and a sweatshirt at night. While I was there, I learned to eat bananas every possible way: boiled, broiled, fried, steamed, etc. The locals also taught me how to husk a coconut with a machete (*my* machete, the one that now lives in Alabama).

One Saturday, the guys came in from the ship and we all went back on the river in our rubber boats. This was an incredible place, you couldn't see the tops on some of the trees. Papaya grew everywhere, vines hanging down to the water, you kind of looked for Johnny Weismuller. We did our Tarzan thing after we found a deep clear pool, we'd cast off on the vines and release over the center of the pool. There seemed to be snakes in every tree as well as a few swimmers. There were areas of the river you couldn't have penetrated, the growth was so thick. There had to be plants and trees in that jungle that hadn't been named yet, there were so many of different colors and shapes. You couldn't count the amount of different plants, and the same goes for the birds. There were monkeys swinging through the trees or just staying in one spot screaming at us. After a full day in this unbelievable river paradise, we went back to the trading post and drank warm San Miguel beer.

The nomads came through that day. They had real bushy hair and their teeth were the color of deep mahogany from chewing beetle nut, a local favorite narcotic. It wasn't a sneak behind a tree thing, they chewed it openly, and by the looks of their teeth, they all used it. The tight curly bushy hair was very different from the other Filipino people. They seemed to have come from a different part of the world. They would set banana stalks on the beach and shoot them with their bow and arrows with a casual dead-on accuracy. It seemed they were putting on a show just for us. They also carried arrows with prongs for getting their fish. They wore only loin cloths and didn't speak the same dialect as the locals. I've seen them throw their machetes and cut a papaya out of a tree so accurately that the knife would end up stuck in another tree so it wasn't lost in the thick growth.

Danny Dever (Cunningham) had fallen asleep in the corner of the store after the long day up river and several bottles of San Miguel.

Solid Brass

One of the nomads came in with a baby boa and wanted to trade it. There was some thought of putting it on Dan and waking him, but we didn't want to carry him all the way back to the boat after a coronary. That evening, just about everyone went back in our team boat, but a few of us went back in a borrowed outrigger. After dropping them off, I took the outrigger back and spent the night on the beach as usual. In the morning, I woke to something touching my eyebrows. A very small hand with tiny little fingers was checking out my nose, my ears, my lips. I opened my eyes to peer into the inquisitive eyes of a busy little monkey. Standing not too far away was his best friend, a young boy from the village. I'd talked with him before about the little wooden goggles he had around his neck. Although we couldn't speak each other's language, I had understood, through our gestures, that his father had made them and would make me a pair. Some days later, through another person's translation, the boy said his father was finished with the goggles, but he was having trouble finding eyes—which turned out to be glass. But this morning, he held out goggles carved of mahogany with the eyes intact. He had his goggles around his neck, so we swam out to check mine for fit. A nice way to start the day in the warm water of Dingalen Bay. Mac hadn't found these goggles while rooting through my treasures, so I still have them.

That night a few of the guys paddled in and some of the locals roasted a pig over a big fire on the beach. They also cooked a few barnyard strutters accompanied by adobo and fried bananas—it was a meal fit for a Frog! Anytime I went back to the boat for a few hours, I'd take stalks of bananas and coconuts to hang in the diving locker. Before I had to leave the beach and head for sea, we had several weeks supply for us and the ship's crew. I had a little spot on the back deck where I husked out the cocos. My new skill was a crowd pleaser.

The only bad thing that happened at Dingalen took place a few days after I took our guys back to the ship in the outrigger. The ship let their off duty crew come to the beach and have a picnic beer bust. Our shark-toothed boat acted as a taxi. Some time after the last boat went back, two guys from the ship's crew took one of the outriggers from the beach like we did. Halfway out, the boat filled with water and they

Solid Brass

started swimming for the ship. Only one made it. What they didn't know was when the fisherman pulled their boats up on the slanted beach, they pull a plug in the stern and let the water from the day's work drain out. They should have stayed with the boat because they don't sink even if they're full of water.

We spent all that night and the next three days looking for him. He floated in several miles down the beach and was found by a Filipino soldier. Bob Worthington, one of my closest friends, and I were miles down the beach in the opposite direction when we got the call on our walkie-talkie. We walked back to the village and sat down on the beach. Dog Breath Allen came over and asked if we'd ever seen a drowned man before and headed us down the beach to experience something he felt strongly about. There were lots of people there by now and our Corpsman, Doc Beaver was doing the fingerprinting on what was left of this body. A body in the tropical water for three days is something I won't describe, but I'll never forget. After Doc got his prints and tags, he said, "OK, let's lift him onto the stretcher." Bob and I looked at each other's pale face and vanished into the crowd, then we ran all the way back to the village. I had thought a long time about why they were in that outrigger in the first place.

After the fleet was all in place, our job, beside surf observation, was to sink 'em. And sink 'em we did—the whole fleet, some ships several times. We lost track of how many times we sank the flagship, our favorite target. During the war games, we would make underwater attacks on a given ship. If you got in, undetected, you pulled a water-proof flare, which meant they'd been hit. We'd maneuver around the target ship at an undetectable distance in our pick up boat. We'd drop over the side, take a compass reading on our target, submerge and swim our course until we heard the hum of the generator and follow it right to the ship's keel. We were using both aqua-lung bottles and oxygen rebreathers.

With the clarity of the water, we didn't have to swim too far before we'd pick up the glow of any ship lights left on. Then we didn't have to use our compass. On a moonlit night we could see the sea snakes swimming by us. One ship had so many lights on at the gangway, it attracted all the snakes in the area. They were boiling at the water, like so much spaghetti. The gangway was let down so we could get out of the water and wait for our boat. This time we climbed on their picket boat which was out trying to spot our bubbles, rather than climb through a thousand snakes, many of which were poisonous.

The games had a starting time and a finish, so it was known we could attack at anytime from 0600 on Monday to 2400 on Friday, for instance. In a similar game, some years before, our fleet sat at anchor as the games started at 0600. The captain of the ship the team was traveling on at that time, had to go to a meeting on the flagship, as did all the captains, so at 0630 the Frogs took the captain's gig crew captive. They put on the crew's dress canvas, waited in the captain's gig until he came aboard, took him to his rendezvous, tied up with the other boats and went aboard like everyone else for coffee. As soon as the meeting started in the wardroom, the Frogs went in and passed out assassination slips to the brass of the whole fleet. All without so much as a wet towel in the house.

We used every method from forged papers to grapnel hooks to get on board in different situations at various times. Once getting ready to swim on a less sophisticated ship, we were going to get on board and disable them. Hamilton was putting tape around the flukes of a grapnel and putting cans of paint on his belt. Joe Hutch, one of our Henny Youngman types, knowing the rails on this ship would be too far from the water to throw a hook, explained to Hamilton that he was about as sly as a rhinosaurus sneaking up on a house cat over a bed of Rice Crispys.

After the fleet went their different ways from Dingalen, we left for some work closer to Manila. When we got to Manila Bay, we dropped the hook and went on liberty. God knows I needed it after so many days climbing coconut trees. We caught a Mercedes cab to our first order of business—some cold San Miguel beer. We drank so much warm San Miguel at Dingalen, I had kind of gotten used to it. After consuming a righteous amount of beer, we found it was cockfight day just down the road, so that's where we headed.

The cockfight pit was a very large place, with a big crowd passing money around. There were several roosters in several stages of kicking ass—it didn't take long to get into the spirit of things. It didn't hurt that there was no shortage of beer here, either.

Somehow Joe Hutch talked some local out of his rooster. We paid for the bird and arranged for a fight. We bought some heavy duty cigars to smoke now that we were fight promoters, and had our own cock to boot. A couple more beers and half a cigar later, it was time for our bird to show what he was made of. We all gave him a few strokes for luck, Joe blew smoke up his tale feathers and tossed him in at the same time as his opponent. The other bird made one pass over ours and laid him flat. The smoke hadn't cleared before our bird was dead. If we had a stop watch, we wouldn't have had time to start it.

Off and on in the Philippines, we trained the Philippine Navy Frogmen. We did a lot of drop and pick-up from our boats and this day we were getting ready to jump from one of their helicopters into the clear tropical water. We had schooled them in class and now we were ready to take them out the door. We gave our directions to their pilot, who did not speak english, but nodded and smiled as the translator relayed our instructions. We asked to be flown thirty feet off the water at thirty knots. At the drop area the red light went on and out the door I went with Davis right behind me. You're not suppose to look down as this throws your center of gravity off and you could belly flop. I had made this jump hundreds of times but this didn't feel right, so I took a peek down. Not only were we too high, we were too fast. Almost straight below us were two of the largest sea turtles in the world. We just fell short of hitting them. If we would have landed on one, we would have gone through eternity as a grease spot on a sea turtle off Corregidor. We could think about this later; now we wanted to catch a ride on one of them. As we approached them, it was just in time to watch the two giants sound and swim out of sight.

After being picked up by the helicopter, we knew that something had been lost in the translation. We were at sixty feet, doing sixty knots. We had asked the pilots, after studying their gauges, to look out the window to make sure that there wasn't a tramp steamer or large reef below before they gave the signal to jump. I guess we should have added giant sea turtles to that list.

Solid Brass

The Philippine officer in charge was a pleasant, young gentleman. He was telling us that his government knew of an illegal logging operation of Philippine mahogany trees. They knew it was deep in the jungle but couldn't find the exact location. He wanted us to help, so we made this our next project.

After a few days, we took our boats up the large river that went through the area they suspected. We went up river until it was too shallow for our boat. We then launched our rubber boats and continued paddling up river. The overhanging trees and dense jungle blocked out much of the sun. There was plenty of light, but it was very eerie. It was a quiet place, but yet it wasn't. There were jungle noises all around us. I'm not sure just how many hours we were back there but just when we would have bet no man had ever been here before, we spotted a wooden bridge. Then, on the bank through the trees, we could see a clearing. In waist deep water, we pulled the boats to the bank and tied them. We checked our weapons and headed to the jungle to the edge of the clearing. Unbelievable, here in the deepest, darkest jungle, was a first class logging operation.

The first thing we saw was stacks of giant Philippine mahogany trees, all carefully rowed and numbered. Also, some very up-to-date logging equipment, the size you need to move trees this large. There were well-made offices and barracks. The bridge wasn't just a quickie to get by, it was well engineered and professionally built. Some engineer had to feel bad about this place being illegal, not being able to show it off. There were millions of dollars just in equipment.

We cautiously moved through the area obtaining information needed to estimate how much explosives would be needed to destroy this operation. We then put off downriver to our awaiting boats, then back offshore to the ship. After a couple of days of preparation, we headed back up river with more rubber boats, the Philippine Frogs, and loaded with explosives. This time would be a little different, we would be required to be in the open more than before. In the open with more of us, some being Philippine trainees. We decided to do this one in the dark.

Our explosives were in our Hagerson sacks, which fit over our head and shoulders like a poncho. The jungle was playing a different tune, all the night creatures seemed to be making more noise and more things

slithered by and brushed against our boats. In the daylight, we had paddled by snakes longer than our boat.

We knew approximately how long it would take to get there, but now
being in the dark we would have to use the bridge as a landmark. We
finally tied the boats and with our packs on, got out into chest high water.
Some of the Filipinos had to stretch their necks to get air. We couldn't
pull up to the bank because the vines and limbs grew out much farther.
We had some distance to travel to get to the bank.   One boat continued
up river to load the bridge.

After getting through the clearing we split up, taking our trainees
with us. We loaded explosives to everything that didn't belong there. We
put shape charges on the engines and a cratering charge in the road. A
good cratering charge would keep a war tank from getting through, so it
would keep a logging truck from going to work. The jungle was so thick
here and the trees so tall, it was easy to understand why this wasn't spotted from the air. It certainly wasn't in any kind of a flight path.

Our bags were empty and the fuse was lit. We set a fuse long enough
to allow us time to get out of the jungle and back to the ship, so we would
be sitting offshore when she blew. If you're the kind of person who
appreciates well-made machinery, you would have to feel bad about that
fairly new equipment that was about to go high order. We used one of
our favorite charge calculations; you figure exactly how much you need,
then double it. For a brief moment the sky lit up. The jungle creatures
let out a protest for the rude awakening. Then it was all over.

We got some sleep and early in the morning, started back up river.
Our calculations were right on. There wasn't a piece of the bridge left
big enough to pick your teeth. The road could be used for a water reservoir and the heavy equipment would become part of the jungle, as did the
instruments of war some years before.

When we traveled around in our small boat we used for drop and pick
up, it was easily identified as being ours, even though it was painted
Navy gray, it had a large shark's mouth painted on it. This was long
before *Jaws*. The story goes that during one of our war games, a very
famous Admiral, looking out from the bridge of the flagship and spotting
our boat, asked, "What the hell is that?" "That's UDT, Sir." "That figures."

Solid Brass

One day, we were passing a curious looking diving barge at a safe distance, but trying to see what was going on, when a guy in Panama whites hailed us over to one side of the rig. He knew by the shark's mouth that we were UDT and just wanted to say hello as he too was an American diver. We tied up to the stern and talked a bit.

During WWII, as the Japanese moved into Manila, the banks took their money offshore and dumped it. These guys had a deal with the government to retrieve the money at a 50/50 split. The year before, they pulled four million pesos, pesos were two for one American exchange, so that puts their take, after the split, at a million dollars. A peso was the size of our silver dollar and they were just getting a few a day now. So why were they still doing it? Gold bars were also dumped and none had been found yet.

UDT Team 12 Shark-mouth boat in action, circa 1950.
Official U.S. Navy photograph

Solid Brass

His parting words were, "If any of you guys are qualified for heavy gear, look me up when you get out and I'll put you to work." "Danny, Mr. Richards and I are qualified, how about if we get leave and work with you now?" I blurted out. "If you can get off, you've got a job. How about it, Mr. Richards?" "When we get back to the ship I'll see about getting off," was his reply.

The possibility was mind boggling; not even out of the Navy and I'd have my first commercial diving job. I couldn't care less about the money. The adventure and maybe getting to keep a handful of the blackened silver coins would be plenty. After getting back to the ship, before the excitement had a chance to wear off, we found out the team needed volunteers to go on a diving and demolition job in Pusan, Korea. I volunteered, Danny Dever did, and so did Mr. Richards. We all three volunteered away our chances of going on our first world-class treasure hunt.

Korea was still cleaning up after their war, in fact, it was still easy to get killed. There were still plenty of people around that didn't honor the cease fire yet, because the whole town of Pusan was off limits.

We lived in a portable Army camp, within walking distance of town. The whole camp could be folded up, put on barges and gone in a few hours. The galley was on board one of these barges. We slept in small plywood rooms. The one I stayed in had a big mural painted on all the walls. Trains, cars, horses...very well done. This type of creation came from the lack of recreation, being this was an off limits town to our troops. Our host for the job was the Army Corps of Engineers and the man in charge was also in charge of the base. One hell of a guy. The job was to remove obstacles on the bottom of Pusan Harbor. At low tide, ships coming into the harbor would bottom out.

Our first look showed that there were more than reefs here. There were munitions dumped while unloading ships during the war. Bombs, mortars, cases of ammunition, grenades, etc. There was enough stuff here to fully arm a small country.

This survey and mapping out of how many explosives were needed took many days. Some days we couldn't work, for one reason or another, like ships coming in to unload, for instance. So we checked out the town.

Solid Brass

We would, from time to time, duck into what looked to be a friendly bar. We would take turns at what today would be called a designated driver to keep an eye out. If the MPs came, the girls that waited tables would run us upstairs where we could hide. The MPs knew we were there somewhere but couldn't find us or just didn't want to find us bad enough.

There was one alley that was fun to tour through. It was dubbed *Thieves Alley*, and there was every imaginable thing ever issued to American troops; ship-to-shore radios, all Army issue clothing and boots, walkie-talkies, typewriters, etc. There was a Korean law then that no vehicle could be driven by anyone but a Korean. This also held true coming out of the base, so it was impossible to stop the thieving. I read one report of how many gallons of diesel fuel had been taken, it was hard to believe.

Danny was telling a true story of a big heist he'd heard about. A train was somehow removed from the main track and stolen, never to be seen again. The ultimate in thievery. Everyone was listening, but didn't show enough surprise or excitement in their face for Dan, so he changed his description to "choo-choo train." He repeated the story with hand gestures and a much louder voice, "They stole a whole choo-choo train!"

The Commanding Officer of the base, Mr. Lint, would invite us out on his boat to go fishing on the weekend. This was no military scout, no sir, this was a very nice forty-foot yacht type. He'd have a couple of trash cans full of iced beer. We soon introduced him to Dupont fishing, which was the art of stringing out explosives across the ocean floor, touching it off, and going back and scooping the fish off the surface with a net. He was hooked, so every weekend we went fishing with our Dupont spinners.

The food in the Enlisted Men's Mess wasn't all that great anyway but if we came in late, after a long diving day, we'd get warmed up hot dogs and that would be that. The second time this happened, we stayed in our wet suits in an effort to get there on time for a full meal, but that didn't work. We went to the intercom and called Mr. Richards at the officer's mess. He told us to come right over. In we went in our diving gear to just a bit of a difference from our usual steam table, we sat down.

Solid Brass

We chose one of the entrees on the menu and had excellent service. That's where we ate for the rest of the trip.

Another invasion of officer country came after we'd been invited to a masquerade party on the base Enlisted Men's Club. They knew we didn't have anything with us but work clothes, so they asked that we stay low silhouette and enjoy the refreshments. A few of the soldiers borrowed our gear and went as frogmen. After several hours of consuming adult beverages, Mr. Richards came in from the officer's bar. He was accompanied by a merchant marine officer dressed in civilian clothes. He was telling us of the great spread of food and drinks they had next door. We all wore the same marine greens in the team, except the officers wore their silver gold emblem on their hats and bars of rank on their shirt, that was the only distinguishable difference. So Mr. Richards pinned his bars on me, we changed hats, Danny used the merchant's overcoat and through the doors Danny and I strolled. The only officer who would recognize us was Mr. Lint and Mr. Richards already told us he wasn't there.

We sat right down at a table of several officers and were promptly brought into the conversation. They wanted to know all about UDT and the Merchant Marines. Danny had a little more trouble winging it. One happy sort of guy offered us a smoke, and then lit it for us. Neither one of us smoked, but we couldn't pass up the opportunity. There was no way they'd let us buy a round, they had tabs and we were guests. More people came to the table because of all the laughter. Danny was one of the key speakers, he could tell a great story. I had to kick him when he started to tell a team story. By then everyone was so screwed up, I don't think they would have caught it anyway. All the time, the drinks were stacking up. We also enjoyed some first class hors d'oeuvres that were constantly being set down in front of us. Lots of kim chi, the Korean dish I took a life-long liking to (kind of an oriental sauerkraut). Before we left, a Korean girl brought us a large container full of kim chi to take with us. By her big grin, I'm sure she recognized us from the Officer's Mess. She was the only one there onto us.

I just happened to look up as Mr. Lint walked in. He spotted us immediately because of the large crowd we'd drawn. Now the young lady wasn't the only one onto us. He smiled, shook his head in some disbelief, but not really. I could see the "Ah, shit" look in his eyes. We knew he'd have to come to the defense of his officers. We excused ourselves to the disappointment of our new friends, and slipped out the door back to the masquerade party, much to the relief of Mr. Lint.

There was another run-in with officers by Danny worth mentioning. I wasn't there, but I like the story. Danny was coming through a restaurant somewhere, feeling no pain, when he spotted an old Navy commander who'd been an important heavy gear diver himself. He was also famous on his stand against scuba bottles, which then were just called aqua-lung bottles. He spoke out against them from the day they came into the diving world. Danny staggered up to the commander's table. "Excuse me, Commander, I just wanted to stop by here in case you haven't seen the new report out on heavy gear. I know you would like to know if you hadn't already heard, they're going to melt all the Mark Vs and make aqua-lung bottles out of them." He didn't wait for a reply, just staggered away.

We worked hard in Pusan Harbor and set off some really big shots. I'm sure with the first, everyone within twenty miles must have thought "Here we go again." It was the Fourth of July for sure, all those munitions on the bottom of the harbor were set off by our explosives. We made sure we took a wrap around every piece of munition on that bottom. When the main charge was set off there came the finest display of fireworks and aerials shooting and whistling every which way. The explosions were so deafening, the sound lingered in your ears long after the smoke cleared. With all the reefs flattened and the old war toys blown up, we were flown back to our ship. What the hell, one more adventure.

We loaded up in one of the oldest flying boxcars in the world. The plane was sitting on a dirt strip in the middle of a bunch of rice paddies. We should have gotten suspicious when they handed us parachutes upon boarding. They were manufactured for some war a long time ago. We put them on, they closed the door. We were sitting side by side with our backs to the windows, we put shoulder straps on, but we could still see out. The pilot revved up the engine, waited until they were full throttle, took his foot off the brake and we proceeded to rattle down the runway.

Solid Brass

He had everything he could get out of that old World War II engine, but it wasn't enough to lift off. He got her stopped, just before we dumped in the rice paddy. We taxied back to the other end, dumped a few boxes of cargo, and headed down the runway again. We got off, but anyone in the paddy would have had to duck as we flew over, we were barely off the ground for quite a distance.

The ship we were traveling on all through the Philippines was a small destroyer escort (DE). All this ship had to do during our tour was taxi us around. The crew loved it. When we were off the ship for long periods of time, they would be in port waiting for us. They got more liberty than most ships. The only one that wasn't too crazy about us was the skipper. I don't know if he didn't like being a taxi or what. We also had certain requirements, like turning his ship's library into our diving locker, where three of us also lived. Or maybe he didn't like us walking around deck in swim gear. But for some reason, he didn't like us.

We even changed their eating habits after several weeks of complaining about the starvation spread. We came in from an island we were working on, with a couple of our officers who came with us to check it out. We'd called ahead to have dinner held. When we started down the line, there was grilled cheese sandwiches, that's it. No soup of the day, salad, nada. The guy behind the steam table told us that was what the crew had for dinner. Mr. Richards flipped on his hat displaying the only sign of officer rank among our swimtrunks and sweatshirts. "Get your Chief Steward down here now." Some indignant guy came down in a tee shirt, who'd obviously been eating better than us. He started right in about the sound sleep he was in before we got there. "I don't give a shit about your sleep, my men have been working hard all day without lunch and they're not eating grilled cheese sandwiches for dinner." (Actually, most of that day we were learning how to make coconut hats from Henry and Apu, two of our guys from Hawaii. It was our day off to partake in hot San Miguel beer on our mission to the beach. But I didn't feel it was necessary to divulge that information.) This evening was well overdue about the food. "How you feed your men is not my business, but you'll feed mine as you should anyone that works hard. They can't continue busting their asses day to day on the lousy food you're feeding them!"

Solid Brass

He went on until we had all kinds of food to eat—from that night on, actually. I think that was one more strike against us with the old man.

One night in Okinawa, the ship's old man got his revenge. We'd taken the liberty launch to the beach to try out the new Enlisted Men's Club that had just opened. It was a nice place and we proceeded to help the success of their grand opening celebration. A couple of hours before closing, a few of our officers, Mr. Richards and Whiskey Jack, came over from their Officer's Club. They came to our table and said, "We decided that the first Frog we ran into, we'd buy for the rest of the night, so being you're all together, I guess we're stuck with all of you." They ordered a round and started to sit down, when out of the john, Guinea started waving to us to come in, he was in hysterics. He led us into a stall where there was—there's no polite way to put this—a turd of world record proportion. It was lying in the bowl, all by itself. Someone had tried to flush it. No one had a camera, so there's no way Ripley or Guinness would believe us. One thing, for sure, no one from our ship could have done this before we got their diet changed. Finally, everyone was coming in to see what the attraction was. There were roars of laughter, and soon the money was out and the bets were on as to how many flushes it would take to get it swallowed, or not. We went back to our table, wiping tears from our eyes and broke up each time a yell or cheer came out of the men's room for all the "Almost!" shouts until the final, winning flush.

After closing the place, we walked to the dock to catch the boat but it wasn't there yet. A few of us decided to swim back. This was one of the few times we were in our dress canvas. We gave our hat and shoes to the others waiting for the boat. The ship was quite a way offshore, but what the hell, it was a warm balmy night, full moon. My commanding officer wouldn't be mad; he was swimming right alongside me and Mr. Richards and the rest of us.

When we got to the ship, everyone got on the gangway and on board before the watch made much notice of us, but Brown and I swam around for a while. We were out there long enough to make gestures to the guy with the spotlight. They knew who we were when the morning's plan of the day had Brown and Wick spelled right under next week's Captain's Mast.

Solid Brass

Our commanding officer called us in his room, said he couldn't be sure, but he thought if he held his own Captain's Mast, possibly the ship's captain would honor it and that would be the end of it. We were severely reprimanded and our punishment would be to make coffee when needed for the next two weeks on alternate days in the diving locker. I'm sure this wasn't the report turned in on our mast. The ship's captain didn't pursue it further.

We had other close calls with keeping our service records clean. We got a call to move to another ship that would take us and our equipment off to Borneo. There was some kind of uprising, they were to evacuate the American citizens and wanted us to be there just in case there was trouble.

We circled the island of Borneo over thirty days before they settled the matter and sent us home. We went to Subic Bay and the ship's crew was instructed to be very cautious while on shore. There had been several cases of sailors getting hurt by our own Military Police. Something to do with getting everyone under control while on liberty, or else. There was going to be an investigation, but so far it was just talk.

A few of us had gone to a club to meet Bob Worthington's brother, who was coming in from another ship. I was walking up to the bar to order another round, when I heard a sailor say something about some guy outside getting the hell beat out of him. I walked to the door to see the fight, instead, I saw a sailor on the ground behind a paddy wagon, getting beat by the MPs. I ran out and jumped the guy doing all the damage so the sailor could crawl away. That's all I remember. I've been hit in the head a few times in my life, some requiring stitches, but I've never been knocked out. I was that night. Hit from behind with a club. I woke up in a bunk and by feeling around, knew it wasn't mine. I had a hard time clearing my eyes. When I reached up to wipe them, my face got in the way. My head was swollen to the size of a basketball. Someone was trying to help me up. It was a CB that came to get one of his people out of the brig and recognized me from the ship (God only knows how) and told them he'd take this one too. I couldn't wash all the caked blood off my face, so I just cleared my eyes. I couldn't stand without help. My wrists were raw and swollen so bad, I could hardly move my hands.

Solid Brass

I was hit from behind, handcuffed, and beaten while unconscious. I must have come to enough to fight the cuffs. We were wearing our whites. The jumper was ripped off and the bottoms soaked in so much blood they had to be thrown away. Of course, my people didn't even know this had happened until I got back to the ship. The guys I was with figured I'd wandered off and would be back.

The guys on the ship took me to sickbay and cleaned me up as best they could, than helped me to my bunk. In the morning I struggled out of my bunk, with some help. I was told to put on greens and to go see Whiskey Jack as soon as I felt up to it. I went to his room, he said they had found the other sailor I was trying to help. He was also in the brig and he told the story of me being knocked out. They drove me to another location, pulled me from the wagon unconscious and beat me with their clubs and kicked me. "We can't get an answer from the MP station, so we're going to do a little checking on our own," Jack told me. "Do you think you would know the guy if you saw him?" "Yes, the one I jumped, I'd know." "There's a few of the guys waiting for you at the gangway, so you can go to town and look for him. This time there'll be someone to watch your back."

All these plans and accumulated information was obtained that morning, while I slept. I walked out on deck, and there stood several tons of Frogs. I was the only one under 200 pounds. I was one of the smallest and youngest guys in the team and they knew me as the happy type when we were on the town. I always tried to stay away from arguments and trouble, unless absolutely unavoidable.

This was one of those times when you have a difficult time finding things to say, like "Good morning fellas, I got hit from behind." We went through the gate with our special pass to be out of uniform. I never, ever, had that "get even" attitude or carried a vendetta, but this time, as sore as I was, I was certainly looking forward to finding this MP and his cohorts. I didn't care if they brought their clubs this time. They must be animals anyway, the way they beat my face.

We spent two days and nights, going in and out of every bar in town, walking the streets, stopping patrol cars and paddy wagons, and looking inside without much explanation. Soon it seemed everyone in Subic Bay knew what was happening. About the third day, it was found out these MPs had been transferred out of the area to avoid any further problems. They had already been getting flack about their self-enforced laws to beat anyone in town that staggered while on liberty. There were any number of military situations that would have finally stopped this and when the team came through the gate with one of their own in bandages and permission to be out of uniform, it must have seemed like a good time to start.

There was another time we were, in part, responsible for a man getting transferred. Poker was a recreation that we thoroughly enjoyed. Frank was this little guy from the ship's crew who was kind of a poker playing legend. Nobody won big like Frank. After a few of our guys sat in for a night or two, Joe Hutch told us Frank was using marked decks, both Diamond and Bicycle. Hutch took one of the decks and read the cards off to us from the back. Joe was the only person I had ever known that could actually stack a deck. He got our guys together and taught them how to play Frank's game and where to be seated around the table that night. They were going to take Frank to the cleaners. Each guy was told when to bet, when to raise and most importantly, when to get out.

They played a few hands before the deal came to Joe. As usual, Frank was lucky that night. Joe dealt the first cards followed by a flurry of betting. The pot built to a lofty proportion. The key play was John Dadian's, he had to drop out before the last card was dealt. Instead, he not only stayed, he raised the pot. There was disbelief on everyone's face. This changed the way the cards came out, Dadian's failure to drop out canceled the winning hand, and the good hand Hutch dealt Frank to keep him raising, won the pot.

That night there was a good chance Dadian was going to die. "What the hell did you do, forget the plan? You had to drop out to set the cards right, asshole." John's reply was, "I couldn't get out—that was the best hand I'd ever been dealt!" They finally did get Frank, and for a handsome chunk of change. Not until then, did they reveal Frank's skill at card manipulating. He was transferred off the ship without anyone knowing it, which possibly saved his life.

When we weren't traveling around to do these various jobs, we stayed in an old Japanese barracks, Camp McGill in Takiama, Japan. The

Solid Brass

locals called us Takiama Swim Sailors. This was where we lived and based while overseas. Takiama was a beautiful place, a small farming community on the coast. It was a perfect place to run through the country or on the beach for our daily workout. There were large pits on the farms which we all feared falling into when we'd come back off liberty at night. It's where the honey buckets from town were dumped. Back then, a big part of the residences had buckets under their binjo (toilet) that, when full, were set outside and the honey wagon, as it was known, would come by and empty the small buckets and deliver them to the farms to be used to fertilize the crops.

We also did a lot of diving off the coast. There were several types of edible shellfish, including a good sized abalone, which looked a lot like our pink but more the size of a red. We would make a gift of our catch to the locals, which kept us beloved members of the community.

Life was good at this barracks. If you had the watch, that meant you pulled your bunk over by the phone for the night. On the weekend the trash cans were full of iced beer and the table used to powder the diving dress was turned into a craps table. Whiskey Jack had brought a couple of cases of whiskey to our barracks for safe-keeping. For some reason, he didn't want them in officer country. During one of the big crap game sessions, it was decided to open a few in lieu of rent due on storage. I wasn't a good drinker of any sort, let alone whiskey, but this was the event for the evening. After a dozen toasts to Whiskey Jack, I decided to get in the crap game, which I knew nothing about. They showed me where to put my money, and as it turned out, where to pick it up. Under the influence of Whiskey Jack's private stock, I broke the house.

Unlike most hangover mornings, my pockets were bulging when I woke up. It doesn't take much imagination to figure, they had me in every sucker bet possible, but I could do no wrong. All bets turned into my money.

Outside our gate, we could catch the ten yen bus to Yokosuka. There were a few of us that, no matter what we had planned later at night, we'd first take the bus to Watanabe's Dojo for our judo lessons. The bus ride

Solid Brass

alone was an experience. By the time it got to our gate, there was standing room only. We'd come to the next stop, look out the windows and see several more people and think, Oh no, they can't get on...but here they'd come. They would step on, bow, turn around and start backing up. This went on for several more stops. No place for a claustrophobic. No place for a pickpocket either, you couldn't get your hands in your own pocket.

Our sensei (instructor) held one of the highest belts in the world. An old gentlemen in his seventies would come to our dojo once in a while. He also was one of the top-ranked belts. When he came in, everyone would move back and sit alongside the paper wall and watch these two put on a show. It was truly remarkable to watch this elderly man move as fast as a cat.

After a good workout, a few of the Japanese guys would take us to the public bath house. These were off limits to military personnel. We wore civilian clothing and nobody cared since we were accompanied by locals. These baths were co-ed, men and women of all ages, in a very long pool made of stone.

We went to a favorite restaurant, also off limits. Put off limit by the Japanese, rather than our military. Every night we ordered the same thing, gohon and asoba (fried rice and soup). The very best. The girls who served us watched sumo wrestling on TV with a real reverence. If they were able to touch their favorite Sumo, they then would be prepared to die. They were equally enthused about seeing the Emperor. We sat at the counter facing the TV, the girls would explain all the ceremony in broken English, then giggle at something, then get excited and start talking to us in Japanese, then giggle because they did that. The same situation took place every night we were there, and I looked forward to it.

The town had a lot of little alley-sized muddy streets, with tidy little shops on both sides, and lots of bars and pachinko parlors. I can remember more than once, the military trucks rigged with loud speakers telling all Navy personnel to report back to their ships. There'd be a typhoon coming and the ships would have to get out of port and go to sea to buck the storm.

Solid Brass

On these trips to and from the Orient, we would get a few days liberty in Hawaii. On one such stop, we must have been coming back because no one had much money, we went to Don the Beachcomber's to hear the sounds of Quiet Village, played by Arthur Lyman and Martin Denny. Arthur Lyman still lives and entertains on the Islands today. The lounge was large, open-aired, thatch-roofed, and very Hawaiian. You could have a hibachi brought to your table to cook your own bamboo skewers of meat called Bora-Bora, kabob style. The famous tropical drinks with such names as Cobra's Fang, Angel's Tit, and Fog Cutter were draining our small supply of greenbacks. We decided to pool what little we had, buy one more round, and send Ace out to buy a bottle. We would just nurse our drinks while enjoying the show. Then we'd refill our drinks with the now stashed bottle under the table. Sometime early on, I got up to make a run to the john. I got a sick feeling in my stomach as I felt my foot hit something under the table followed by the sound of breaking glass. I didn't stop or turn around, but when I returned, everyone was standing up, while someone was mopping up the remaining liquid. I stayed in the men's room as long as I could, but finally had to show my face. Even with the trade winds blowing through, I could smell the liquor from the other end of the room. This was not a good night for me, but it didn't compare to what happened on another trip to town.

I was a follower of modern Jazz and blues and had heard of a place a block or so off the main drag of Waikiki, called Clouds. It was everything I'd hoped it would be, so I got there every chance I could. There was a very large Hawaiian (300 pounds or better) playing stand-up bass. He had noticed I'd come back several times and had enjoyed the music, so he would nod his head in recognition each time I came in. Finally, some of the other guys had asked where I'd been disappearing each night. When I told them, they decided to take a look. It was real crowded that night and somehow, after we were there for awhile, a fight broke out. I'm not sure how it started, but we were right in the middle of it. This was like one of those Hollywood productions, guys landing in the middle of tables, chairs being broke over heads, one guy tossed through a window, old Western style. The band was offstage when the fight got up there and somehow that bass got smashed. When the large one

Solid Brass

showed up back on stage he grabbed the first person near the remains—
Bob Worthington, my running mate. He came from Bob's back and put
a killer bear hug on him. Now Bob was a big man himself, solid muscle,
but at that moment looking like a helpless Tiny Tim. His feet dangled off
the floor by two feet. I saw this and started yelling, "He didn't do it!"
Then the large Hawaiian recognized me and seemed to let up on his grip.
Somebody jumped out the broken window and ran, so the big guy ran out
the door in pursuit. But the guy running was probably getting out
because someone put out the word the HASPs (Hawaiian Armed Service
Police) were on their way. These guys were all highly trained to handle
riots, were world famous, each one black belt or better, and they all had
big guns. With no desire to spend the night in jail, we made it out the
same window.

I've never been sure what had happened to the bass, but some twenty years later, I had a chance to talk to the big man. He was sitting down
playing a much smaller electric bass, in a jazz spot where all the good
musicians go to jam after-hours in Honolulu. He told me that his
destroyed wooden bass was a family heirloom. His whole life may have
changed that night had he caught the person who broke that old bass.

We hardly ever wore a uniform while on liberty, so no one knew the
Navy Frogs had helped destroy the furnishings of various establishments.
Wearing civies also came in handy in places like Hong Kong, where part
of the town was off limits.

While in Hong Kong, I'd seen a very old, long Chinese pipe and
knew I had to have one. There were some hustlers on the street that, for
a couple of bucks, would guide you any place you wanted to go. I asked
one particularly energetic guy if he could take me to a place to get one of
these pipes. We walked a few blocks to a giant tobacco store. Inside I was
shown new pipes, the kind you could buy anywhere. Through many minutes of translation, the man behind the counter told my guide in Chinese
where we could get such an old pipe. We went out and caught a rickshaw, went some distance to a place known as the 1000 Steps, which was
off limits to the military. We left our rickshaw and started up. At the top,
it was like stepping into a different century or at least a Bogart movie.
No more tall buildings as below, instead, a muddy street that wandered

Solid Brass

between a group of old shops and wooden buildings. A fog-like smoke filled the air from all the wood fires in the street used to cook or as just a place to stand around and warm your hands. There were many people coming and going. Everyone in traditional Chinese clothing. No western influence here as in main town Hong Kong. Most men had their heads shaved to a long single pigtail. Everyone seemed to be hurrying along with short little steps. I was certainly aware of myself, being the only round eye on the hill (as we were known in the Orient at that time). There were chickens and ducks hanging in the windows of one shop, some smoked and some just plucked and hanging by their feet. There were pigs and things I couldn't identify, hanging in other shops. Small cages of live monkeys and snakes, stacked on one corner, also to be used for someone's meal.

We came to a small store and stepped in. There was one of everything ever made, somewhere in that store. A type of used goods store. There is no way, in one day, you could have seen everything that was stacked in this place. There was a very old man behind the counter, who was tending to an incense burner sitting on a glass case full of urns and jars. I'm sure they contained herbs and powders. There were pieces of what I could identify as reindeer and rhino horn. I had heard that ground up reindeer or rhino horn is used by the Orientals as an aphrodisiac, but this was the first place I'd seen it for sale. After some Chinese conversation with my guide, the old man left to return with two very old pipes about twenty inches long. At one end of the hard thick bamboo was a brass bowl, at the other end was a tobacco-stained ivory piece. He explained to my guide there was no way to know how old they were because they were handed down through the centuries. If the bamboo would get damaged then the old end pieces would be fitted on another piece of bamboo. A very fair price was struck and the old man wrapped both pipes in old newspaper, and tied it with string.

I was to meet some of the guys in a popular restaurant in town soon after, so I bid my guide farewell after giving my guide his small fee and I headed off in a rickshaw. At the curiosity of everyone at the table, I unrolled my pipes and, of course, everyone wanted one and asked where they came from. I explained my journey and also told them if they had dates tonight, I could get them some ground rhino horn. I had obtained local dealership of this fine oriental aphrodisiac.

Whiskey Jack proceeded to tell me that the Steps were off limits for a reason. In the old Chinatown, where I'd spent the day, round eyes have been known to disappear and never heard from again. These people did not like intruders. I remembered the guide telling me he could get into trouble just being there with me.

The divers we were meeting in Hong Kong were the English version of us. Instead of Underwater Demolition, they were called Underwater Clearance Teams. We would go to a barge anchored in the harbor and use each others' equipment after an indoctrination and demo of our gear. We had a very cold reception by the UCT. It was clear they were only doing their share because they had to. They were very standoffish and cold. Kind of like they were dealing with their bastard child. As the days wore on this changed as they found out who we were and started to laugh with us. They decided we were "all right blokes." Over some ale they told us why we had such a cold reception and what their opinion was of American sailors. They said all Yanks were from Texas, drove Cadillacs, had lots of money and big mouths. So when the American sailors hit port, all the English could see was the flashing of big rolls of greenbacks. We explained that when an American sailor knew he was going to Hong Kong, he saved up as much money as possible because clothes and shoes or whatever you wanted were so cheap. I bought my first Rolex in the China Fleet Club for $72 American dollars, for instance. I still wear it today. This explained, along with a lot of laughs, we developed one hell of a bond with each other. We then told them the story of Limey Auston.

I met Limey when I got to Team 12, he was a career Frog, possibly since World War II. He had been sent to live and train with the English UCT as an instructor to teach them a few of our methods while learning some of theirs. After being there for a long period of time, it seems the U.S. Navy forgot about him. He got an American paycheck, but that was the only outside contact. He eventually started wearing UCT work-clothes. Then when his dress canvas wore out, he started wearing their dress canvas. He lived and ate with them, and of course, drank with them. One night when totally drunk in a pub, a big fight broke out

Solid Brass

between the Brits and some American sailors that were in port on liberty. As the MPs came to break up the blood fest, they all ended up in the brig. They were put in separate cells so they couldn't glare at each other, the Brits in one and the Americans in another. Limey was put in with the Brits, of course, because of his uniform. There were a lot of obscenities being passed back and forth with each group trying to out ugly the other. Finally, as might be expected, from the American cell came a blaring "Fuck the Queen." After a short silence came "Well fuck Babe Ruth."

The barge we worked off was some distance out and far from the hundreds of sandpans anchored in a nest of a sort of floating village. We were told some people were born and died on a sandpan and never stepped foot on land. Even as far out as the barge there were still things floating by that defied description. At night we would have mock attacks on the war ships. We always swam in pairs for safety, not necessarily so with the Brits. They would get in their gear after the briefing, "See you later mates," jump over the side, and make the swim alone in many cases. We jointly sank every ship in the fleet, both fleets. The flagships, the ones with the Admirals on board, were sunk again and again.

After we came back from the attacks, cold and hungry, we looked forward to the giant pot of tea that never ran out, made by our Chinese cook. He'd also whip up magic concoctions with eggs and canned Spam. The ocean was cold, so we Yanks learned to love the big mug of tea and hot food waiting for us after climbing the ladder to the deck. He brewed his tea in a giant porcelain clad iron pot that took both hands to pour, the kind used at campfires in the old westerns.

We all felt the Brits' equipment was superior to ours, in simplicity, if nothing else. One Italian rebreather we used was beautiful to look at, but was just too much gear, too many buckles and straps to put it on. The mask was large and complicated with all kinds of fitting and hoses. The Brits had a small unit UBA (Underwater Breathing Apparatus) that fit over your head like a poncho and had a lightweight mask. The poncho had one quick release buckle to hold it on and a little pouch in the back that held round lead balls that released by pulling a ring in the front, if you needed to drop your weight in an emergency. This eliminated the use of a separate weight belt such as the one we wore. We had to

Solid Brass

painstakingly take our Soda Sorb and run it through a hand sifter to remove the dust, carefully measure and pour it into a canister inside the rebreather, than button everything up before each dive. The Soda Sorb removed the CO_2 as the oxygen was exhaled back in the bag for reclaiming. The Brits opened a can of premeasured granules directly into their unit without all the dusting ceremony and they were ready to go.

All this ended too soon, we were scheduled to leave Hong Kong for other assignments, but not before the Brits threw us a great going away party. We started in the Great Hall, where we all sat around a large oblong table as the pints were delivered. First, the stories went around the table, then the jokes and songs, and finally the drinking games began. We drank and sang and learned new games born in a different country. The Prince of Wales Has Lost His Tail, Buzz, and many others. When your turn came and you screwed up, you chugged your drink. It became the Brits against the Americans, who could hang in there the longest. Already said, I was a lousy drinker, but I'd have to stay with the best of them that night, in the name of honor. Here came my turn once again, I chugged, it came right back up. I managed to stop it in my mouth and thinking nobody noticed, got up and headed for the john. After tossing my cookies, I washed up, soaked my head in cold water for a bit, slapped myself around some, and stuck my nose out the window for some fresh air.

This, for me, would usually be it for the night, but the thought of letting my country down just wouldn't do. So I headed for the Round Table and back to the other knights. I took my seat at the table like nothing happened. I looked up right into the eyes of Wiggie, my English friend sitting across from me. He filled his cheeks with air to let me know he knew. He started laughing, but didn't blow the whistle on me. We finally broke up the games, went outside, caught a whole fleet of rickshaws, and decided to visit every bar in Hong Kong, two men to a rickshaw, a Brit and a Yank. The competition continued, Bob Worthington challenged our rickshaw to race to the next bar. Those Hong Kong runners were in such good shape they didn't even break a sweat. Going down hills, to take a quick rest, they would pick up their feet and balance themselves on the bars using our weight in back as a counterbalance.

Solid Brass

Some of us stopped by the famous Pinky Tattoo Parlor, just in time to watch the finishing touches of a perfect two-masted sailing ship on the chest of a very large English sailor. It was quite detailed including all the rigging, blocks, and anchors. The small detail and so much freehand is why Pinky was world famous.

We were dressed in our Navy whites, instead of civies, because of the party and sailing in the morning. But by this time we were dressed half and half—U.S. Navy bottoms and British jumper and flat hat. The Brits had on the other half. Luckily, we didn't get spotted by the Shore Patrol, because the English wouldn't just lose a little liberty, when they get in trouble, they got fined, lost liberty and leave, and for being out of uniform in a foreign country, we'd all have gone to the brig. The last stop the rickshaws had to make that night, was the fleet landing where we caught the boats that took us back to the ship.

We felt we had known each other for years. The moment of the English and American Frog's farewell, knowing we'd probably never see each other again, left us without a dry eye on the dock. What started out as a cold beginning a few weeks ago, was now as warm as it gets between men. These are memories I have no trouble bringing to mind after some forty years.

Earlier that evening, as a going away present, our British comrades gave us all a copy of Davis's book, *Deep Diving and Submarine Operations*, which at the time was, and perhaps still is, the bible of diving.

Our ship set the special sea detail early the next morning and left the harbor with her new paint job. I don't know if they still do, but back then, when a Navy ship was in Hong Kong for a few days, the ship got the entire hull painted by Mary Sue and her girls.

Mary Sue had a series of little boats that would scull (row) to where the ship sat at anchor, come alongside, roll canvas out to protect their teak decks, the boatswain would pass several five-gallon pails of Navy gray, and the girls would move to the bow and proceed to paint the boat from stem to stern. They used paint brushes tied to long bamboo poles. They would paint around our numbers and a sailor would cut them in later. They did this in return for our garbage.

Solid Brass

Not as bad as it sounds. After each meal, as we came from the galley, we'd dump scraps in a large trash can before putting up our trays. While in Hong Kong, there would be a girl standing outside the galley with several five-gallon coffee tins. We'd hand her our loaded trays and she would carefully put the meat scraps in one can, the potatoes in another, the vegetables in another, and so on. These were later lowered to one of their boats and taken ashore to be sold in the cardboard, tin, and bamboo village. This village made up a big part of one section of Hong Kong, very visible while sailing into the harbor.

Mary Sue was known to become a wealthy lady from this enterprise. Her boats were small and very clean, as were the girls who ran them and did the painting, every hair in place and spotlessly dressed. There were several other vendors allowed to come aboard while at anchor. One man sat on deck with his portable sewing machine to do any tailoring that was needed. Another sat with his cobblers equipment, ready to half sole your shoe or do whatever shoe repair you needed. The deck was covered with people ready to offer their services, and throughout the day, there was a constant flow of bung boats coming alongside, with anything you can imagine for sale. We also used these small boats for transportation if we missed the regular boats scheduled for liberty run. I can remember several nights some of us rowing back while the boat owner sat and held a lantern.

I made port in Hong Kong several times through those early years, each time there was a new adventure. Each time something from the past to experience and stir up the imagination of a young sailor. Somewhere in Hong Kong, you could buy anything that was ever made. There were opium dens, whore houses, waterfront bars which you wouldn't dare enter alone and as we later found out, you could have someone killed for a couple of bucks. There were so many shops with beautifully carved ivory, jade, gold, silver, and precious gem pieces made to order while you waited. You could find, throughout Hong Kong, restaurants of every culture serving the finest foods to suite your appetite. A most interesting cross-culture of people and time which almost defies description.

A UDT diver making a coastal landing. *Official U.S. Navy photograph*

THREE

Abalone

Ed was an excellent diver and a very educated man, speaking several languages fluently. He should have inherited a small fortune at the age of twenty-one, but was such a horrible drunk when he wasn't working, that his mother and her lawyers kept the money and the villas in a trust. They hoped someday he would see the light. Ed lived with me and Dirty Tom, another abalone character. We lived in our beach house in Ocean Beach, fifteen minutes from Dana Landing, where we all kept our boats.

Walking in the front door, to the immediate left, was a coke bottle sticking out of the wall just above an overstuffed chair where Gene had been sitting when Nasty Ed threw the bottle. Not far from that was a spear from a spear gun that had the detachable head protruding on the outside of the house. On the right was a TV with my Mark V diving helmet sitting on it and the entire overhead was covered with a sea-bass net. As you walked ahead, favoring the left, there against the dining room wall were three twelve-gallon crocks full of green beer, and two refrigerators, filled with half-gallon bottles of beer stacked like cord wood on their side, ready to drink. Chuck Snell had furnished the crocks, bottle-capper, hydrometer, and so on, for our brewery. We had thirty-six gallons of home brew cooking at all times.

If you took a right, coming in the front door, there were two bedrooms—one was mine, and Ed and Tom shared the other. My bedroom had a nice Navajo rug hung in place of the hollow-core door that use to be there. One night Gene took off to my room, with the last of a gallon

Solid Brass

jug of fine wine. Bob tried to get in, Gene tried to keep him out and somehow they ended up with Gene's head on one side of the door, and his body, with jug in hand, on the other. John Raines backed up to the tub in the bathroom, straight across from my room and made a run for it, hit the door with a body block and took the door out in three pieces.

Inside Tom and Ed's room was a very large closet with sliding doors. Inside, stacked, from floor to ceiling, were dirty clothes belonging to Ed. Each time Ed had a meeting with his lawyers, he would, as he put it, go down and buy a new set of socks, a new set of skivvies, new shirt and pants, only to wear them until they too made the "great pile." I can still smell it.

During the foul weather, this beach-house became the party place for all the abalone divers in San Diego (or any other divers passing through). During one of these gatherings, we had just cooked up a table full of taco fixings when Nasty Ed staggered in (after several attempts to find the door). He had come from a meeting with his lawyers and afterward went out to drown in his sorrows. We headed him to the tacos, he seemed to be doing all right as he put several together. As he came into the main room where everyone was sitting, he caught his nose on the sea-bass net that had fallen from the ceiling during the party. His tacos became airborne and came to rest on top of some spilled wine, sand, and whatever was drug in onto our uncarpeted floor. After speaking to himself in one of his many tongues, he got on his knees, picked up one of the soft tortillas, placed it on the floor, like a dust pan, and pushed the splattered cheese, tomatoes and salsa back onto the tortilla. He folded it up and got half of it eaten before we could stop him and head him back to the table to make one minus the wine, sand, and debris.

Another experience involving Nasty Ed happened in Mexico. It was off-season in the San Diego abalone patch. I was fresh out of the Navy about a month or so and had already partnered up with my skin-diving friend, Les, and bought a boat. I went right from the barracks to live on the boat while we geared up for the next commercial abalone season. I got out of the Navy just as the two-month close of the season started. Our boat was at the end of the dock beyond all the other "ab" boats. I found it strange that not one of the other divers would warm up to me.

Solid Brass

I thought they just didn't want more competition. Nobody said squat. It was later explained to me by Bob Wompler, the first ab diver to say hello. He told me year after year there was always someone who hears about the "big money" to be made diving abalone. Many a scuba diver came into the business unprepared and ended up getting killed. The ab divers followed the rule of not getting to know you on a first named basis until they were sure you knew your stuff and would be around for some time. The following year, I broke the rule myself and paid the price. Bob further explained that every season in San Diego there would be as many as fifteen boats start up and by the end of the season there'd be the same old six or seven. So after I got accepted and they asked if I wanted to go to Newport with them, I jumped at the chance.

The trip to Newport was to pick up some diving gear. The abalone fleets in those days worked mostly out of San Diego, Newport, Santa Barbara, and Morro Bay. After collecting our diving gear, we all stopped at Snug Harbor to have a few horns with the local ab divers of Newport. I was the only one who didn't know everyone. These divers mainly worked the California Islands and when the red tide hit the coast, the San Diego divers would also work the Islands. A processor from Newport ran a pick up boat to the Islands every other day to buy the pickings and hauled them for 25 to 50 cents a dozen. They'd also fill and deliver grocery orders and supply ice to all the boats.

We made several more stops on the way home and with last call in San Diego, Nasty Ed said he was going to Tijuana, Mexico, where the bars are open all night. Everyone there, except me, gave a firm NO. I said I didn't think it was such a bad idea and "father-like" they proceeded to tell me if I stayed with Ed, I'd end up in jail. I knew he was getting a little rowdy and I should have thought more about how he got his nickname, Nasty Ed, but it had been a fun party day for me and I felt real good about being out with these guys. Despite all the warnings, I was in a cab and on the way to Mexico with Nasty Ed. I knew my way around TJ from all of our bullfight trips with the teams. With this trip we didn't need to leave the main drag of wall-to-wall bars. Sometime during the night, I was talking to someone other than Ed, when a local came up to tell me my friend had gone outside to fight. I had no idea how it started. I was having a good time and had just lost track of what Ed was doing.

Solid Brass

I walked outside, and standing in the middle of the street was Ed and several really pissed off Mexicans. I was wearing my favorite leather flight jacket, the one I had in high school and throughout UDT. I loved that jacket. I had stuck my ID in the pocket because I was proofed in every bar we stopped at from Newport to San Diego. It was my military ID. I carefully laid the coat on the curb before running out to join Ed's fight. At first, I seemed to be fighting everyone in town. I had one down and one weakening, when I took a hell of a shot to the kidney. When I turned around to get the back stabber, he was gone. At that point I noticed my coat was no longer folded neatly on the curb.

Nasty Ed was also nowhere in site. Someone grabbed me from behind, I swung around full of anger from the sucker shot and now really pissed at the loss of my jacket. I packed in a right punch which laid flat the arresting Policia. Before I knew it, I was looking down the barrel of a very large pistol. He never took the sights off me, even while he laid there. The look on his face told me he didn't want to hear the part about me not knowing it was the police and how sorry I was about his broken nose, which was oozing blood into his ears by now.

I was thrown into a waiting paddy wagon with some guy who hadn't seen water since he was christened. I knew all the stories about the Tijuana jail, how you never got out, as then sung by the Kingston Trio. Now here I was going to jail in Tijuana with some smelly old man who wasn't potty trained.

I got lucky, they put me in a cell by myself. Sometime later that night, they brought me into an interrogation room and the Capitan asked me why I'd hit one of his officers—the one that was down at the hospital getting his nose set. I decided to tell a short, not so true, version of what happened. Someone had stolen my jacket, I was after him when his friend sucker punched me and ran. At the same time someone grabbed me from behind so I turned around and swung, not realizing it was his officer. I told him how very sorry I was about that.

Not only did he believe me, he was going to get his "secret service" officer to take me out looking for my jacket. He called in some guy with three days worth of growth on his face along with his side kick who

Solid Brass

looked a lot like my smelly friend from the paddy wagon. Just as we made the hall on the way out of the jail, here came Ed, busting through the front door. He had a bottle in one hand, waving the other, and yelling at the top of his voice. He was shouting horrible things about everyone's ancestry and they'd better let his friend out before he'd call his people at the American Consulate.

I ran to Ed and told him to keep his mouth shut. Through clenched teeth, I told him that I was getting out if he didn't blow it. We walked outside and got into a vintage Plymouth and headed for the part of Tijuana the tourists never see. We went into the dingiest bars I'd ever seen. They all smelled like the head in a bus depot and you couldn't see one end to the other, there was so much smoke. There were questions asked each place we stopped, but no jacket.

All this time Ed was going on about the girls he fixed us up with. I figured he made these arrangements while I was out in the street fighting his fight. I let him know I'd become very sober and I didn't care what he did. I was going back to the boat, in fact, I asked the police if they'd drop my friend off and take me to the border. I no longer gave a damn about my jacket, I just wanted out.

Ed ran alongside the car trying to change my mind as I bid him "Adios." They dropped me off on the Mexican side of the border. As I passed through the gate to the American side, the MPs stopped me. One of them noticed the UDT stencil on my shirt and asked if I was in the teams. I explained I was just discharged. "Could we see your ID?" "Well, you see, my jacket was stolen and," etc., etc. "We believe your story but just come along to our office," etc., etc. I told the story again, this time to the American officer in charge. Of course, my discharge papers were in my pickup truck at Dana Landing and my ID in the pocket of my favorite jacket somewhere in Tijuana. This took another several hours. I'm sure they were detaining me to make sure I was sober before heading me back out in the world.

I gave the cab driver my last ten dollars and walked down to my boat in broad daylight and crawled into my bunk. My next contact with reality was the smell of fresh coffee. Bob was passing the mug under my nose. I opened my eyes to his knowing, we warned you, smiling face.

Solid Brass

They were right about the jail thing. I proved it twice—once in each country.

This reminds me of another run-in I had with the Mexican Policia a few years back when I was still with teams (unfortunately I couldn't blame this one on Nasty Ed). Every Saturday night was pre-bullfight night, another good excuse for a party. These parties were usually held in Admiral's Row at one of our officer's rented homes. One in particular was a very nice mansion that several of the team bachelor officers had rented in Coronado. Everything in its place and very proper, except the current inhabitants. I'll just use one person as an example; Lt. JG Dave Carse, an officer, gentleman, and friend.

Dave was a tall, muscular type with long piano fingers, which he could put to good use as a beautiful piano player or end for our football team. He was a versatile, well-spoken, refined gentleman, who dated well known socialites, could play Bach and Beethoven at will, or get drunk and shit in the Admiral's pool—as he and another phantom did. The phantom part didn't fly, because the next morning they were at poolside with their cleaning gear.

At our pre-bullfight functions, he played and sang every foul song known to man. This soft well-spoken gentleman was horrible when drinking. If, by chance, you brought a girl or a married couple came to the party, they had to be briefed about Dave before arriving.

These parties weren't just for the teams, many bullfight enthusiasts came, and many civilians. On Sunday, we'd caravan to Tijuana or at least meet at this liquor store, where the proprietor knew us and would fill our botas, beach balls, and all sorts of containers with concoctions of evil spirits, mostly Cubalebras. These were taken to the fights and consumed throughout the day.

But, one Sunday, we got stopped at the arena gate and were told no containers could be taken in. The reason (a good one) being the Sunday before, some jerk threw a beer bottle toward the arena, it fell short and hit a small girl.

So, here we were, with the day's supply of personality and we can't take it in. We had quite a bit of time before the fight began, so we

Solid Brass

formed a circle, sat on the ground just outside the gates and proceeded to solve the problem by drinking it.

It was a very hot and beautiful day as the crowd started coming in. We soon became a tourist attraction. More and more of our friends showed up and joined us as well people we didn't know who had the same problem. Pretty soon, it was difficult to move around our party, it was so big. Here came the pushcart taco stands, vendors selling blankets and pillows to sit on, jewelry and bullfight souvenirs, we had created our own mercado.

By the time we'd all moved inside and the trumpet played, it wasn't important any more, until the first bull ran in. Then we shifted into bull-fight mode. About the first casualty of our record downing of a full day's supply, was a young Coronadian, who had also been at the mansion the night before. The first bull that came running out, sent some demon to this guy's head, he jumped in the ring, pulled off his shirt and waved it directly in front of himself. The bull charged and hit him right in the middle of his body, one horn on either side and threw him up over his back. While he flew through the air, the matador distracted the bull and were able to pull this guy out of the arena. All of that and he emerged from the hospital with just a cast on one broken foot.

A fight or so after that was exceptional. The crowd was really getting excited, shouting "Ole, Ole!" with every move of the Matador. But some creep sitting in front of us kept turning and looking at us with disgust every time we yelled. He was trying to impress his girlfriend about the damn fools yelling Ole every time the bull ran by the Matador. He couldn't stand it any longer and stood up to grab at me, I was closest. I stood up, although he was bigger, I was higher, which made us even. I got off my best punch ever, which rolled him down through the people and caused quite a commotion.

There's always plenty of Policia on the sunny side, so we had them all over us in seconds. I was proud, everyone boo'd the Policia and asked for them to let me go. I was also proud they had to carry out the guy that started it all.

After leaving the arena out the front gate, there were kids everywhere watching all of this. As the Policia took me to the Paddy Wagon and opened the door, another guy I recognized from Coronado jumped up and tried to get out, laughing the whole time, trying to fit his large Mexican hat through the door. All of a sudden, I realized everyone's attention was on this guy's commotion and no one was holding or standing by me. I ducked down and headed back to the arena through the crowd. The kids standing on the rails, saw all this unfold and came to my aid. When the Policia realized I was missing, they started running around like the Keystone Cops, looking everywhere for me. The kids all crowded together and hid me in the middle, moving around the whole time. We did this until the wagon and Policia left.

Once the fight starts, the gates are closed and try as I did, could not get back in and didn't get to see the fight that Sunday. I headed back across the border to where we had R.E.'s red convertible parked. This seemed smarter than staying on the other side where the Policia were looking for me. I woke up in the back seat to the laughter of my friends and the smell of a fresh baked boleo, stuffed with fresh sliced beef and salsa. Lolly Worthington had brought it back for me. After they checked the jail and hospital they knew where I'd go after my escape.

I had a partner the first year in the abalone business, Les Davis. I knew Les several years before I got out of the Navy. We had made many skin-diving trips to Mexico. He knew when I got out of the Navy I was going to dive abalone. Les was a foreman in a fabrication shop in El Centro. He thought he'd like to make a career change and tend me. So we did a 50/50 thing on a boat, the *Mrs. D*. She was an old Navy spoonbill with too much cabin but a good work area on the back deck. It was off-season when I got out of the Navy. The ab season is closed for two months out of the year. I'd saved a little money and had my mustering-out pay, but when you start putting a diving boat together it goes fast. Les kept his job and came out to Dana Landing on the weekends to work on the *Mrs. D*.

I was living on the boat and had checked into a locker club to take showers. I had water on the boat but just a small sink. Most of my time was spent working on the *Mrs. D*, installing the dive compressor, the winch and davit to haul the baskets, and some major alterations on the house. I managed to go out on a fish boat a few times to fill in for a missing crew member, which gave me some beam money.

Solid Brass

Bill Johnson, co-owner of the San Diego Divers Supply, was a very good friend in those hungry days. I knew Bill from the Frogs, where he used to bring equipment out to the Strand every Thursday and sell to us at a super discount. During this first off-season, I'd occasionally drop by his store just to shoot the shit. Before I'd leave he'd have something to give me he thought I could use on the boat. He'd even offered to get me a job painting his ex-wife's house because he knew, without me saying, times were skinny. Before the season finally opened, I counted my change before going into a store so I didn't embarrass myself.

Another good Navy friend was Joe Bassett. We spent a lot of time together in the Navy and out. One weekend when Les came to work on the boat, he told Joe and I to come over the first of the week if we wanted a shot at making some good money. The watermelon season would be over and he knew of some fields where we could get second pick.

Joe and I headed out before first light on the long trip over the mountain to El Centro. Somewhere along the way, I got pulled over and ticketed for speeding. I couldn't argue that one. When we finally arrived, Les told us the bad news that someone else got our field. "But don't worry, I know where there's a cantaloupe field and we'll get them."

By the time we got there that desert was 110 degrees and Joe hadn't picked six melons before he went over with heat exhaustion. I'd just commented on it being too damn hot and he answered, "This is just the way I like it"...crash. We pulled him under the truck and poured what water we had all over him. When we finally got him talking again, Les put him in his pickup and headed for air conditioning. I finished filling the back of my pickup. I had to drink hot cantaloupe juice because Joe had all of our water on his shirt. Les came back with ice cold beer and helped me finish. "By the time you guys get home, all the stores will be closed, so spend the night here. We'll go frog gigging, eat dinner, and you can get an early start in the morning and sell the cantaloupe all the way home." That sounded just right.

I'd eaten frog legs a few times in my life. They seemed, for the most part, to be served in finer restaurants, which explains why I'd only eaten them a few times in those days. At times you could buy them at the San Diego Fish Market, frozen in wooden boxes, imported from a foreign country.

57

Solid Brass

I'd heard stories about frog gigging. It was something that happened in the southern states, so I was pretty excited about getting to do it right here in El Centro, California. I'm not sure if the California interpretation of gigging frogs keeps within the traditional method of the South. Our gigs were three-pronged spears. I've been told by a friend from Louisiana that the gigs used there are mechanical devices on long wooden poles used to grip the frog.

That night we loaded up the skiff and headed for the reservoir and irrigation canals. We had lights, frog gigs, beer, and a long pole to push the boat around. We must have pushed that boat for an hour before we even heard a croak. "I'll be damned, we should have had enough for dinner by now," Les complained. One hour later, "I can't figure this out, two hours and only one frog."

We poled and poled, moved to other ditches and only got three frogs for the whole night. "There's one," a whisper went up. I was poling, Les had the light, so Joe got the gig for the first time. Maybe he hadn't gotten himself together yet from his stroke, but he took a lunge at the frog and over the side he went. By the time we got him in the boat, cleaned the moss and mung off him, Les and I were laughing so hard, there couldn't be a frog left for a mile around. First heat stroke, now we had to worry he didn't freeze to death. Joe's chattering teeth were an endless source of entertainment for Les and me all the way back in the skiff.

It was time to head back. We threw our gear in the truck. Les felt really bad, he'd been bragging for months about the great frog gigging in the valley. "What's that? Stop the truck!" It was a big frog. "Now we've got four...there goes another one!" We didn't need the gigs, we were catching those fat, long-legged suckers with our bare hands (kind of like every kid does in his lifetime, but without the wart fear thing). We didn't get fifty feet when more frogs were in the lights of the truck. They were all over this old dirt road coming out of the reservoir. By the time we got to the bottom, we had two gunnysacks full. All night poling that boat and we got two sacks full in thirty minutes on a dirt road (in the lights of the truck) with our bare hands. It had been that kind of day, but we ended it with an enjoyable frog leg feed. Les's wife, Jo, cooked them up like you would good 'ol Southern fried chicken.

Solid Brass

We headed out early to beat the heat and get to the first fruit stand about opening. "Ten cents a piece, are you nuts"? "No Sir!" That's the way we handled the first couple of stands but by the time we got closer to home, that's what we sold them for, ten cents a piece. By the time we paid the speeding ticket and got gas, we had just enough money left for coffee and a hamburger.

With the boat finished, the diving gear ready to go, the abalone season finally opened. I dove abs all my life, skin diving, so I knew what they ate and how and where they lived, which was a lot of help that first year. After some months, the other divers let me in on the exclusive shell market where they sold their dark meat red abalone. The processor in San Diego preferred only the white meat reds which, after processing and packaging, appealed to the eye more than the gray or dark meats. Whereas, the shell market in San Pedro sold the abs live, without processing, and paid us $6.25 a dozen. So all the divers took turns driving them to San Pedro, a couple of hours away. Those same abs today bring over $125 per dozen. If it was your night to deliver, after a day's diving, you'd load the abs in your pickup, drive the hundred miles to San Pedro, come back and be ready to dive in the morning.

Mrs. D's house had too much surface area to be a good work boat. If the wind came up it acted like a kite and kept moving with each change of breeze. Once I was working in ninety feet in a very heavy kelp. I felt all the slack go out of my hose and then begin to drag me off the bottom through the kelp. We had the edge of our abalone iron razor sharp to cut kelp when needed. I was now cutting faster than I thought possible. Every once in awhile my hose would get enough slack so I could stand on the bottom and cut the kelp off me and my gear, only to be snatched off my feet again. The anchor wasn't just dragging now, it was off the bottom and no help what-so-ever. This went on for over an hour, and my arms were incredibly tired. I'd would just finish cutting off one mess and then get dragged into another. It was hard to believe how hard the boat was dragging me. I tried to rest my arms a moment to get circulation back and some other incredible mess would occur. I could never get my feet under me long enough to bail out, but I was still getting plenty of air. I was then drug through even thicker kelp that got caught in my quick release buckle and disconnected it. I wasn't in a position to be able to do anything about it. The belt weighed about sixty pounds and as it fell toward the bottom, it started to pull my brass mask off. It was connected to the belt by my airhose. With about 50/50 water and air, the problem now changed to extremely severe.

Through the years of diving, you prepare yourself for these kinds of problems and instinctively go into mental gear to keep control over the situation. Being a young cocky diver, I remember telling myself, "Here you are, you smart little shit. You thought nothing like this could happen to you." Finally my mask completely filled and I had just come to the end of the kelp. I started pushing to get the mask the rest of the way off, but with the belt pulling down and me not standing on the bottom, it was very difficult. Plus, I didn't have much strength left.

Finally, it came off and I started up, only to meet with another problem. I had on some new chaffing gear over my diving dress to keep it from getting worn out. The chaffing gear was acting like a sea anchor, not allowing the water to exit as fast as it was coming in. It was keeping me from getting to the surface as fast as I would have liked. In fact, for a time I wasn't sure if it was letting me gain or not. Of course, there were no fins to help because I walked.

While on the bottom, fighting and cutting the kelp, I used up all the energy a man has. But trying to get to the surface, I dug up some of that unknown energy you hear about. I broke the surface, gulping to fill my lungs to replace the air I had to dump on the way up. It had been several minutes now since I had been able to do that. I came up a little distance from the boat, and saw Les frantically trying to get the boat under control. He looked at me as if he didn't know what to say, and then he yelled "You have to decompress!" That was the next problem.

We had to get the gear up and out of the tangle and get me back in it and over the side to decompress. To someone reading this who doesn't understand the physics of diving, it probably seems strange that I'd be hurrying to get back into the water. I was on the bottom (a little off the bottom, most of the time) two or three times longer than the decompression table allows at ninety feet. Plus, you certainly shouldn't go to the surface as fast as I did. You would normally have decompression stops along the way up to combat decompression sickness, or "the bends." For the amount of time I was on the bottom, it should have taken an hour to make my stops coming up at different depths. With the drag from my chaffing gear, I still made it in less than two or three minutes. Les and I pulled as hard as we could to retrieve my gear, until the bubbles started talking to me and I had to let Les finish alone. By the time we got it up, me back into it and over the side, I had zero time to spare from the way I was feeling. We use a perch to sit on (a piece of pipe with a line to the surface) while decompressing. I sat on it, tied myself so I wouldn't fall off, and slept for the next few hours while Les pulled me to my stops.

It had been a long day and was night before we got in. In San Diego the water is fairly warm as compared to other abalone areas, so we used the lighter gear. Everyone wore dry dress with wools but I was using the wet suit I had used in UDT. At first it wasn't well received by the other divers, but later became the standard of light gear abalone diving. The divers from Santa Barbara north to Morro Bay, almost all used the warmer, more comfortable, heavy gear. That's where I'd be someday.

That first exposure came by chance rather than by careful planning. The year they lowered the size limit of the red abalone from eight inches to seven and three-quarters, opened up all kinds of possibilities. We had what we called short beds, which were large areas of abalone just short of being legal size. Every year you could go in and pull a few legals, but now the size limit change made many more legal abalone available.

One of the fleets that worked out of Newport Beach was owned by a processor, Jimmy Magg. They primarily worked San Clemente Island, where the abalone are greens and pinks. Jimmy wanted his boats to head up to the Santa Barbara Islands (where the reds are) to be ready for the size limit drop. He had a pick-up boat, the *Marko Boy*, running back and forth with fuel, groceries, and hauling the abs, so the diving boats could just stay at the Islands and work the beds.

Nasty Ed was diving one of Jimmy's boats, the *Wetback,* at the time at Clemente, and took it into San Diego instead of Newport Beach. He was going to meet his mother who was visiting from her villa in Spain. Ed was split diving with a diver named Whitey Rampage. I saw my chance here; Ed wanted to be with his mother but the *Wetback* was supposed to go north. How about Ed working with my partner in San Diego, where he'd be in every night, and me going up north with Whitey on the *Wetback*. Everyone agreed and away we went, headed for San Miguel Island.

This was incredibly exciting for me. I would be going where the famous Black Fleet and all the other heavy gear boats worked. These guys all live boated. Once dressed and on the bottom, the boats followed the diver the rest of the day. They have a three-man crew: diver, tender, and boat operator. The tender stood on the bow and used a large pole with a sickle on the end to cut kelp off the diver's hose. The operator kept the boat over the bubbles. He'd come down off the flying bridge to help get the basket of abalone up and over the bow, after the tender pulled them to the surface.

Once I saw this operation, I knew I'd have to make some changes back in San Diego. In heavy gear you couldn't just bail out of the gear if you were cut off by the boat, so the diver carried a small bottle across his hip which could be used to blow you to the surface in an emergency. The Black Fleet usually worked close together, which was a built-in safety feature.

The water here was noticeably colder, and the weather was a little more unstable than I had been used to in San Diego. The boats we used for abalone were big enough to cook and sleep aboard, but didn't have many creature comforts. So when you did your morning constitutional, you couldn't read the newspaper with your butt hanging over the rail, the wind blowing a stiff twenty knots, and the temperature in the low forties.

For the first time, I felt out of place getting in my wet suit, while the Black Fleet got into their wools and heavy gear dress. Whitey was using light gear, but with wools and a dry suit. He was one fine person to work with—very bright and had lots of interests, a real prince of a man. He was pretty set in his ways and only wanted to dive so much time and come up, if he had a good day or not. This gave me more time on the bottom, which allowed me to pick more abalone. Whitey was getting paid for claiming just his abalone, but I insisted the processor add our entire load together and split 50/50, since he gave me more time on the bottom which enabled me to pick more.

Solid Brass

Besides my normal competitiveness, I had a big desire to pick as many abalone as the other boats, to kind of defend my "Mickey Mouse" diving equipment. When I'd dive the whole day by myself, as I normally did, a lot of the time I'd put in over eight hours in the water. So there is good reason to be as comfortable as you can. This was my only time split-diving and I knew it would be close to my last as an anchor boat.

One day we were working the foul area of San Miguel, when I got three sharp pulls on the hose, followed quickly by three more frantic pulls. That's the signal to come up. I worked my way back to the boat and climbed the ladder. Whitey pointed to a pod of killer whales coming

Herb Harris being tended by Willie Stratton with Greg Pratt in wet suit looking on. *H. Harris photo*

Solid Brass

very close. I've never left the water for sharks, but when the killers are near the boat, we give them some time alone. I never worried about them on a one-on-one basis, but their eating habits made me anxious. If they started feeding in the area and got into a feeding frenzy, I'd be concerned. Laddy Handelman was diving just a little further up the island toward Castle Rock, so we headed over to tell them.

Lad came up and sat on deck. His tender was Herb Harris who, twenty years later, was to be my best man. Lad's operator was Willie Stratton, who eventually became my tender for more than thirty years; we three were meeting for the first time. I had met Laddy before, his brother Gene, was one of my running mates in San Diego. Laddy has since become a very good friend and we went on to do many projects together in the commercial diving business. But that day we just sat on our boats and watched the orca doing just what we worried about. They were circling in front of Castle Rock, which is a sea-lion rookery. One killer would take off straight at the rock, slide up half out of the water onto the

rock, create an enormous wash while thrashing from side to side and knock most of the half grown seals in the water. The other circling whales moved in. The stronger and larger seals managed to climb higher, briefly delaying the inevitable. The air was filled with the sound of barking seals and waves crashing across the rock. Over and over they continued this pattern, until there were no seals left on the rock and the water boiled frothy red. Then suddenly everything was still. The whales had their fill and were on their way, leaving the sea birds to pick through the untidy mess they left behind. I couldn't help feeling bad about the seals, but at the same time couldn't help being in awe about how efficiently the whales went about their task. I think you feel less of an intruder of the sea the more you are allowed to witness these marvels of nature.

I'll leave the Santa Barbara Islands for a moment to tell another tale of the orcas that happened the following year. I was live boating off of

Laddy Handelman and Kevin Lengyel getting ready to head down off the California Coast. *K. Lengyel photo*

Solid Brass

San Diego, my boat (which I will describe later) was designed to enable one man to operate and tend. We both made more money that way. We still didn't have phones and I was using light gear, working fairly deep for reds. I had just set down my full basket and had moved over to look under a ledge, when I got the signal on my hose to come up. I started back to get my basket and just before I reached it, got another signal and simultaneously was pulled right off the bottom. All the time I was pulling trying to reach my basket of reds. Jim was a very big and strong individual and he was pulling me off the bottom with everything he had. He actually pulled me out of the water and half way up the ladder. With my mask set face down on the gunnel Jim released the spider to get me out of of it. I raised my head to start yelling about the basket I just left on the bottom, but instead I looked across the bow at the largest dorsal

Solid Brass

fin I had ever seen. It was a big bull killer whale. He blew and sounded, seemingly to avoid hitting the boat, right down on my bubbles that were still coming up. I looked at Jim, who was now a sickening, pasty white color and trembling with fear. Fear, not for himself, but the certainty of me being on the menu. After the long suspenseful sounding, the bull surfaced so close that it blew water into the boat. He then swam out to join the cow and calf that we had a watchful eye on while we waited for his reappearance. We watched as the calf would build up speed, come clear out of the water and fall to one side repeatedly as they headed away from us, up the coast and out of our area.

Jim told me he had been bent over measuring abs when he looked up and saw the whales. By that time, they were already too close and heading right toward my bubbles. That's when he decided I needed to be off the bottom. By the time the show was over and Jim got his composure back, I had to go back in the water for a short decompression. But not before I went back to look for my basket of three dozen or so reds. I took an empty basket and picked more while I was looking, until my time was up at this depth. I didn't find my other basket until a couple of days later when Gene Handleman found it and gave it back to me—EMPTY!

We had an excellent trip at San Miguel, but the weather was getting real snotty, so every one headed for Santa Barbara Harbor. I had learned a lot of little boat tricks while we were out. Whitey had been at sea many years and didn't mind sharing his knowledge. He'd spent time in Santa Barbara before and knew his way around. He knew of a Swedish sauna that an old boat builder had in his boat yard. So, once safely moored up in the harbor, we headed for the Lindwall's Boat Yard. Charlie Lindwall was an interesting old guy, a little hard to understand at first. His tongue was cut out during the war, before immigrating to this country. Little did I know that fifteen or some years later one of his sons would be one of my partners on a large crane barge. Charlie's boats were very famous in the fishing fleet, he built mostly large wood fishing boats. There are still some out fishing today. After a long time spent in the sauna, we headed for a watering hole. Not an original thought, the place was packed with divers.

Solid Brass

The laughter and stories were out of control. One of the stories told that night is worth repeating. Jerry and some guys were headed for his house to continue a party already in progress. They were in Jerry's yellow Cadillac convertible when they spotted a goat staked next to a barn. They decided that's just what they needed for their barbecue that night. They were able to drive right up to it, pull the stake out of the ground, and throw it and the goat into the trunk. They pinned a twenty dollar bill on the barn and drove off. They got out on the freeway and headed home. They had driven a couple of miles up the road when the flashing red light appeared behind them. Jerry pulled over. "I'd like to talk to you boys about that goat back there." "What goat?" "The one you're dragging behind your car." It seems the goat they threw in the trunk was chained to another goat they hadn't seen, the one now being dragged down the highway.

I was later to dive abalone again with these guys, as well as the oil patch, but for now, I had to go back to San Diego to our boat. Ed would go back out with Whitey. We had been having a good season in San Diego, but red tide came in and stayed. Red tide being a plankton which is so thick that it actually cuts out the sunlight in the water so you can't see. The weather can be perfect for diving but you can't work. So eventually we were forced to go to San Clemente Island to work. I didn't mind at all, this was another adventure for me, being single, but for Les, it was a long time away from his family.

The Islands were great. Clear water to dive and just a nice place to be in a boat. The first day out was usually a meat run. We'd go on the island and shoot goats, hang them in the rigging for a couple of days, then have some great barbecue. Bob Wompler's tender was watching one goat that had his rear end out of view. He thought by the way she was humped up she was taking a dump. He fired and went down to get his goat, only to find she had just given birth to twins. He brought them out in the skiff, not knowing what to do. Les and I had the biggest boat, so we took them on board. We cut the finger out of a rubber glove and fit it over a wine bottle, warmed some milk, and became Godparents.

You'd think we were feeding them a bale of hay a day, for the amount of crap they bestowed on us. They crapped on every square inch of the

68

Solid Brass

deck and when that was covered, they jumped up to the next level and crapped there, too. On the table, the radio, everywhere.

I slept in the bottom bunk and the first night I was up a dozen times giving them milk. Thirty minutes would go by and they'd *bahh* again. Finally, I stuck my hand down to stroke them, each one grabbed a finger and started sucking. I finally got some sleep.

When we got in from this trip, Nancy Handleman was the adopting parent, because they were "so cute." They were so cute until they were tall enough to walk in her house and eat the drapes.

I worked at driving Les nuts about live boating and looking for a better boat. I explained how this would make us money and save us money, etc. We started hitting all the docks in San Diego, reading out-of-town papers, boat magazines, etc. We went about our business, but my free time was spent looking for another boat. One day, we thought we'd recheck a dock in San Diego for new sales, and there she was. There is such a thing as love at first sight. My Fairy Godmother must have done this, she was perfect. She was about thirty feet, planked hull, bow loader, cabin in the back, every fastening was brass or stainless, and she was in perfect repair. There'd be a few things we'd have to add to make it a diving boat, but no major changes. We got a hold of the owner of the *Prima Donna*, an old Italian fisherman, who turned out to be a perfectionist. He built the boat himself for gill net fishing the Sacramento River in California. When the river was closed to commercial fishing of this type, the state was obliged to buy the fisherman's boats or they could sell them themselves. Since he lived in San Diego, he just ran his boat home and put it up for sale.

The boat had steering and a throttle in the bow right where we needed it. We ran a linkage up there so we could put the transmission in and out of gear. She had an open bow, so you were standing on the bottom of the boat. It had to be bailed out with a pump, so we put in a beautiful self-bailing deck. The watertight compartment in front of the house built to house the gillnets, was a perfect spot for our compressor. We put a small hand crank winch, made especially to fit our starboard side, next to the wheel and in front of the diving ladder. It spooled one quarter-inch stainless steel wire. We could lower a hundred-pound ball to about ten feet off the ocean floor with it. On my way down on a dive, I'd snap my hose into the ball. The snap was set about twenty-five feet from me which gave me slack on the bottom. A tender could then pull the slack up and tie it off, making it impossible for the hose to get back in the wheel, where it could get cut off. With all this completed the *Prima Donna* was a dive boat, ready to go live boating.

Archy Fox and Corky bought the *Mrs. D.* from us, and the old girl launched another abalone diving career. There was some reservation about the lead ball trick from some divers, but from the first day out, it was a success. And anyone could see how much more bottom I could cover and how much more time I'd have on the bottom. This year we were the only boat doing this on the coast, but the next off-season found several boats rigging up lead ball systems. But now we were still dealing with red tide, so we motored back to San Clemente.

With the pickup boat coming out every other day, I wanted to have a minimum of a hundred dozen abs on the boat. Sometimes we'd have almost twice that amount. I took Les to the area we dove when I was a Frog in training. We had a hundred dozen day in that spot alone. I couldn't help flashing back to us rushing to fill our rubber rafts with more abs than the other boats, only to be filling the instructor's freezers. With the water so clear at the Islands, the beauty of the ocean floor jumped up at you as soon as you headed down. There were the ever-present kelp beds, and the hundreds of different kinds of bottom growth, long waving eel grass, and more colors than there are names for. There were so many fish, they became a problem. The female Sheep Head would stick her buck teeth through your basket and with one good bite, make an abalone unsellable. So you had to pack the abs "shell out" most of the time.

I did see one of the largest sharks I've ever seen at Clemente. I was working behind a reef when I had that feeling something was watching me. I looked up and coming my way was one hell of a big shark. He looked to be a blue, but I couldn't be sure. He swam a course that was directly at me. The closer he came, the bigger he got. When I was well in his vision, he slowed down, but never changed course. Finally, he got close enough to see he didn't want my company and turned and swam away at a much faster pace.

Solid Brass

The harbor seals used to swim in kind of slow, make a few passes, then lay on the bottom not too far away and watch with those big liquid-filled eyes of theirs. The sea lions would come in faster and do a lot of fancy maneuvers around me and I always looked forward to these. Well, almost always.

I had just stood up with my bag after working a ledge when a very large sea lion came swooping by with her mouth open. She made a quick turn and came closer again with her canines bared. She now had my full attention and I watched her go just about out of sight and then back she came. This time she was so close the claws on her fins caught up in my basket and tore it from my hands. I dropped it just in front of me. At this point, I used the disconnect at my mask to release the whip that went to my bail-out bottle to give her a big blast of bubbles when she came back.

This time she went up for air, came back down in front of me, picked a ball off a kelp leaf with her mouth, spit it out, and charged me again with fangs bared, blowing bubbles through her throat. It was as if I told her to give that kelp a try and she didn't like it. I gave her 2200 pounds of air bubbles, but that just slowed the charge. She moved a little but the bubbles didn't have the effect I wanted. It was getting harder to stay away from the teeth and hooks in her fins. Just the brisk commotion of her swimming around me was knocking me about like an inshore tidal action.

This went on long enough that I knew there wasn't going to be a happy ending unless I got off the bottom. I started pulling in my slack and walking under the lead ball very slowly. The next time she goes up for air, I'm going to climb my hose as fast as I can. I had noticed there was a little delay when she surfaced, until she got back on bottom. I didn't want to get caught half way up. My chance came and up I went, unsnapping my hose as I passed the lead ball.

When I climbed the ladder, Les was standing there with a 30/30. It seems those delays on her coming back down was because she was circling the boat, baring her teeth and barking at Les. We didn't have phones then, so he could only guess what was going on below and was getting ready to shoot her. Even after I was aboard, she continued to circle and bark at us. It was getting late anyway so we decided to head back to our anchorage. We had only gone a hundred feet or so, when we spotted a dead seal pup floating in the kelp bed. We weren't sure if she was still trying to protect it or was full of grief, but we now understood what caused her unusual behavior. We were glad Les hadn't shot her.

It was an eight-hour trip from San Diego to San Clemente for us in our slow boat. We didn't have ship-to-shore radio or any navigational equipment. A compass was about as sophisticated as we got. I know now how lucky we were to make the crossing as many time as we did, without incident.

The worst thing to happen that first year was extremely unfortunate. There was a little boat half way down the dock that everyone had to pass as they went to and from their boats. She was getting rigged up to go diving by some scuba divers that had heard there was money to be made. One night the friendlier of the two came to the *Mrs. D*, which I was still living on, to talk. He knew his partner was a know-it-all and wouldn't listen to anyone. I told him what any diver walking down the pier would tell them; the exhaust on the engine was too close to the intake on the compressor. He came down several nights to talk diving. He told me they were about to go out to work and he was a little nervous.

Solid Brass

The morning after they went out we came to the dock to face his family. They asked if we would go out and look for his body. It seems they were anchored up where none of us were working, he was on the bottom and passed out from carbon monoxide. His partner pulled his mask off trying to get him up.

Sometime later the Coast Guard came out, buoyed that spot, then took the boat in tow. It was Les's anniversary, so we told him to go home and I'd go with Bob on his boat along with Rex and we'd make the search. On the way out Bob pointed out how I broke the "don't get to know him" rule. Rex drew the short straw and made the first dive. After only ten minutes down, he hooked the body to the basket line and we brought it on board. On the way in, I only hoped his family wouldn't have to see what happens to a human body after spending the night on the ocean floor. Other than that, we had a good first year, especially it being our learning year. But Les decided it was too much time away from his family and he'd find something else to do. Jo, his wife was teaching and they liked where they were living, so they decided to stay in San Diego. I bought Les' half of the *Prima Donna* and the coming season I'd hire a tender and be on my own.

Off-season is spent working on your boat and equipment, hauling out and painting the bottom, etc. You need to fix all the little things you didn't do all season because you don't want to take the time off. Gene had a sheet steel mask, which someone did a good job making, but it would always be a big ball of rust. Gene was famous for not taking care of his gear. A small petcock valve broke off one day, which wasn't something he used anyway, so he took a pencil that was about the right diameter, drove it in the hole and busted it off. He dove many days like that. Off-season, he said he was taking the mask down to be metal sprayed with zinc, then it would never rust again. When he brought it back it looked beautiful painted all shiny silver, but it still had the busted pencil stuck in the hole. No doubt, if he still has that mask today, you can bet the pencil is still there.

Gene, Bob, and I had talked about going to San Diego Bay to dive for brass for a few days so we could make a few bucks off-season. We got a permit to dive under the NEL (Naval Electronic Labs) docks.

Solid Brass

Everywhere else in the bay, we'd just help ourselves, depending what ship was away from their buoys. For instance, one of the sub tenders had left the nest with all the subs, so we went out and jumped the area. We took turns diving, tending, and running the boat. We found a pile of fire nozzles as big as our boat. Evidently, they were swinging a full cargo basket and lost them overboard. We spent two days picking brass fire nozzles. The bay was muddy and after walking the bottom for a time, you couldn't see anything, so we carried a magnet. If we walked into something, we'd put the magnet to it, if it didn't stick, we'd send it up.

After unloading our biggest load at the junkie's, where we got paid in cash, we decided to go to my friend, Tiz's bar, and have a few horns. Tiz from the teams and his wife, Bobbi, a delightful lady, owned several bars in San Diego. Tiz, right away let everyone at the bar know we were his friends. We would normally have been known as honkeys. We had a hell of a time. Huey, another Frog, and formerly one of our instructors, came by and we had a few more horns. On the way out, Huey's car was just outside the door. It was a very small car, so we thought it a good idea to put it on the sidewalk, between two signs. We got help and lifted it up and moved it. We were still laughing as we walked to my pickup, when a car with three very large guys slammed on their brakes, jumped out, and started running at us. The one running at me was big enough, so I knew I had to get the first move in. I caught him in the gut as he rushed me. I stepped aside as he hit the sidewalk and immediately jumped on top of him with both knees. Someone yelled, "Cops!" and the three of them were up and running. Gene was holding his mouth and running after them.

Personally, I was glad they were gone. I looked at Bob and said "What the hell was that all about?" Bob shrugged his shoulders. The police were asking us the same thing when Gene came back. "Aren't you going after them?" he asked, "Look, they split my lip." One officer got a first aid kit from his patrol car and worked on Gene's lip. "Aren't you going after them?" he insisted. "No, you boys are in the wrong neighborhood." We got in our truck and drove back to the boat. It wasn't until twenty-some years later did Bob admit to me, he flipped them the bone. He saw them before we did and said they were giving him the bad eye

Solid Brass

because we were in their territory, so he produced the finger. We gave Gene light duty the next day while he mumbled (through his split lip) more complaints about nobody going after those guys who punched him.

I'd heard some years before that there was a lot of brass under the mothball fleet. The story went that when they changed screws or totally removed them, the divers would back the nuts off and put a couple wraps of primer cord in front of the screw and blow it off, letting it fall to the bottom. It seemed like a worthwhile rumor so we headed for the back bay. After arriving, it looked OK, so we eased in running the little dive boat between two piers. There was so much on that bottom, we had a line on one piece of brass and hands on another when the U.S. Navy arrived in force. No less than three jeeps and two cars, even guys on bicycles, all with sirens and red lights flashing. Each one had a gun aimed at us. We were invited to come on the dock and introduce ourselves—at gun-point! It was very hard to explain how we missed all the security signs every ten feet coming in. For quite some time, we were in deep shit. They put us AND our boat through a thorough check. We showed our permit to dive at NEL, and after several hours of interrogation, were allowed to leave. We were not invited back.

Gene's lip wasn't getting any better and we did have work to do on our boats, plus we made a few bucks, so we headed for Mission Bay to our own docks at Dana Landing. We were fairly certain there would be a Navy patrol boat on our tail until we left anyway.

The off-season before, sometime between the great frog hunt and the start of the season, we did some other off-season work. Someone brought a gallon jug of wine to the boat (one gallon because two gallon jugs weren't made). We were sitting on the back deck, when Les came down the dock to tell us the boat in front of us was sinking. Everyone stood up and took a look, and sure enough, it was. Now this boat had been sitting in that slip for months. Nobody ever came down to pump it out or start it or even look at it. It had bottom growth at the waterline a foot long, so everyone thought it must be heavily insured and they were just waiting for the day—and here it was.

The boat had to have had something just let go and start the rush of water coming in. We would have spotted it earlier if it was going down slowly.

Solid Brass

It was down to where we knew the engine was under and everything in the house was ruined. The damage was done, but had we run down the dock, we probably could have gotten a pump in her and kept her afloat. But then they wouldn't have needed a diver, so we had Les walk down the dock to tell someone to get a pump down here. Before he left we talked it over:

"We should get someone down here."

"Yeah, at least see if there's someone in the yard."

"Actually, take another look at the boat."

"Actually, all the damage is done."

"Yeah, that's true."

"The cantaloupe money's all gone."

"So's the frog legs."

"Take another look at the boat."

"Well, if we need the money or not, we can't just watch a boat sink, not men of the sea."

"That's true, I'll head up there now," taking one more hit of the wine, Les looked back several times and when she was on her last few bubbles, turned, and ran up the dock.

"Anybody seen Betty, Howard, or Tom? There's a boat sinking at the end of the dock." Betty, in the office, gave us the name of the insurance company. We called, explained we had a boat with gear on it, right there at the dock so we wouldn't have to charge for mobilization, then struck up a price and he'd be here first thing in the morning.

We located some fifty-gallon drums, welded some bails on them, and pulled our anchor chains out to use with the fifty-gallon drums. Now we were ready for the big salvage job in the morning. Bob and I both dressed in our gear, the insurance guy would stand on the dock to protect us, so the owner couldn't say he had hundreds of dollars worth of stuff on board that was taken. Good idea. Of course, if there was anything we wanted on this old tub, we could have set it on the bottom and got it later. We both jumped in to flood the drums until they laid alongside the bow. Then we worked together to chain them securely to the bow and two more drums at midship. After filling the drums with air, she just started to lift at the bow but not quite enough. This was a heavy old steel boat,

with who knows how much weight in barnacles and mussels. It did have
a beat up old wash deck, so we stuck the air hose under it and tied it off.
She slowly started to rise, a short time later, she broke the surface. We
threw a hose from a salvage pump we had sitting on the dock and soon
we got ahead of the water coming in. The insurance guy threw in a little
extra money for us to tow the boat over to the launch ramp, and put it on
a trailer. He was a nice guy. After we completed the job, he wrote us a
check, thanked us, and was on his way. The boat was quite a sight out of
water with enough shellfish on it to feed a small village.

That first off-season, Bob and I would go to the back bays of Ocean
Beach and shoot brant, as another source of food. Although brant look
like a small honker (Canada Goose), they don't taste like a honker. After
they've been feeding on the coast for awhile, they taste like fish. Mary,
Bob's wife, was an excellent cook and she did some tricks to disguise the
taste. I love seafood, but something you pluck feathers off, shouldn't
taste like tuna.

Our brass and salvage operation were all we did to support our
income that off-season. We had to finish work on our boats now and get
ready for opening day. The season started off a lot like the last ended,
lots of red tide. Like I said before, I like working San Clemente after the
eight hours to get there, but there were other problems. Some of the
processors that we sold to in Newport, took forever to pay. Sometimes
the checks bounced. Out at the Islands for weeks at a time, we couldn't
check the poundage, when they gave us some story about why our load
didn't pound out good. While I was out, I had one processor send my
checks to my bank in San Diego to be deposited in my account. After a
month's diving, I came back to San Diego and bounced checks all over
town. The processor hadn't sent one check. They were running their
business on our money. One shop was full of druggies, or as we called
them, loadys. Everyone in the crew seemed to be high most of the time.
Once when the pickup boat came out, this one really strung out guy
jumped on my boat after I'd tied up. "Hey man, Pat sent you this little
present," he said, with kind of a shit-eating grin. "What is it?" "I can
only guess, man." I walked around deck, while I was unwrapping the
plain brown paper on the box, this guy followed me around like a puppy.

Solid Brass

The longer I took, the more anxious he got. When I finally opened the box, you couldn't believe the disappointment that registered on his face. It was a "Peter Warmer" (I believe that's what it was called). The description and directions on the box were for the man who hunts and fishes (she had penciled in "divers") to keep it warm without holding it in your hand all day. It was colorful and knitted out of wool, with two little draw-strings. This guy thought for sure, that box was full of dope.

There were a lot of colorful people who worked the Islands, with boat names like Fuzzy Cup, Sea Daddy, Fort Mudg, Wetback, Awabi Maru, and A.W. Grub. Not to mention characters with names like Weisel, Lurking Larry, Flippy, and others. There was Bobby Gill, a known drug-user. Before he became a druggie, he was a good diver. I was pulling into Seal Cove one night, Bobby's boat was already at anchor and all you could hear bouncing off the rock walls was the sound of a well-played trumpet. Being a jazz fan myself, I knew this had to be a top horn man. Sure enough, it was Chet Baker, recognized as one of the best jazz trumpet players in the sixties. He'd come out on a trip with Bobby. I went to sleep that night with the soothing sounds of Chet Baker's jazz trumpet— live. Some months later, Bobby was found dead in a Mexico City hotel. The coroner's report stated that it was an apparent overdose.

I had a tender wake up one night with an impacted wisdom tooth. He could hardly stand the pain. We had an eight-hour boat ride to take him in. I went by Bobby's boat for a pain killer. The best he had were "Bennies" he made himself from Benzedrine powder and Nestle's Chocolate.

Then there was this guy they called Flippy. I'd never met him, he was always somewhere else when we worked the Islands. He used to dive out of a skiff. He had a box on board that he slept in if it started to rain. He'd just pull the cover over himself. This was known as Flippy's coffin—and it almost was. Flippy used to work fairly deep and didn't pay much attention to the tables, so he'd get bent now and then. One night when he didn't show up for the pickup boat, they went looking for him. They spotted his skiff and inside Flippy was lying in his box. He'd been bent real bad this time and he couldn't see. They moved him to Wilson Cove and got him to a Navy decompression chamber. He didn't get his eyesight back for a while, but did eventually. After that, Flippy went to work in the family brokerage firm.

Another bad bends case that happened before I started working the Islands, was Rolly Thompson getting hit real bad while on deck after a dive. They put him back in the water to treat him. Whitey Stefens was on his boat and called the Coast Guard. The nearest chamber was in Willmington, so the Coast Guard flew a seaplane out and took Rolly on board. Whitey told them not to fly very far off the water or it would kill him. So they knocked the top of the waves off all the way across the channel.

One of the more memorable barbecues at San Clemente involved cooking albacore instead of goat. The day before I had taken some large bull lobster to the St. Christopher, where Weasel was working. The next night at the same anchorage, they brought us over some large albacore. We cut those suckers into hibachi-sized pieces and cooked them until they turned from clear to white. It was as good as any fish we'd ever eaten. We were tied in a nest of three boats. I had my small portable radio on the stern as well as the hibachi. After everyone turned in, some-time during the night, the boats swung and one of the stern lines knocked everything off the stern into the water. In the morning, when this was discovered, I put on my mask and jumped over the side (skinny dip style, which will wake you up without coffee). We were anchored in forty feet of water and it was so clear, I could see the radio and hibachi as soon as I left the surface. Once on deck, we ran freshwater through the radio, and as a joke, before it was even dry, I turned it on and it played!

After all the laughter was over, we decided to work the lee side because it was too rough around the island to go out that day. Rolly said he wasn't going out, so he would dry the radio for us. When we came in that night, we found he had melted the radio beyond recognition. He had put it in the oven and forgot about it. When he handed it to me, with a smile (a smile that turned to laughter), I turned the melted knob and the damn thing started to play. I was always going to tell GE about the radio that spent the night in 40 feet of saltwater and then sat in an oven until it melted only to continue to play sweet music for us out at the Islands. That would have made a good commercial.

Solid Brass

When I think back on how we use to cross from San Diego to San Clemente, from San Clemente to Newport in those small ab boats, no radios, not much in the way of survival equipment, it's hard to believe we were really that stupid. A few times we had to put our abalone on the bigger boats, as we ran from a storm that even the big boats had no business being out in. Later, my bigger boat served the same purpose at other islands. We would try to cross in numbers during bad storms. We wouldn't be able to see each other for long periods because the sea was so big the other boats would only come into view at intervals.

Finally, we tried to stick it out in San Diego. We couldn't let the red tide beat us. It almost did. Gene and I had made a trip in the past to see his brother Laddy in Santa Barbara. I enjoyed this trip, up again where the big guys were, but one day Gene just shipped out of town on his boat and we eventually found out he'd gone to Morro Bay, where the Black Fleet had all gone to pick abalone. Gene had been told to keep it quiet. My curiosity got the better of me, so I jumped in my pickup and headed north to find out what was happening. It didn't take long to see they were all doing quite well picking reds and getting twice to three times the money—and no red tide. Like I said before, we almost waited too long. I was damn near broke, but I got my boat ready and stored all my things in a rented garage. No one else from San Diego would be going and I would miss them all. Bob and I were like brothers, lots of good times. I would be seeing more of Chuck Snell as he would be stopping by my place in Morro on his way to his mother's in Humboldt County. I wouldn't see Sulley and my old teammates for sometime. Sulley was still in the teams and a very close friend. He was a career Frog and lived just a few blocks away in Ocean Beach. The locals called his home "Father Flannigan of Beacon Street," because of his large family. Kay somehow managed all nine kids while Sulley would be away on maneuvers. We used to surf together and eventually fixed him up a nice little Monterey hull. I gave him my compressor I bought from Red Doyle and Sulley was ready to dive commercial abalone on weekends. Sulley had a way about him that commanded attention. Once while I was away, there was a long-term party going on at my beach house. Sulley went over looking

Solid Brass

for me, he told everyone to clean up the damn place before I got home and made sure it was done before he left.

It was difficult for me to leave, emotionally. Also, Morro would open a whole new way of life for me. An old fisherman I knew told me before I left to be careful when I got to Point Conception. "Just stick your nose around the point and if there's any wind at all, spend the night at Government Point and continue on early the next morning," he warned. "Then after Conception, it's a whole new ocean."

I spent the night plotting course on the new charts I had bought. I had a friend drive my pickup, loaded with my personal gear, up to Morro Bay and my tender, Jim, and good friend, Archy Fox and I headed up the coast in the *Prima Donna*.

We had plenty of food and the weather was good. The company was superb, lots of laughs and something new to see every day. Archy had a crazy sense of humor so there was never a dull moment. We'd chase sharks and sunfish at times and had a good show from all the porpoise that seemed headed our way. The day finally came when we had to stick our nose around Point Conception and as promised the seas changed, the swell grew and the wind picked up 20 knots, so we found Government Cove and spent the night.

We headed out at first light and found our compass had taken a dump, so we headed for the next point. We came into Avila with carb trouble. We cleaned the carburetor and spent the night. Early the next morning we headed out, next stop would be Morro Bay.

Everything seemed changed after Conception; we were even seeing sea birds we'd never seen before. The lobster didn't exist some distance past the point and the pink and green abalone also stop somewhere in the same area. The reds were the only abalone picked commercially. We had monkey and wolf eels in Morro, which we didn't ever see in San Diego and we didn't have a lot of moray eels in Morro like we had in San Diego. And the weather in San Diego generally is the same when you come in as it was when you went out in the morning, with some exceptions, of course. But, past Conception, you can go out in no wind, glassy conditions and by noon it can be blowing forty knots with five-foot seas.

Solid Brass

We arrived in Morro Bay in the afternoon. We stuck close to some pretty rugged coastline since we lost our compass. About an hour after arriving in Morro the fog came in and stayed. What unbelievable luck. Without a compass, out in the fog, along a coast loaded with large wash rocks and rock beaches in unfamiliar territory, no telling what might have happened. The sea has been good to me.

The man who ran the commercial dock where I tied up for the first few weeks in Morro, to my surprise, was Red Doyle. He was the retired pilebutt, heavy gear diver I had bought my first Mark V heavy gear and

Solid Brass

portable compressor from in San Diego. The one I gave to my old buddy Sulley. Small world.

I remember Bob Wompler and I going to Red's house to look at his gear after we raised the boat at the dock. We had cards made up and figured we would get some commercial work, for extra income, while we dove abalone. Red told us to forget all the glory crap about commercial diving, it was just dirty hard work. How many times that proved out!

Coming into Morro Bay had something else to get use to. It ran like a river here, something else you didn't have in San Diego, with a very swift current. The fog letting me get to Morro before it came in wasn't my only good luck. We got a few good days diving before the weather set in which provided the money to pay for a place to rent. With two guys on the boat, the boat had two bunks on either side of the engine, I'd go down to Morro Rock and sleep in the back of my pickup. The rock didn't have all the tourists visiting it then. It only had one dirt road going out to it at that time. Finally, I got a small motel room, it was so old, the hot water heater was in two parts. Half was outside on the weather side of the house. I had one army cot for a bed. Later, I heard of a house for rent, next to the oyster plant. It became home for a while.

It was a big clean home with hardwood floors. It was old, the backyard went off down a hill and so did the septic tank pipe. The top half of the pipe was rotted out and above ground. If you flushed the toilet and ran to the back window, you could watch your load heading down the hill, which was always good for a laugh. The house was just above the bay, which was a real plus. The shower had a little toweling off area that used the same drain as the shower. I had a hook in the ceiling of this area to hang deer. I had a big tree in the back to hang deer during the hunting season, but during hard times you shoot a buck when you need one, not just during the season. I remember one year, when money was tight for some older people we knew, another diver, my very good friend and hunting partner, Kurt Berger and I filled several freezers. We used to get two deer tags, so if Kurt and I filled out one, that gave us two deer to give away. We would also get the two deer for the old folks that could buy a license, give them one and give the second deer to someone that couldn't afford a license. I'm not trying to sound like Robin Hood, we just enjoyed the hunting, and it was a good bail-out for some poor people.

One year we snuck into Hunter Liggett Military Reservation. Kurt, another friend, and myself. An hour after first light, we had five legal bucks in the trunk of Kurt's old turtle back Plymouth. We hadn't gutted them yet, because the military police were right behind us. Finally we started down an old dirt road, that would have been scary on horse let alone this bald-tired old Plymouth. We not only had to get away, but had to clean our deer soon. After several miles on this steep, windy road, at the edge of nowhere, we might have had to clean our pants also. The loose sand and dust on a very steep downhill, sometimes just free-wheeling with no control, was just like driving on ice. I had a picture in my mind of the five very crowded deer bloating and blowing the trunk lid off. The hill led us right down to the Coast Highway just near Jade Cove. We'd usually clean our deer as soon as we got to them, except for that night and one other.

We'd been hunting on a ranch that I had a special permit to enter. It hadn't been hunted in forty years. We really brought some big bucks out of there. One day, for some reason, Kurt didn't get his and when we were driving down the road from the ranch, in the dark, a huge forked horn jumped in front of us. Kurt jumped out and shot him. He was hit, but didn't fall dead, instead he took off running and ran right on the porch of a nearby farmhouse. A wooden porch with about a cord of nicely stacked firewood up against the house. Kurt and I were tripping over the wood that was everywhere but in the pile by now, trying to get the deer off the porch. It was like a Portuguese bullfight. His horns on both sides of me, while I hung on to his neck trying to pull him down, rodeo-style. Before we finally captured him, all the lights in the house went on. We managed to grab him, throw him in the pickup, and get the hell out of there. Those people are probably still trying to figure out what happened on their porch that night.

About forty-five minutes down the road we stopped by the Whale Rock Dam turn off to clean our deer. We were working in the headlights when a car came by, stopped for a minute and then continued on. When we finished and drove to the bottom of the hill, the only way back to Morro Bay, there was a sheriff's car. He stepped out in his bathrobe and slippers

Solid Brass

and walked over to us. We knew him, we'd seen him around town. He said he was sorry to stop us, but he'd gotten a call about some poachers at Whale Rock Dam, cleaning a deer. Well, we couldn't tell him it was us, how could we explain, doing that so late. We told him we'd been at the ranch, showed him my permit, and were just getting home with our two deer. He looked in the back at the two large bucks and from where I was standing, I could see the liver lying in the back, still smoking. If he looked there, we were goners. He said, "I can tell by these big racks, they're not from around here. Good night Gentlemen, I'm going back to bed."

When I first saw Morro Bay, it was love at first sight. As you came into the harbor past the great rock, on the starboard there's the long sand spit that separates the ocean from the bay. It is the outside parameter, the breakwater of sorts, that makes the harbor. On the Port, below the PG&E stacks, start the many wooden buildings, people fishing or maybe setting crab pots from several public piers. Every kind of fishing boat imaginable was tied along the many docks and piers, or moored in mid-channel. There were several unloading docks where the commercial fishing boats unloaded. I eventually got a dock I considered the best dock in the bay. It was just long enough for my boat, so it was private. Off my stern was the fuel dock and a crane for unloading my boxes of abalone, and five minutes down the road was the processor.

When you left the harbor in the morning you could either go left to the south or right to the north. If you did go north, you could stop at some areas along Cayucus, but you usually went past Astero Point to start diving. If you went south by Pacho Rock, there was good diving all along that area, clear to Avila.

One of my favorite places was San Simeon. We used to anchor in San Simeon Harbor. We'd drive there in our trucks in the early morning and take the duck (amphibian vehicle) out to our boats. We couldn't use the old pier, but Snow Soto had the only permit to drive across the beach, so we'd load our gear in the duck and go through the surf to our boats. When we came in at night we'd anchor up, unload our boats onto the duck, and go back through the surf to our trucks. Out of San Simeon, if you went left you would be working offshore Cambria and if you went right you could work or as far north as you'd care to go in one day.

Solid Brass

One year Laddy had gone up to Jade Cove and brought back a few pieces of jade. He unloaded them when nobody else but the duck driver was there. Snow used to have an old fellow, by the name of Slim, drive the duck. Slim was known to tip a few. Laddy swore him to secrecy about the jade. The jade from the cove is not top gem quality, so the market could only handle so much. One night, Slim let his little secret out to a few friends at the bar and in a short time the jade market was flooded. There were big boats coming in hoisting jade boulders they could hardly swing onboard with their booms. One guy slabbed a big piece with a diamond saw for someone in Arizona made a whole wall out of it in his den.

Working out of San Simeon was one of the nicest experiences in the diving business for me. The small bay was protected by a point of land on the north side and on the beach there were a few buildings left from the whaling era. Randolph Hearst would unload here and store his treasures for his castle, which stood as a sentry overlooking this anchorage. There is still an old pier and behind it is a small state park.

Most of the area north is accessible by Highway 1, which goes through here on the way to Big Sir, Carmel, and Monterey. There are miles of little coves, reefs, and at low tide miles of tide pools, full of lush sea grass and sea life usually only seen by divers.

No matter where you dove, there was always a kind of competition of sorts among the divers, at least a few of the high liners who competed for the fullest boat. No one officially entered a contest. I know Gene and I used to make money for each other in San Diego with this feeling of competition.

I remember one day when I first got to Morro, I had my gear on and was about to go over the side when I saw Gene's boat bearing down on us full bore. Gene was standing on the bow, waving his arms frantically, trying to get our attention. As they came nearer, we could hear Gene yelling, "Don't let him in the water! Don't let him dive here!" Finally, they came alongside and told us this was part of the reserve, the closed area to abalone diving. Now, I know Gene, and I know he wasn't as worried about me getting into trouble as he was of me landing in the biggest bed of abalone in the area. If there was no one around and you found a

Solid Brass

good area, you would do all sorts of things to hide it. There would be times you couldn't hide your abundant load when you came in at night. One way other boats would try to find your area was by not going out in the morning and driving up the coast to spot you. There was always an unwritten law that you would stay at least a hose length away from another diver. It was a built-in safety factor to have boats in the same area, in case the diver got into trouble.

Here's one example that happened before I got to Morro Bay. A diver named Francisco had gotten cut off (when your hose gets caught in the boat screw). His back bottle was empty so he couldn't blow himself to the surface. Don Gallagher was nearby and got to him in time. A few days later Francisco was cut off again, this time there was a piece of rubber in his check valve, keeping it from closing. His air from the bottle just ran through, this time they couldn't get to him in time. I just mentioned Don Gallagher; I didn't know him before coming north, but he soon became my mentor. He is truly one of the real gentlemen in our business and one of the best abalone divers ever. He worked a fine boat named the *Hornet* that belonged to Frank Brebes, one of the processors and a retired abalone diver who worked the *Hornet* himself many years prior.

The story goes, once Frank was sitting on deck, taking a rest, when another diver jumped his spot. He got so excited, he jumped over the side without his helmet. Luckily, we snap a line on us after removing our helmets, for that very reason, a dog leash as we call it. That dog leash kept him from getting too deep before the crew could get him back to the ladder and back on board.

When I first got to the bay, I was still using my wet suit. Ninety-five percent of the divers there used heavy gear. I was going to switch as soon as possible. One reason was the comfort in cold water and I also wanted to be recognized as a heavy gear diver to eventually be considered for the oil patch. I finally located a set of abalone heavy gear some guy had in his garage. He never dove himself. He was a businessman that had been talked into buying this gear and a boat from a would-be diver. He was told he could make a ton of money if this diver did the work and they split the profits. It didn't work out so he sold the boat and stored the gear

Solid Brass

in his garage. Lucky for me. It was all first-class stuff. Helmet, floating hose, brass shoes, back bottle, breast weights and dress—all the best. When Don got in that night, he went out to this guy's garage with me. It turned out Don knew him and he also knew the helmet. It had belonged to Freddy Steel, a retired ab diver, when he dove. Don spent quite some time horse trading with this man, until he got me an excellent buy. Also, for the next few weeks, Don stayed near (without saying)

Diver up in heavy gear in Cook Inlet, Alaska. *J. Jackson photo*

just in case something happened. In fact, one day, after I jumped over the side, he had his boat come over to mine because he thought they hadn't snapped me in. I had a light trolling cable that my snap was hooked to and he couldn't see it from where they were.

Working out of San Simeon, I would, on occasion, tow a skiff a friend of mine worked so he could save on fuel. That was OK, but then we couldn't get rid of him. I was working some beds I'd found and it wouldn't be long before I'd run into him on the bottom. I'd move to another location, leaving him in good picking and after a while, there he'd be again. After moving several times, leaving good abalone, I yelled to his tender that we were moving one more time and not to follow us because someone was going to get cut off. He finally got the message.

Solid Brass

At San Simeon, we'd usually get to the beach before sunrise, drink our coffee around a fire, eat cactus apples that George the Greek showed us how to peel, and head to the boats at first light when the duck operator got there. One morning I got out very early, in perfect weather. There was no wind, no swell, and the water was crystal clear. I jumped in a little cove by Cambria and hit an area that had never seen a diver before. Just as fast as they could unload and send me another basket, I'd have the other one filled. I had about fifty dozen onboard when my crew called me up. They could see Buzz off in the distance, heading our way. We moved offshore, and I was sitting on deck drinking coffee when they arrived. Buzz's look of disbelief was followed by a barrage of questions. "Where have you been? You couldn't have gotten so many this early!" I pointed to a little bit of stringer kelp off our bow. He had some reservations, but was frantically putting on his gear (he dove light gear). Just to make our story to him more believable, I had my tender put my hat on and I jumped in the kelp before Buzz was fully dressed. I couldn't believe what I was seeing. There was the reef, totally surrounded by clear white sand. You could see by the half buried palm kelp, that some storm had moved the sand in and all the abalone in the area moved up on the reef to higher ground. They were everywhere, in clusters and on each other's backs. I started sending up basket after basket, as I moved around the reef. I'd sent up better than twenty dozen before Buzz got in the water. He jumped right where I'd been and before he got to the area I was working, it was all over. There were so many scars where my picked abs were, he certainly believed this was where they all came from. Scars are what's left after an abalone works an area on the reef, rock, or bottom until it's almost polished flat. It's where he lives. This way he can get the perfect suction he needs, making it almost impossible to get him off. It's his defense mechanism against predators, be it ab divers or sea otters. They will move out of their area to feed but always come back to their scar.

After Buzz left in disgust, I went back to picking but had to quit before noon because the scuppers were below water part of the time. We actually took kelp over the bow in a small swell going back to San Simeon. The next year I got a bigger boat.

Solid Brass

Another fun time that we had Buzz buzzing, was on a day I left out of Morro really early in the morning to do a little exploring. I knew before going out the weather was going to be real snotty. Just as I was about to turn and go back to port, I saw a kind of slick inside Lyon Rock, so we headed that way. Somehow, the closer we got to the rock, the calmer it got. There were points of land that made this some kind of anchorage. By now, just outside a few hundred yards was a tremendous swell and the wind was blowing at least thirty knots.

I dressed in and hit a hot spot and picked thirty-five dozen before the wind shifted and blew us out. It was one hell of a trip back to the bay. When I got in Buzz ran right down to my dock to see where we had been. No one went out, so he couldn't believe the load we had onboard. He could see by the sea growth on the abs that they didn't come from deep water and it was too damn rough to work shallow. "So where the hell did you go?" I loved it, and to this day, I still haven't told him where we went.

Once, Chuck Sites and I had found a little spot down by the windmill where we could be found by no one. It was off of a private property, so we couldn't be seen by land. It was behind a point in an area we didn't work often, but found good picking for at least a week before being discovered. Chuck worked a boat called the Sea Bird and also worked light gear. We'd occasionally run into each other on the bottom, not knowing the other was in the area. That was fun, when it was just our two boats working the same area.

Solid Brass

One time, while on a dive, Chuck ran into a boat on the bottom—his boat. It had sunk while he was busy on the bottom. There was enough air in the volume tank that he didn't notice his own boat sinking until he saw it sitting upright on the ocean floor. He pulled in his slack, followed his hose until, sure enough, it hooked to the volume tank on the boat sitting on the bottom. He dumped his gear and swam to the surface, only to join his tender treading water. They swam ashore.

There have been several close calls that turned out to be something to laugh about. Skinner was working near a wash rock when his hat came off, he climbed to the top of the reef until he was out of water. When his tender saw him standing there without his hat, he quickly pulled in the slack of his hose, pulled him off the reef and dragged him underwater to the ladder where he attempted to pull him up. He pulled him under the bottom rung and repeatedly dinged his head before giving him enough slack for him to climb up himself. The next ten minutes were spent running around the deck, Skinner chasing his tender trying to pop him one with his abalone iron.

Solid Brass

Another time, Earl McCutcheon was working shallow when he got cut off. His hose got in the screw. The only choice he had was to walk into the beach and wave back to his tender and boat operator. He waited as his tender swam ashore to get him out of his gear. He took off Earl's helmet, but forgot his T-wrench to take the breastplate off. So, with Earl in his dress and breastplate and his tender fresh from an afternoon swim, they carried the helmet, breast-weights, and brass shoes and hitchhiked back to Morro Bay.

One real close one was when one of our elder divers, Lanky Tippton, came up on the ladder while his tender took his hat off. Before getting his dog leash on, the ladder broke off and Lanky sank to the bottom dressed in all his gear, minus his helmet. The tender threw the basket line down, which is weighted, and hit Lanky—shithouse luck. Before Lanky swallowed half the ocean, he managed to grab the line and pull himself to the surface. Lanky was somewhere between sixty and seventy-years old when that happened.

I'm sure somewhere in Morro Bay, perhaps at the Circle Bar or Happy Jack's, there might be someone who still tells these stories. The abalone business no longer exists there today.

When Morro Bay was a little smaller, there was always someone at the Circle Bar that could tell you where almost any diver was or what he was doing. Chuck and Donna Snell came by and picked me up in the middle of the night and we went to Humbolt County for a few days. No one knew this, so after a few days of seeing my truck at the house and my boat at the dock, they broke the door down to see if I had died.

Solid Brass

Just a few weeks before, Hog's Head and his whole family went to the hospital with food poisoning, so perhaps they thought I'd had something similar happen. So many of these people are gone now. They had names like Mattressback Mary, Hog's Head, Albacore Al, Little Bit, Bumps, George the Greek, Indian Dick, Blanket Ass, One-Eyed Ronnie, Rodent, Big John, The Rat, Windy, The Bum, Duck, Dutch, The Chink, and Skinner, all part of the business, either pounding abalone, working the ab boats, or diving.

The Circle used to jump when times were good. On one stool there might be a fisherman without a boat at the dock and next to him a cowboy with 10,000 acres outside of town. Snow Soto, who had the Duck at San Simeon, also had several thousand acres of coastal property. It was given to his family through Spanish land grants. Snow was also a cowboy who worked for the Hearst Ranch. His family had always worked for the Hearst family. His mother worked at the small store in San Simeon. One night at the Circle this plump lady came in, nobody knew who she was. She got very loud and obnoxious. Someone took down the marlin that hung on the wall, came up behind her, and stuck her right in the ass.

One weekend Jerry Todd and Ed Woods were shooting pool at the Circle when some half-drunk college kids came in. The girls were just as loud and foul-mouthed as the guys. They stumbled up to put their quarters on the pool table to play the winner, bumped the table and upset the balls, and continued laughing and carrying on. Ed and Jerry opened the doors because it was getting pretty hot, and they preceded to take off their shirts, then their pants. Pretty soon all their clothes were neatly piled in the corner as they continued shooting pool. Not long after that, only the locals were left in the bar.

Kurt Berger, who might still be bartending at the Circle, has so many good stories attached to him. One happened at his home rather than at the Circle. He and his wife had a big argument which heated to the point that she went out, got into her car, and started driving off. Kurt came to the front porch and shot out her tires, all four, flat.

Once during a big gathering Kurt fell from a window, and check this out, was pronounced dead. The ambulance was taking him to the morgue

93

Solid Brass

in San Luis Obispo. Somewhere between Morro and San Luis, Kurt came forward to ask the ambulance crew if they'd stop this thing so he could take a piss. They all took a piss before getting the ambulance stopped.

Once Berger's dog was taken from his front yard by the dog catcher, because it wasn't tied up. The next day when the pound crew came to work, they found all the dogs had escaped. In fact, all the cats, the ducks, the chickens, and horses all expertly picked their locks. There wasn't even a bird left. One can only speculate what might have happened.

We had a few Fish and Game people in Morro who were on the enforcement side of the group. They went a little overboard when it came to abalone divers. I certainly want to express my feelings towards the Fish and Game with my most full-hearted support and love for what they've done for our wildlife. But, as with any group of size, there are usually a few assholes that even their own people dislike. We had one in Morro, in particular, whose mother must have been bitten by a diver when she was pregnant with him. Every Wednesday, it was a big event to go to our courthouse to watch the abalone trials. Most of the cases were for shallow water (less than twenty feet). Although it was considered a medieval law, when you dove shallow you were breaking the law. The one we divers looked down our noses at was when a diver picked shorts. Divers in the business year after year, knew better and would never pick short. Shorts were the abalone we would make a living off next year, after they became legal size. We used to have large short beds we could go back to each season—take the legals and leave the shorts for the coming year. But unfortunately, our friendly fish cop was determined to spend his every waking hour setting up triangulation points to catch divers in shallow water. Triangulation was a method of measuring two points from the beach to the third point, the diver's bubbles, to pinpoint the dive spot. He would later take a boat to the calculated spot and take a depth reading. There could be a margin of error here, but not when he got the Greek. He took a picture of the Greek's hat skimming the surface of the water as he walked along picking abs. Gotcha!

After I dropped off a very large load of abalone, sometime during that night I got a call that a new officer came by the shop and confiscated my load because they were short. I came unglued, told the processor that this new officer, Mr. Goodrich, better keep them refrigerated, because he'd somehow made a mistake. "I don't run shorts and everyone knows it. I'll be right down!" I went by my boat on the way and picked up my gauges and ab iron. After arriving at the shop, I was still ready to pop. Standing by my abalone was a young, good-looking, polite sort of man, who proceeded to show me how he measured the abs with a tape measure by stretching it across the foot and eye, eyeballing the numbers. I gave him my gauge, had him measure it, then take an additional measure with the gauge in my iron. When he could see they were right on, I used the gauge on the rest of the abs and every one was well over the legal limit. He quickly said it was his mistake, apologized, and we became friends from that time on. I understand he's one of the top people in California's Fish and Game today. However, regarding our local Morro creep, we used to see him sneaking through the brush, hiding behind rocks, and other obstructions in hopes of catching us in the act. It was always good entertainment. He never got snake bit, I guess because he was one of their own.

Kurt had run into this creep one day and told him he'd seen the funniest thing the day before. He saw a mountain lion (which at that time had a bounty on them) sneaking through the brush just up above where he was diving. Kurt went on, "I almost shot him because he was so unique. He had tennis shoes on!"

I mentioned the Greek before, getting caught with his helmet out of water. While George came from Florida, his family were all from Greece and were diving sponges out of Tarpon Springs some years earlier. The sponge had gotten some kind of blight and many beds died off, forcing boats to stop diving or work for a smaller living than they were use to. George came to California to dive abs. He said if he ever went back, he'd dive the sponge the way we dove abalone. Their operation for sponge was much bigger for the same results, with bigger boats, more people, etc. Once, I found a four-foot octopus on the bottom, in the open, just before I made my ascent. I put my foot out and he crawled onto my shoe, then I blew myself to the surface. I told my tender to be ready to grab him as soon as I got on the ladder. Just as I got there, he slipped off and

Solid Brass

went back to the bottom. The Greek was on deck, close to my boat and heard and saw all this. He was very upset that I'd let it get away. He already had that octopus figured for some great Greek dish.

George didn't mind sharing the abalone you found, with you. In fact, he was a notorious hose jumper. I'd been called up more than once because our boats were too close for safe operation. Either boat could cut you off. We were all at the foul area at San Miguel, when he jumped a spot I'd just found. I promptly developed engine trouble. While working on the engine, I'd stick my head out of the engine compartment in time to see him pull another basket, I went back to work on my engine, threw a few tools and swore a lot while George kept picking my abalone.

At the Santa Barbara Islands, instead of goat, like San Clemente, we would hunt pigs and sheep. On one end of Santa Cruz where cattle were raised, sheep were chased out or killed to keep them from grazing the same land. Some remaining sheep would be several generations wild and super good eating, no matter how old, because of their diet on the island. The pigs were different, you had to take the young ones back in the canyons, the older pigs that had gotten down to the ocean, ate sea birds, dead seals, etc. and smelled and tasted like low tide smells. There were also the island quail,that made several nights of fine dining. The Islands were always a pleasure to dive. The water was as clear as it gets, with large kelp beds spreading across the water. There were many beautiful little coves to anchor up in for the night with just enough tide action to rock you to sleep. With each weather report, we would determine which anchorage to spend the night. Hopefully any anchorage would do, but once in a while, we would get caught in the wrong place at the wrong time.

One night we were anchored near Willow, at Santa Cruz, just my temporary tender and myself. The rest of the crew was coming out on another boat. When we turned in, the water was flat and glassy, with just a light breeze freshening up. Sometime in the middle of the night, I woke up to the sound of my anchor dragging. As I came up on deck, a very stiff wind met me. I could see, even in the dark, there was a swell and whitecaps outside. I could also see we were in the wrong anchorage for this wind. I woke my tender and started making ready to pick the hook. As we pulled out of this little shelter, it started building fast. I was

Solid Brass

headed for Smuggler's to round the point to Potato Harbor. I have to wonder, what would have happened had I slept fifteen minutes longer? We hardly got the anchor up, when the winds picked up to about sixty knots. We just cleared the cove and the swell started breaking across the entrance. The black silhouette of the island was about all we could see now as the water exploded off the boat when it hit. Before it was over, we had gusts of wind over a hundred knots. I was beginning to think we were losing ground. I had to have the engine idled down most of the time while falling off the large swells. We slammed down so hard, it sent a trembling vibration through the boat.

After many hours, which seemed like days of torturous pounding, we got to Smuggler's. Even though this wasn't the anchorage we needed for that blow, we threw the hook. There was no guarantee we'd get around the point to Potato and unlike a large ship, we didn't have another crew to relieve the watch. We were soaked to the bone and we just got our ass kicked.

We planned to spend a few hours here, perhaps until first light, and see what the morning would bring. Sometime during the night, my tender got violently sick and for the next three days couldn't eat, getting weaker and weaker as the storm was merciless and didn't let up for a minute. I made contact with the Coast Guard trying to get him off and to medical attention. I thought of running my boat up on the sand, noticing the surf wasn't that big on the beach, then run broaching lines from my stern to some trees I'd spotted. Then the helicopters could rescue my tender from the beach. But the wind was too strong for the helicopters to fly. They couldn't even get alongside me with the cutter or couldn't launch a whale boat because of the wind and rough sea. I even offered to put him in a wet suit with more floating gear and set him adrift for them to fish out of the water. That night the Coast Guard called to inform me that as soon as the weather let up a little, they'd be alongside to take us both off. I said I'd have my tender ready to go but I wasn't leaving. "We can't order you off, but we strongly recommend you leave," came a firm full military voice. "Roger on the part where you can't order me off. If the anchor line breaks, I can save my boat, but not if I'm on the cutter, snug and warm."

Solid Brass

On the fourth day, my tender was seriously weak. I had managed to get some hard-boiled eggs, bread and water down him while we waited it out. My radio was in a good dry spot. I was receiving "moral support" calls from friends in Santa Barbara on their ship-to-shores.

I received the same kind of weather report for the coming days, so I made the decision to cross. I told the Coast Guard my plans and would appreciate if they'd follow me in case we lost the boat. I wasn't sure my tender could last another day. With the still gusting winds, I had to buoy and had to leave my anchor. I nailed the bow hatch down and put the abalone shields over the starboard window. Not having another piece of wood to cover the port windows, I knew I'd probably lose them.

The Coast Guard suggested going in front of us to try and knock the swells down a bit. The sea was unbelievable after leaving the lee of the island, the swells made the cutter (maybe 210 feet long) completely disappear. It was just a short distance in front of us. We were tossed around at will. At that point in my life I'd never been in seas like that in a small boat. While in the Navy, we rode out some typhoons, which my mind was comparing to this crossing. The old fisherman's quote, "The sea is so big and my boat is so small," sure fit.

My old *Jeffery* was a good sea boat and it hung in there as best it could under these conditions. It had a flush deck and a good Jimmy diesel, so water coming in wasn't a problem. The windows that weren't covered came out at some point from one of the waves that crashed over the house. The water went raging through the cabin where I had my tender tied into a life jacket and wedged between the table and bulkhead. When the water crashed through the cabin, it was just another indication that he was going to die. I was on the flying bridge, using what steering I had to keep us heading in the right direction. Except for my pickup at the dock, everything I owned of monetary value was jumping from under my feet and taking a terrible ass kicking by Mother Nature. And no, I did not have one nickel's worth of insurance. I can mention that now, but at the time I'm sure that the financial end of this nightmare was never a thought. With all the anxiety this sort of situation brings, I could write two more chapters on my thoughts at that time, but about two miles from the mainland, the winds started to let up, the swell started to lay down and the kinks in my gut started to unwind. We had made it.

As the cutter crew started out on deck, waving "Good for you" gestures, I saw one young pasty looking guy with his hair cut short, top and sides, looking at the bow of my boat, taking notes. It turns out, he was writing a citation, because a couple of my Coast Guard numbers were missing. If he wasn't such a young punk who didn't know any better, I would have pointed out that the windows were also missing, and my working radio died right after the windows blew out. On the plus side, the crew had dry cover waiting for us and blankets, lots of hot coffee, plus an ambulance waiting at the dock.

The story had a happy ending. My friends Chuck and Donna Snell, who were supposed to meet us at the Islands, came to Port Huyneme to pick us up. By now, we had become media stuff for the local radio and TV. Plus Chuck and Donna followed our Coast Guard conversation on their ship-to-shore along with many of my local fishermen friends. It was a delight to see their smiling faces.

Not all boat problems at the Islands turned out so well. While one of the Black Fleet boats sat at anchor, another boat anchored a short distance away threw a seal bomb near the waterline to get their attention. It did. It opened a seam and the boat promptly sank. A seal bomb has other names, but it is basically a small cherry bomb-type explosive, used by fishermen to chase seals from their nets.

About the time it was getting too damn hot to keep pushing the load at our present rate, Nancy's mother showed up with a case of beer. A similar story of destruction happened on land. We were moving her belongings from one apartment to another. By late afternoon, we had finished moving and finished the case of beer. Gene suggested we go to the landing and check the boats. The weather had been bad and that's why we had the time off. We hoped that a few days more would bring good weather that would take us back to the abalone patch. Bad weather is always an excuse to kick back.

Gene stopped off to check his boat, and I continued down the dock to check mine. I stepped inside my boat and the first thing I saw was a note on the cabin. "Hi, we're on our way to the Halfway House.

Solid Brass

Sorry to have missed you. We'll be there all weekend if you can make it." This note was from my high school friends that I hadn't seen in five years. They were all married and were going back to Mexico, camping in a place we'd surfed and skin dived as kids.

Having the bad weather, kick back time anyway, I knew this is where I had to be. Having told Gene the story, we hopped in the pickup and headed for his house to tell his wife that he would like to accompany me to this high school reunion. Nancy wasn't home, so he left a note, "Gone to the Halfway House with Bob."

We got back into the Nasty Ed's pickup, which Gene had borrowed for the move that day. This pickup was brand new. The reason Ed wasn't driving it was because he lost his license. I don't want to lose track of our trip to Mexico but I think Ed's license being pulled fits here. Ed had pulled in enough 502s (DWIs) that the judge didn't want him driving anymore. But one night when he had an important meeting at the local water hole, he met some beauty, and shared in some late night, weak vision, romance. On the way to "your place or mine," Ed hit a parked car. Ending up in court, Ed brought his "lady of the night" to be his star witness for this case. The prosecuting attorney had her on the stand, "Did Mr. Deneuville stop, get out, leave a note...just what did he do? Reply, "Yes, he stopped, he got out, pulled the fender away from the tire, and said, "Let's get the hell out of here on account of I don't have a driver's license."

So, Gene and I are on our way to Mexico in Ed's brand new Ford with the even newer right front fender. After crossing the border, we stopped to get some gas at twenty-five cents a gallon, and eyeing a liquor store across the street that sold alcohol at about the same price, decided to pick up a big bottle of wine and a good-sized bottle of tequila. This combo could surely save our lives if we were to get a snake bite on the Baja.

Back in days gone by, there were several places along the old highway that were nightclub type bars and restaurants. After about half a bottle of wine, we came upon one of those places. In front of us, for several miles, we had followed an old four-door Chevy with Mexican plates. They decided to turn into the parking lot of this place without any warning. No turn signal, no brake lights. They were into their turn when we

Solid Brass

gave them a small shove. The driveway down to the parking lot was very steep and in the middle of this lot was the largest tree ever grown in Mexico. With the send off we gave them, the old Chevy shot down the drive at a speed just short of flying. They hit the only tree within eyesight, dead center.

Our first thought was to get down there to see if anyone was hurt. As we started out of the truck, all four Chevy doors opened. It looked like one of those circus cars, people just kept coming out. Before we got too far from our truck, they started picking up rocks and slinging them. They were out of range at first but rapidly gaining. We jumped back in the truck with Gene trying to restart it. Ed had pulled the ignition that was faulty so you had to play with it to get it started. Rocks started hitting the truck. We cursed Ed. Why didn't he exercise his warranty and have the damn ignition fixed? The closer they got, the bigger the rocks they threw. The rocks were coming through the cab now, because they had already taken care of the windshield. Finally, she fired and away we went. Just in time, because we were outnumbered and in their country.

A quick check told us there wasn't one panel in the truck not dented and of course we didn't have one piece of whole window glass. We were wearing all the glass in our hair, in our laps, and down our backs. There were several rocks in the cab that barely fit through the window. There was a moment of disbelief and stupefaction, then we both cracked up and felt comfort in the fact that our bottles didn't get broken. We did some evaluation on the damage while under way and decided the truck Ed wrecked and left in Mexico another time probably didn't look as bad as this.

In Ed's Mexican crash, he was by himself, some distance from the border, somewhere in a farm area. No buses, no taxis, so Ed walked to a farm and bought an old work horse and road it to the border. Bareback! His crotch was so raw, it was weeks before he could put wools on and make a dive.

We continued with the truck opened to the world and just the clothes we left town in. The campfire was a welcome sight. It was good to see my old friends. Gene got out, shook hands, crawled back in the pickup and we didn't see him again until we left. Sleep sounded more important to him than sitting around the fire listening to our high school stories and singing. Not that much was said about our bombed out new pickup and how it got that way. I guess this kind of fit into my acquired image. I was kind of the black sheep of my friends. I left school and joined the Navy and when I got out bought an abalone boat and didn't come back home to live. I didn't get back very often, not because I didn't miss my family and friends, but there just wasn't much of a demand for commercial divers in my hometown.

We were really enjoying our reunion when I noticed the sun starting to peek out. I fired up Gene and the truck, after my good-byes, and headed out. Our trip home wasn't at all eventful, just a lot of turned heads at the sight of our vehicle and a lot of stops to get more coffee.

We used to have a bar in San Diego named The Halfway House, so when Nancy read Gene's note about going to The Halfway House, she naturally thought we went to the San Diego bar, not that we left the country. Then to top it off, we didn't come home until late the next day. Luckily, Gene dropped me off at the boat landing where my truck was parked. It was several months before Nancy would even look at me. There was never any thought given to Gene being a few years older than me, and a man who thinks for himself. Just that I was a bachelor and led him astray. She'd walk right by me at the landing and never say a word. Finally, one day she walked up and asked me over for dinner, smiled, and broke a very thick piece of ice.

Some of my favorite memories having to do with both UDT and abalone were with two of my very close friends, Bob Worthington and Dick Kruger. We went through training together and were able to keep in touch through the years. Bob worked for Disney in those days. He went on to become a top special effects man in Hollywood and one of my closest friends. Dick was an electrical genius. He worked for a company that sent him around the country checking the stations that tracked the first manned space shots. They would come together to visit me in Morro Bay and later in Santa Barbara. Bob and Lolly, Dick, Sue and their son, Rick. It was a fun trip for them to come north on the weekend, especially if the weather was bad and I wasn't working. On a Saturday

Solid Brass

morning I'd wake very early to the smell of coffee perking. I'd walk out to see everyone sprawled out on the floor in their sleeping bags. After some years of this they declared they wanted to dive abalone themselves. It seemed they were totally burned out living and working in the Los Angeles area. Dick told me of one morning while he was sitting at a stop light on the way to work, and he looked over at the car next to him and realized this was the same guy he sees there every morning sitting at the same light with the same coffee and eating the same kind of donut. This seemed to be the straw. He realized what a rut he had gotten into. It became very obvious to me that this was not just some idea or conversation to pass the time. These guys were ready to toss it all and go diving.

I proceeded to tell them some facts to maybe avoid a possible mistake in the making. "You guys come here on the weekends after a hard week at work," I started out, "we have some nice cookouts, lots of fresh seafood and venison. We go down to my boat with the diving gear hung up and the helmet sitting in its place close to the bow. We might putz around fixing a few things that need attention before we drive to San Simeon or maybe hunt a deer if its the season, dig a few clams at low tide, do some crabbing in the tide pools or go to the local pubs to have a few horns with the other divers. This is an unbalanced picture, I want to tell you the other side that you may not know about. The bad weather that comes in and stays for weeks at a time or how about the breakdowns that happen when the weather finally gets workable. The engine work that has to be done when you can least afford it. Standing on the boat, before the sun comes up looking for your tender who doesn't show up because he fell in love the night before. Or getting up at 0300 to bail someone out of jail. Putting nine hours in the water on a bad day and only make enough to pay for your fuel. Chasing a processor to get your check only to have it bounce. Your reward for a long day's work might be a good limp or an arm that doesn't work well for a few days because you got bent. Or a festered sea urchin spine somewhere handy. And there's no retirement plan with medical for the family and no sick leave." I told them much more, but trying to paint an ugly picture of a business I loved wasn't working. There wasn't a worried look on their faces, it was more like they were waiting for the real bad stuff. We laughed and I said, "If all this doesn't worry the hell out of you then let's get a list started of all the things you'll need to do this right. I went on to tell them a story stressing the importance of obtaining the best equipment for reasons beyond safety. The story was about a couple of divers who went after gold on the Feather River and decided before they packed all the gear in, to take the best equipment money could buy. They wanted to do it right the first time, to give it everything they had. So, if it didn't work out, if they didn't strike it rich, it would be out of their systems, and they would not end up sometime later thinking, "Well, maybe if we'd have had a little better gear or worked a little harder..."

There was no question, Bob and Dick's minds were made up, so they left at the end of the weekend with a list, some drawings, and other essentials for their plan. They bought a good sound Spoonbill, put on first-class diving gear, got their permits and headed for San Clemente. They both took a leave of absence from their jobs. They worked the Islands for some time and were probably still trying to decide if this was for them, when their boat sank some miles off Catalina.

The anchor gear was stored in an area near the shaft and vibrated until a bit of the chain got caught up around the shaft. It turned with the shaft until a large ball of chain formed and went through the hull. They barely had time to get off a shot from the flare gun before it disappeared from the surface. Some boats several miles away saw the flare and rescued them from the cold Pacific. They both went back to work with some great stories.

Dick still had to get out of that rut so he and his family did a lot of research, sold their house and cars, stored keepers, and bought a Land Rover with a small covered trailer and headed for South America. After making a trip of a lifetime, he got involved in the cotton business and was doing quite well, but South America also had a large ball and chain. These were the days revolution was in style. It was almost impossible to do business or live a normal life there. Most of the Americans were selling their furnishings ten cents on the dollar and leaving or just simply leaving without the ten cents. Dick and Sue were in town one day when

Solid Brass

the front of the hotel across from their's was blown away. Finally, it got so crazy they had to pack it in and come home.

Bob, Lolly, Dick, Sue, and Rick would come to visit on the weekends again, now, in Santa Barbara. On one such trip, Dick spent the weekend nursing a bad headache. Just before leaving, Sue told me he'd had this headache for several days before coming up and it hadn't let up. He refused to see a doctor. So, as they loaded up, I took him aside and told him if I found out that in a couple of days, he still hadn't seen a doctor, there were some things I would tell Sue. Things I knew he'd rather I not share with anyone, much less his wife. "You wouldn't do that, would you?" came his tentative reply.

I'm sure the headache drove him to the hospital rather than my threat. The first doctor felt something wasn't just right, so he sent him to another. This doctor was suspicious and told Dick he wanted to run more tests and made him stay in the hospital.

Three days later, Sue called from the hospital to tell me Dick had died. Some little weak vessel had ruptured in his head, he'd probably had even as a kid, according to the doctor. If someone in your life has been sick for a long time, you prepare yourself for what might happen or at least know it's a possibility, but Dick was so full of life and we weren't afforded that luxury of preparation. Every day was a new adventure for Dick, a chance to think good thoughts. I had a hard time with this and knew the emptiness Bob and Lolly would feel after time passed. Murray Black, who had lost a friend suddenly, told me it happened so fast, he didn't have a chance to tell him he loved him—that works here for me.

A couple of months later, Sue drove to the ranch with Rick. She told me in private Rick was having a hard time and asked if I would have a talk with him. Sometime during the day, Rick asked if we could talk. I led him to a big flat rock up on the hill and we sat in the warmth of the afternoon sun. It seems Sue had him living often with some relatives that were super religious. They made a big point to let Rick know that Dick was an atheist and that meant he'd never see his dad in the hereafter. Here's a young child suffering the loss of his best friend and father, being told when he dies he'll reunite with the rest of the family, but not Dick, because Dick didn't believe in God. Not trouble at school, not someone calling him four-eyes, or not allowing him in the club, not even a girl problem. Instead his withdrawal and misery was caused by the stupidity of some heartless adult family members.

What I said next, in a much steadier voice than my feelings, just came out without a lot of planning. "Do you believe in God?" I asked him. "Yes, of course." "Then, do you believe your God is so narrow-minded that he would not allow a man like Dick into heaven, because of his beliefs, a man that spent his entire life making people around him happy? I feel I'm a better person having known Dick, whatever his beliefs. Those beliefs were for reasons of his own, he never asked anyone else to understand why he thought like this, or try to make you see religion as he did. Without knowing these people that have talked to you, I do know they are not qualified to stand in judgment of Dick. And don't you worry, he'll have things straightened out before you get there."

We talked for quite awhile and it was clear all the clutter in his head was put into some kind of order. Put in order with the use of his own values, values given him by the very person we talked about. I know Dick was there with us that afternoon, if only in his strong spirit within our hearts. Before getting into the car to leave, Sue asked what had happened, these were his first smiles in two months. "Just some man-to-man talk," I replied.

The first year was the only time I used the anchor boat method. You anchor and pick a circle around the boat as far as your hose will extend. When you filled your basket, you'd go back to the line directly below the stern of the boat, exchange the full for the empty basket, and give a signal for your tender to winch it up. Anchor boating had a lot of drawbacks. If you got to the bottom and it wasn't good abalone country, you'd have to come back up, help pick the anchors and move to another spot, over and over, until you got to good picking.

Every once in a while, sitting on the dock or possibly on a bar stool, you would run into someone who had seen the twelve to thirteen-inch abalone. The person who had seen a whole stack of them, but like Big Foot, had no pictures or proof. Certainly not abalone in hand.

Buzz Owen, in the early sixties, was known as the foremost authority on the Pacific Coast abalone. He was the one that proved they were hybrids.

Solid Brass

He used to travel up and down the coast in his Volkswagen, checking all the large piles of shells in search of these hybrids. Mainly Dutch Pierce's pile in Santa Barbara and Frank Breb's pile in Morro Bay.

Buzz had given me and some other divers a bottle of preservative and asked that when we see an abalone with a different mantle, would we save the shell and put the mantle in the bottle for him to study. Which we did. After picking abalone in the hundreds of dozens, we could spot the hybrid immediately once Buzz had pointed out the differences. Differences that you had never paid attention to before. Buzz owned an abalone shell just under twelve inches and made an offer of $100 to anyone that could produce one bigger. He would let you keep your shell and pay off the $100 just to see it. This offer stood for years with no takers. Buzz's shell came off of Swede Armond's mother boat. The shell was dumped in a load from two divers, so no one is sure who picked this large abalone. Chuck Snell is one of the possibilities. Not until a recent find off the Humbolt Country coast of California, was the record broken. The 12 5/16-inch red abalone was found about thirty feet offshore in just twelve feet of water, under a rock. It took two hours to pry loose. Buzz, still the authority and seeker of a twelve-inch red, heard of the score and after so many years, witnessed the significant find. Buzz, a marine biologist, estimated the discovery was between forty and seventy years old and still growing. It weighed 11 1/2 pounds and was the first abalone taken that's twelve inches or larger. I haven't heard if Buzz paid the forty-year $100 bounty.

Now, I look back on the abalone business as the most enjoyable part of my commercial diving career, besides UDT. Many of the guys from the abalone fleet eventually went on to work the oil patch, which offered more options for making more money as a commercial diver. Diving abalone, you had to work hard to make a good living. Most of the peer pressure came from yourself to get the biggest load, to be the high liner, to constantly try to pick the most. It was a pressure you put on yourself. Trying to find new abalone country and keeping your boat running seemed like a heavy, heavy load at the time, but I believe now you can have more pressure getting ready for a thirty-minute commercial dive than you'd have in an entire season of diving abalone.

Solid Brass

A for instance could be the multi-million dollar rig waiting for you to find and fix a problem so they can get their quarter of a million-dollar day spread working again. In the early sixties most of the West Coast commercial diving was still done in heavy gear and most of the abalone was still being dove with heavy gear from Santa Barbara north. The abalone patch was a perfect spawning grounds for future oil patch or any commercial diving position. The diving companies on the West Coast could pull one or more divers from the abalone boats as needed. Knowing which divers were making a good living meant they were well-adapted to working the current, being pretty handy at mechanics, keeping their boats and diving gear in order, and not adverse to hard work, plus they were all in good physical shape.

In my mind, being picked to work with a commercial diving company from the abalone boats, was like being brought up from the minor leagues to the big leagues. That was my biggest goal at that time. Although this was not true for everyone. Some very good abalone divers just chose to remain there and enjoy life at that pace and still do today. These die-hard divers included Bill Bossert, Don Gallagher, Kurt Berger, Lanky, Chuck Snell and others.

I heard that Danny Wilson, a well-known abalone processor and diver, was putting a diving company together. He would be developing and using gas equipment. At that time it was a pretty new concept on the West Coast, at least in actual practice. Howard from the radiator shop and Bob Kirby would help in the design and actual construction or reconstruction of the new gas dive helmets.

I ran into Danny at Joe's one day and confronted him about possibly diving for him. He quickly reminded me that I'd never sold him one abalone, even after he'd asked, several times. I had my own boat and could sell to whomever I wanted, unlike the divers on processor's boats. I didn't have anything against Danny, but I was selling to a processor in Morrow Bay that paid me well and actually, I was the owner's main diver at times. I even let my checks ride so he could pay his help. Danny said something about sending a resume, so I mumbled something and went back to my table. On the way back to Morrow Bay, the thought

Solid Brass

of how bad my interview with Danny had gone occupied and dominated the space in my head.

Back to business as usual, when one day Buzz Owens came to my house with a message that Danny Wilson had called and left a number for me to get in touch with him. That was pretty exciting stuff in those days, as Danny wouldn't be just making a social call, so I allowed myself the thought that this may be the big one. When I called Danny he said he had a lot of diving coming up and asked if I would come to Santa Barbara. I could work in the shop until we went out on a dive. I told him I was very interested but had to finish the few weeks left of abalone season. My crew needed to make a little more money to get them through the off-season. He agreed, and in fact, thought the timing would be good.

We had a pretty good end of the season and as it turned out, it was the end of my commercial abalone days. After I left, the sea otter moved in and eventually destroyed the abalone industry in the north area. The abalone were always my security blanket. Figuring if things were slow in the commercial diving world, I could always go back and pick abalone. Not so after the sea otter migration, especially not in Morro Bay. There have always been a certain amount of people who would blame everything but the otter. There have been claims that divers overdid it. There were only a small group of abalone divers left in Morro Bay and the amount of abalone they picked was not significant to this claim. Some divers worked more shallow than the law allowed, and up and down the coast there were just a couple of creeps that ran shorts. The shorts were next year's living, like money in the bank. The otters picked everything. We had giant short beds we went through every year to pick a few legals. They're gone. I don't understand how even the most staunch otter person won't believe what happened here. They also annihilated the Pismo clam. There is at least one biologist who wrote, "As long as otter are in the area of the Pismo, there will never be sport takes of Pismos, because there will never be one that will grow to a legal size before being eaten by the otter."

While I was diving off San Simeon, Chuck Sites came out and asked me to follow him to an area he'd been diving, closer to the beach. I just rode my ladder over, my tender put my hat on, and I dropped down.

Solid Brass

The water was extremely clear, so I could see, before I hit bottom, what looked to be an explosion. Laying on the bottom of the cove were hundreds of abalone, each with a hole punched in its shell and partially eaten. I was looking at the remains of an otter feed. If they ate the whole abalone, they wouldn't have to destroy so many to get their fill, but they just ate their favorite parts. The rock crabs were having a feast on what was left, which probably helped them to propagate. A large rock crab is capable of taking his own abalone off a rock. They chip away at the shell until they get to a vital area, punch a hole in this spot and wait until the abalone falls off the rock. I've watched this process more than once to know, for sure, this is how it happens.

We've heard otters will send scouts to a new area and if they don't come back, indicating danger, the rest will stay away. I can only speculate on what might have happened if we would have known this to be true when we noticed the first sign of the otter. If we had eliminated the scouts; perhaps the abalone wouldn't have been depleted. I don't think anyone knew just how bad the destruction would be or just how destructive the otters were.

FOUR

The Bends

While diving in San Diego, there was an exclusive shell market where we'd haul our dark meat reds all the way to San Diego to get $6.25 per dozen. We couldn't sell our dark meat to the processor in San Pedro, Eli Redy. There was a limit on how many the shell market would take in any given week and we shared that among five boats. If, for any reason, one boat couldn't make it out, than the other boats could make up the difference. We took turns driving the abalone to San Pedro. As we started working deeper and deeper for the reds, the more chance you had for getting bent. There was a time when you would sit in the coffee shop at Dana Landing, waiting to see who might have trouble lifting his cup or who walked in with a slight limp. If you had a particularly painful one, you would leave at first light and pass on the coffee.

One particular night, before I got to the dock I knew I had a bubble in my knee and it was my turn to deliver. Before I got to San Pedro, I had to let my tender, Jim, drive. Every time I pressed on the brake, my leg started jumping and throbbing, until I couldn't push the peddle. By the time we got back to San Diego, I knew I should go to the Strand and have the Team put me in the chamber. But, the thought of having all the Frogs mustering at the chamber in the morning and laughing at how well I was doing as a civilian, didn't work for me. I told my tender to meet me really early in the morning so we could get outside the harbor and I could decompress in the water. I didn't sleep at all that night with the bad tooth-ache feeling in my knee. It was still dark when I got into the water

111

and headed down. Normally, when you get to pressure, the bubble decreases in size and you get relief, but instead, it felt like my knee was going to explode. I pulled myself up a little and tried once more to get down, but again my knee was going to explode. There was no way to explain this, all I knew was I had to get down so I dumped my air, gritted my teeth and headed down. The pain was the kind I'd never dealt with before. My knee didn't explode and I finally got the bubble out, but not the pain. I started my slow ascent to my first stop, finished my decompression, and finally got to the surface. The only thing that made any sense of it was as the bubble got smaller, as it had to be doing, it must have moved off into a nerve causing the pain which felt like the bubble was getting larger.

After the homemade treatment table, I went to the area I knew I could pick pinks and greens in shallow water for the rest of the day. A Navy diving doctor would tell you to stay out of the water twenty-four hours or more after a bend. I probably rationalized that diving shallow would be like taking a long twenty-foot stop to get all the loose and nasty bubbles out. Actually, I was just there to build a good payday.

We didn't get bent because of not paying attention to our decompression tables. When we first start a dive, the tender checks water depth with a basket line, or later, when we owned one, a fathometer. That depth reading would determine what table we would use, but the bottom has its ups and downs. Sometimes we'd be higher on a reef, but many times we'd walk off into deeper water. Of course, we did spend more time down there than we should, on occasion, trying to make a good day out of it.

A couple of tenders with some time to kill before the next tide, decided to crawl in the chamber and blow themselves down a couple hundred feet to see what it's like to be a little narced. Was it really like being drunk?

Everyone else aboard was napping, so they decided to go for it. Sometime later one of the divers happened by the chamber and heard laughing coming from the chamber phones. He noticed the gauge at 220 feet. He keyed the phones and yelled, "What the hell are you doing at 220 feet? How long have you been there? How long did it take to get there? What the hell is going on?" After waking the rest of the dive

Solid Brass

crew, a quick decompression table was put together from whatever sketchy information was gathered from the two happy people in the chamber. They didn't know exactly how long they'd been in there. They had started telling stories and laughing so hard that time and good sense got away from them. They got out of the chamber just before their divers had to get dressed in to make the tide.

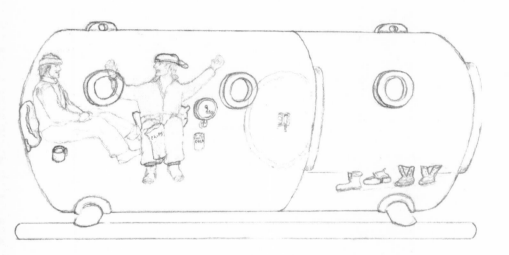

An hour later, when the diver climbed the ladder after his dive, fortunately for the tenders, he didn't need to decompress. Both tenders were on deck with the bends (nothing serious, just a lot of pain). One had a good bubble in the shoulder and the other had some bad pain in his arm. So now they would have to get back into the chamber to go on a treatment table to relieve their pain and get rid of the bubbles. This time there was a lack of humor and less storytelling as they were blown down to pressure. Although they did have the rare distinction of getting "bent" without going under water.

Solid Brass

FIVE

Tenders

As a commercial diver, your most important asset is your tender. The abalone operation consisted of two men on deck: your tender and your boat operator. They dress you in, kept your times and set you on the proper decompression table. If you got bent and spent hour after hour in the chamber, they took care of that also. They'd have coffee waiting after the dive and if you needed to go in the chamber for additional decompression they saw to it that your pillow had been fluffed. And, after your tender came in the tank to blow down and dress you out in the outer lock, he had to blow himself back to the surface, while you sat locked in the inner lock and sipped the fresh cup of coffee he left for you. He also yells and talks crudely about your family over the phones when you ask for just a couple more minutes to work after he's told you its time to come up. They always win that one.

When you're busting your ass on some job, your tender is the one that keeps bothering you, asking if you're OK because you hadn't said anything for a while. They are the ones, when you're on a helium dive, that keep requesting over and over, "Say again, slowly," just because they can't understand divers that talk like Donald Duck. They are also the ones that lie to you about how long you have been down in deep water, so they can steal a couple of minutes of your time to get you up and start your decompression. This being said, they are the ones who have saved many a diver's life or possibly saved him from a serious injury.

Solid Brass

Bud Swain getting some last minute attention form his tender before a helium dive off the California Coast. *J. Jackson photo*

Once, Willie Stratton and I took a helicopter ride from a barge in the Cook Inlet, to a hospital emergency room in Anchorage. The tip of my finger was carefully packed in a baggy full of ice and carried in Willie's pocket.

Your tender is the one that makes sure you have all the tools you need before each dive. When you use your knife on the bottom to cut some big ball of line that you get tangled in, the knife is always sharp because your tender keeps it that way. When a diver is totally bogged down and screwed up trying to accomplish a project, the tender is the one assuring the customer on deck that everything is going well.

Solid Brass

Scooter Treen and Bill McWilliams tending the phones. *B. Wick photo*

One time there was a particularly aggressive engineer that would run across the deck, push the tender away from the phone, and get on the phone to tell or ask the diver something. Willie hooked a wire to the phone with an alligator clip that put 110 volts to it. The engineer got hit by this several times before stopping this grabby stuff. As soon as he would walk away, Willie would release the 110V wire so he could use the phones. The tenders didn't like anyone talking to their divers without permission. Proper protocol was supposed to be used to go through the tender for communication with the diver.

On an abalone boat, if one of your crew couldn't make it, you could use someone not familiar with your operation, but to take out a full crew of green hands was not a good idea. I know of at least two divers that were killed because of this practice. There was a lot of skill involved in

Solid Brass

live boating a diver. Especially in heavy gear. Some of the heavy gear divers used to split dive, diving a half day each. When one diver was down the other operated the boat and they would have a mutual tender.

One diver I knew, who had a small personality problem, used to go through better than a dozen tenders per year. He anchor-boated, so he could get away with breaking in a new tender every time. He was a good producer, so the tender knew he would make good money as long as he could put up with him.

In the abalone patch, I was lucky and kept the same crews throughout those times. Les Davis, my partner in my first boat, and I had a good time working

The perfect tender; Sid Jerik's tender, Tom, administering hot soup on a cold day while working on the Chesapeake Bay Bridge. *B. Wick photo*

together. I felt bad about him opting to get out of the business; I became very close to Les and his family. Jim Lindsey tended me from San Diego to Morro Bay. Jim decided to go back to San Diego, where his family lived and try diving himself for a while.

Indian Dick Vierra and Doggy worked with me on my bigger boat. Once my check valve slammed shut, so I went through the procedure of getting to the surface in heavy gear after being cut off. All I could think while on the way to the surface was, "Ol' Dick wouldn't cut me off." Dick was such a good operator, it was unthinkable he'd get my hose in the wheel. I got up the ladder and started beating on the deck with my iron. Everyone was so busy on the bow trying to get me air, they didn't see me come up the ladder. Dick didn't wrap me up, the hose had blown on deck and in doing so, blew the phone wire out. I had lost air and phone communication at the same time, the same effect as being cut off.

Big John Pierce was one of the best operator/tenders in the business. John's dad was the famous Bill Pierce, who started abalone diving as we know it in Morro Bay. Albacore Al was tending me while Big John was operating. Also, Jimmy McKutchen tended me from time to time. Big John, Albacore Al, and Jimmy worked with me right up until I went to the oil patch.

Albacore Al had been in the business probably as long as anyone. But, there was one problem. His reputation was that he sometimes just didn't show up, but it had never happened to me. Everyone told me to

The Author and Indian Dick with their mascot "Big Red" off the California Coast. *B. Wick photo*

Solid Brass

wait, it'll happen. One morning, Big John and I were waiting in the coffee shop and, wouldn't you know it, Al didn't show. We heard a chorus of "I told you so." I kept my faith telling everyone, "He'll show up." Finally, in walked Jimmy McKutchen, who said, "Al wasn't feeling well and asked me if I would tend today." So Al still hadn't let me down.

Sometimes your tender could get a little testy. Once I was being tended by young Jack Fonner on a bridge job in the Chesapeake Bay. Jack is the son of Lil and Jack Fonner, who were some of my closest friends. Jack Sr. being one of the older divers in the business, going back to the abalone patch.

Our job was on a jack-up rig in about one hundred ten feet, which was the deepest spot on the job. The diver on another area didn't show up one morning, so they called for us to catch a boat and come over to their barge. I was to bring just my dress because they had the helmet and everything else I needed. After getting onboard, I told Jack to check the gear and get it ready, I'd find the foreman to see just what the job entailed. A short time later, Jack walked into the foremen's office. Not being one to hold things in, and without even saying good morning, he blurted out, "I'm not going to dress you in that shit!"

I walked toward the door in an attempt to get Jack back on deck before he said what he really thought. It was totally dark on deck because of the early hour, the weather had been rainy and slushy with lots of hail and real cold due to the fact it was late in the year. With the available light on deck, we looked at a helmet that the Smithsonian would have liked to have in its collection of antiques. The front port was so small you might have to close one eye to look out. The air gooseneck on the back was rattling around and only held on by the rivets, the solder which made the strength and seal was broken. It was the oldest and most beat up hat I'd ever seen.

The diver's phones had one switch, on and off, no volume control. There was a nylon lifeline, which the East Coast divers had tied around their waist and that the tender played out separate from the airhose. They had the standard Navy belt that still had the old jock strap that very few West Coast divers used. Jack didn't want to put me in this pile of junk. He only agreed to dress me in after I convinced him it would just be a

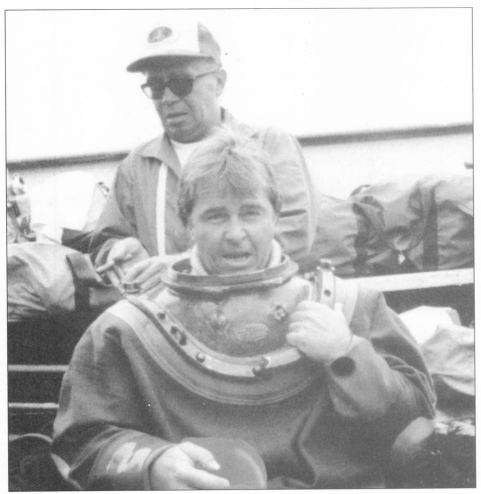

The Author and Willie Stratton, my tender of thirty-some years.
B. Wick photo

bounce dive to make a quick inspection and I'd be right up. As of this writing, young Jack is one of the older divers out there still favoring his heavy gear.

Willie Stratton tended me longer than anyone, from Mexico to Alaska, all through my diving career in the oil patch. Although having already met Willie while diving abalone, our close relationship actually

Solid Brass

started after I went to work with Woody Treen. Willie had tended Woody for many years and was already a respected tender in the oil patch. Willie taught me a lot about the business in those early years and we went on to work together for over twenty-five years.

Once, while having breakfast with Albacore Al, in one of Morro Bay's local spots, something we were talking about prompted Al to tell me a story that was near to his heart. He was probably in his sixties then and the story went back many years. He worked for a diver who was also one of his best friends. This diver was notorious for not keeping his gear in proper working condition. One day Al went to the boat and put all his personal gear in a bag and while walking down the dock, ran into his friend. At this point of telling the story, tears started down his face. His friend asked him where he was going. Al said, "I've asked you to get your gear fixed and you won't do it. The latch on your helmet is broken, the gasket is so worn, the hat wobbles. Your phones don't work half the time and I'm not going to be the one who puts you over the side to die." He then walked down the dock and didn't come back. A few days later the diver took out a green crew, his hat came off and he was killed, the crew not having that little extra knowledge to get him up in time. After all those years, Al had a hard time telling this story. He felt, by leaving, his diver would finally get the gear fixed. Now he wondered if things would have been different had he been there. To make things worse, the crew couldn't get the diver on board; they tied him to the ladder and that's the way they took him to the dock.

SIX

Oil Patch

I left my boat tied up in Morro Bay and headed for Santa Barbara. I left belongings with friends and rented another garage to store stuff. I still had one rented in San Diego at this point. After renting a furnished apartment a few blocks from the harbor, I went to the shop to check in. No one in the shop was expecting me, but there I was, chomping at the bit.

We held meetings at Danny's house in those days, to talk about gas diving, how to work the tables, and a myriad of other diving logistics. Danny Wilson had the most influence on getting gas diving off the ground on the West Coast. At those first meetings of general offshore diving, there was Danny, Laddy Handleman, Whitey Stefens, Huey Hobbs, Jerry Ruse, Glen Miller, and Reggy Richardson. We went out to do a few rig jobs and the word was getting out about the new company. I remember when Danny was suppose to get his picture taken offshore, after his first gas dive, for a publicity article. That morning he showed up to work with a big shiner. Someone punched him at a party the night before. On top of that, the photographer had to wait around on deck before he could take this classic photo of Danny standing in his breast-plate with helmet in hand. Danny's hat wouldn't come off after his dive. We had to take all the nuts off with a T-wrench and take the breastplate and hat off all at the same time. Just to show that the chance of this happening was pretty slim, for this historical dive photo, I've been diving for over thirty years and I've never had a breastplate stick that bad.

Solid Brass

After a time of working offshore (and inshore for that matter), it appeared that the four primary divers of the company could do all the diving. Granted, it's what they had to do, but I didn't see when I'd get a shot. I started to get just a little disenchanted.

Bob Colome, an old friend from the abalone patch, told me about Woody Treen. He was working for Woody and took me to meet him. He had a lot of work coming up and could use another diver. He asked if I had skin gear here so I could meet him in the morning, go out and look at the job they were on and make a dive with him. He wanted to see how I handled myself in the water. Well, my gear was still in Morro Bay. I drove there and back that night, round trip about 300 miles, so I would be able to meet the Treen's diving crew in the morning with my gear. We went out, made our dive and I stayed with Woody for twenty-five years. First working for him, then partnering up with him in three different corporations.

The day after going out with Treen, Whitey told me they had a job coming up at San Clemente. He said he couldn't promise me diving, but if I'd tend him he'd try to get me in the water. That shows I wasn't totally correct about the situation with Danny. I told Whitey that Woody had offered me a job. He told me to go for it with his blessings, which was important to me. Whitey is still a good friend and we still work together from time to time. Somewhere in our history, Whitey managed a large diving company and bought one of our barges.

Woody was about my height, 5' 7" in his thirties, Irish with a good sense of humor, and we hit it off right away. He was instrumental in launching the diving careers of some notable West Coast divers. Woody was well-known in the diving business and had a lot of work, primarily with Texaco at the time. He kept the guys that worked for him quite busy.

Treen's Commercial Diving had a small shop on the Santa Barbara airport, a one decompression chamber-sized company. Woody kept six to eight people on full time and also used independents, or guys from other companies, when he needed them.

Although this happened many years from where I am in this story, it is interesting, so I shall include it now. Woody and I had three partners in our barge company. In the beginning, it worked just fine. We found our

Solid Brass

Woody Treen, my partner for over twenty-five years and the man responsible for launching countless diving careers. I loved him as family. *E. Treen photo*

Solid Brass

barge in a government bid sheet. It was in the Navy mothball fleet in San Diego. We put in our bid and got it. We formed a corporation, putting in equal amounts of money, and went down to San Diego to see what we had bought.

It was a beauty and it looked like new. We could tell by the deck's condition she had hardly been used. The crane was sealed with monkey shit (a sealant used to make everything airtight), so we could just see the outside. To go below we had to use battle lanterns as there wasn't any electricity. We found a new shaft in a cradle on the second level, all stitched up in canvas full of Cosmoline. On the port and starboard sides there were brand new spare screws bolted to the bulkheads. I wandered off to look in another compartment and yelled at the top of my voice for the other guys, as we were the only ones on board. This compartment was full of bins of spare parts. Some bins were just full of brass pumps. There were tons of brass parts.

In the engine room, we found one engine with a hole in the crankcase, where a rod had come through. The other engine looked OK. All the electric motors had been gone through and had paper on the armatures. Everything was painted and in perfect repair. Up in the wheel house, the large wheel was still in place, as was the binnacle, one of the large wooden binnacles, with a very large compass in place. The front of the house was made of brass sheeting and brass angles, so there'd be no compass deviation. This was getting to be more and more like a fairy-tale.

We had to have her towed to the dry-dock as the sea chests were welded closed. We had made prior arrangements at this dry-dock to have her hauled out. We had her hauled out to open the sea chest, paint the bottom to the waterline, and have a survey done for insurance. We had a new engine on its way.

Billy, one of our partner's sons was on the payroll to help us. Scooter and I took him down to Tijuana one night. After driving across the border and parking our truck, we had a few tortas on the sidewalk and hit several bars. We walked into one place feeling no pain and were a bit noisy as we moved through a whole lot of people sitting and listening to some type of Mexican opera. About that time I noticed everyone was

Solid Brass

dressed in their finest and taking this very seriously. Knowing this was no place to have Billy, who had already insulted everyone we'd met that night, I turned around to collect everyone just in time to see Billy dump a full taco on the brim of a very expensive Stetson. It didn't have to fall far, because the guy sat very tall in his seat. He didn't feel it and nobody saw it as he was in the back row. This taco was full of salsa, and it would just be a matter of time before it started dripping. Billy still had the folded tortilla in his hand as we dragged him through the front door.

We hit just enough places after that to assure we'd feel like shit in the morning. There was one incident that finally sent us home that night. Scooter and I were at a table in the back of a typical Mexican pub, when we heard a lot of noise up front. Billy had just started some kind of trouble. We came very close to having to fight our way out. We used some big time bullshit to get out the front door alive. We made ourselves heard by yelling at the top of our lungs, throwing a few chairs, and strutting around acting so tough that nobody wanted to mess with us. We dragged Billy right to the truck, after searching for it for a good two hours. The fact we might have to take a cab out of Mexico wasn't that bad, but we had a company pickup with several thousand dollars worth of compressors in the back end. I hid Scooter's and my Rolex under the dash. Scooter's was welded there, I guess I'd hit some hot wires with his when I carefully shoved it under. It was never the same after that.

Having a full hard day's work on the barge the next day was the second time we'd paid for the tequila we drank the night before. We spent over a month getting our barge ready to sail, which was over our budget, but necessary. One major job was cleaning all the monkey shit off the cracks. After finally getting into the crane, we found it to be in excellent shape with a beautiful Cummings diesel to run things. We got all our insurance squared away, had a survey which turned up a replacement value twenty times what we paid. We paid right at $60,000 and replacement was a little less than $1,000,000, not including all the spare parts. We could have gotten our money back selling all the brass we found aboard.

We finally got underway for Santa Barbara with our new barge, *The Happy Hooker*. A few of us were on board and the others followed the coast in the pickups, in case there was a problem. There was no problem, it was perfect. We'd drawn up some plans on building up the bow to place a skadget for our four-point mooring and a lot of other things that needed to be done. We planned on doing most of the work ourselves in the interest of cash flow. We'd use a professional to make our ideas Coast Guard legal.

We'd only been back in Santa Barbara a few days when we got a phone call from the Suma Corporation (owned by the famous recluse, Howard Hughes) saying they'd like to use our barge. "We just got here, how did you know we had one?" was George's first question. He went on to explain we still had quite a bit of work to do on her before we could take any job. "How long will that take?" George told them perhaps a couple of months. Their reply was to get all the men and welders

Our newly outfitted barge, the *Happy Hooker*, en route to work for Howard Hughes' Suma Corporation off Catalina Island, California. *E. Treen photo*

needed to get it ready in a couple of weeks and they'd pay all the costs, including mobilization and demobilization.

The next day we had the entire Navy Pier in Santa Barbara full of welding and delivery trucks. The barge was crawling with people. With an incredible effort from everyone involved, we were ready to go on schedule.

As Suma directed, we set sail for Catalina with a full crew and a twenty-ton winch on our stern. We were sailing under sealed orders as we still didn't know what the job entailed. We only had a channel to call when we arrived in Catalina. Real cloak and dagger stuff. We were told not to use any photography equipment nor board their ship, the *Glomar Explorer*. It was well-publicized, so we already knew that Howard Hughes was transforming a large drill ship to mine mineral nodules that lay at great depths on the ocean floor. They would be testing their equipment and practicing what most people thought at the time, mining underwater nodules. It turned out we were to be the anchor boat for the *Glomar* while they tested their equipment. We did this for several weeks, then brought the barge back to Santa Barbara, job complete—or so we thought.

We started doing business as usual, looking for work on the coast, distributing brochures about the barge, and doing some small local work. Then we got another call from Suma. "We will need the barge again, in about two to three weeks." George told them we were looking at a contract with PG&E to do some mooring work about that time. "Don't sign any contracts, we'll be up tomorrow." They came out that very day and gave us a contract to stay tied to the dock at their expense plus $500 per day until they needed us.

We had a mooring in Santa Barbara Harbor and only went to the dock when we had to, because of the cost. Now we were tied to the pier where we could work on our new quarters and whatever else needed to be done. All this was being paid for. The fairytale continued. (I couldn't have fantasized one this good.)

After the two or three weeks tied to the dock, we got the call and headed back to Catalina for a few more weeks of work. This time when the job was completed and we went back to Santa Barbara, we never heard from them again. One other nice thing they did for a young company was to fire payment right back with each billing we sent.

Solid Brass

Like everyone else, we found out why there was so much secrecy surrounding this job. The real reason the *Glomar Explorer* was testing their equipment was not for the mining operation but rather to attempt the recovery of a recently sunken Russian nuclear submarine that laid somewhere in deep water.

The barge continued to do well after that little leg up, but the strain started due to the fact there were five partners. Woody and Lloyd couldn't say good morning to each other without an argument. To illustrate how crazy it got, Lloyd took us to the labor board to get his salary. He took his own company to the labor board! The board probably still tells that story over cocktails. We had all voted to let our salary slide for a while enabling us to do more work on the barge. All of a sudden Lloyd got impatient. Once, while Lloyd was lighting off the engine room he, being the engineer that day, got mad at someone and walked off the barge while a very important oil customer was standing on board waiting to get underway.

I'd hurt my back in a skiing accident and walked to the dock one day against doctor's orders. I limped over to the boat with my cane and a damn tight girdle just in time to see Scooter jump out of the crane. He'd just had an argument with Woody, who was on deck directing the crane. Again, we had customers standing on the dock. Scooter was up the ladder and gone. At that time, Scooter and I were the only two that knew how to operate the crane. This was a mechanical crane which took a lot of leg power. It took me forever to climb into the cab cursing the missing crane operator at every jolt of pain. I had to use every tender new muscle in my back to make the levers and brake work to clear everything from the deck. I needed help to get out, after the customer left. I still get apologies from Scooter over that incident, he didn't realize I'd be the one to take over. (Sure!)

The petty crap seemed to be mounting so Woody and I talked it over before we spoke with our banker. We made a proposition of either you buy us out or we'll buy you out. Lloyd went to Whitey, who was managing Ocean Systems at the time. Lloyd knew Whitey would love to have the barge. Ocean Systems bought the barge and Lloyd. He continued on with them with one-fifth ownership. This arrangement didn't have a happy ending because Lloyd's one-fifth finally got bought out.

Solid Brass

At this time I lived on four acres in the Santa Barbara hills above the mission and just a level above the fog. The house was old and had an interesting history, it had been moved from the town of Santa Barbara where it served as a whorehouse somewhere in Santa Barbara history. The hardwood floors and walls were out of plumb, but it had a big fireplace and redwood throughout, which made it a comfortable place to come home to.

I had an Arabian Stallion, which I was paying off at $100 per month. I used him for breeding and bought horses from another part of the state to ride and put a pretty good handle on to sell. This brought in extra money during slow times in the diving business. I had bought a very rank horse from the feed lot in Buellton, planning to make a good riding horse to sell. It had been a long dry spell for diving, not much work at all, so I trained several horses. Ocho, the one I bought at the cattle auction, tried every dirty trick he knew. He tried rubbing me off under a tree a few times, but his worst habit, by far, was his cow kick. He had a few moves that could have earned him a black belt. One day being half-stupid, I put just a warm-up type blanket saddle on him with the stir-ups attached to a stitched on leather strap. I had him seemingly under control, when he decided to start bucking. I don't mean some little crow hops, I mean a higher than the fence, the horizon going out of sight, rodeo big pointer. As I rolled to the back, my legs flung into the air with a terrible jerk and all the stitching pulled out of the stirrup strap. I continued to roll off his ass end. Being we were both airborne, I had a long way to fall and he had the time to get off one more good hind kick, which got my foot with full force. As I picked myself off the ground, I knew that noise I heard was the sound of breaking bone. I had lace boots on instead of riding boots. I made it to the back porch and started to untie the throbbing left lacing. I removed it to watch my foot grow in size. I hardly had time to feel sorry for myself and draw water to soak it when the phone rang. It was Woody; Platform A had just blown in and we had to get to the shop to get gear together and head out on a dive to try to stop the flow of oil.

There was no way I'd be able to go on the job with a cast on, and no way I could miss this job as it was the only one in some time.

131

Solid Brass

So, I wrapped my foot in ace bandages and hobbled to the shop. On the job everyone was busy getting set up, under enormous pressure to try and stop this flow coming out of a fissure on the ocean floor. So, my limping around was hardly noticed. This was the now famous Platform A blowout that caused entire environmental groups to be formed. I could not believe how hard the oil company involved worked (and money was no object) while trying everyone's ideas to get this mess under control. Ridiculous pay scales became standard for people working on the beach doing labor in an effort to clean up. The company didn't need any other bad press or union problems, so they just ate what was thrown at them.

Platform A is in two hundred feet of water, and requires a decompression chamber and use of gas or air at this depth. It worked out to a dive of twenty minutes duration if using air, and a little more than double that time on gas. Still not much time to work. We had a lot of divers out on other jobs so as soon as you were "back in time" from decompressing, you were in the water again. You have to wait twelve to twenty-four hours after a decom dive, depending how deep, before making another dive.

The oil was coming up in several places. I made the first dive to try and determine how big the worst leak was. I was on the bottom walking towards the sound, which sounded like a freight train. The closer I got the louder the roar became. There was no visibility. Sensing I was very close, I slowed down. All of a sudden I fell into a very large crater, having to fight to maintain any kind of control. I had lots of slack out because I was traveling. By the time the tenders got it all up, I was laying in the bottom of a fifteen by thirty-foot hole, with the ear-shattering roar just a couple of feet away. I took measurements, then started for the surface.

On my next dive, I was walking on the bottom with a light and a line that was attached to a drill string, looking for another smaller leak. The idea was to find this hole and guide the drill string over to be placed and sent down the fracture until it bottomed out. Then, pump in heavy drill mud or cement to plug off the leak. My light picked up what looked to be the world record shrimp. He was about the size of a small lobster. I stopped and picked it up and started to place it in my chaffing pants pocket.

Solid Brass

His arms shot forward and cut my thumb almost to the bone. Still holding his back, I decided I didn't want him in my pocket. The front pockets are too close to an area I didn't want him punching holes in. I let him go. Holding on to my thumb, I located the hole, stabbed the pipe in and headed up.

While doing my decompression stops, in the much cleaner water, I would let off the pressure on my thumb and a steady stream of blood would rise toward the surface. The little shit hit a pumper on his first shot. Herb was on my phones. I told him he'd better get some towels, gauze, or whatever he could find to help stop my leak when we got in the chamber. We had blood all over the outer lock before getting me out of my gear and some pressure bandages put in place between sips of the coffee he brought in. I proceeded to tell him about the unbelievable size of the shrimp I ran into, how he cocked his arms and let me have it, and how, after so many years of diving, I'd thought I'd seen it all.

"That was a Mantas Shrimp," he said. Herb continued to tell me how this shrimp looks like a praying mantis when it sets itself up to strike. It strikes from its claws, which have a type of bone crustacean that is razor sharp. He saw the "how come you know so much and I didn't even know its name" look on my face. He explained that he had just recently read an article in a *National Geographic* magazine.

Later while limping down Navy Pier with my thumb in a bandage, another friend asked what had happened. I said, "You wouldn't believe the size of this shrimp." "That was a Mantas Shrimp," he said, and told me how one had broken a 1/4-inch plate glass in the fish tank in the Diver's Den, by striking out. By now, I was feeling pretty stupid, and of course, the doctor wondered why anyone would be messing with a Mantas Shrimp. I was the only one in town that didn't know about a Mantas Shrimp.

I bought a Playtex glove to put over my bandaged thumb and sealed my cuff over that to keep my new stitches dry for the next day's dive. Luckily, I set my foot pretty good in the ace bandages, because we were on this job for over a month. It wasn't until years later a doctor discovered from an x-ray that my foot had, in fact, been broken.

The Author (at left) and Woody Treen replacing clamp on a riser off Point Conception, California. *E. Treen photo*

Texaco had an underwater manifold that had some subsea wells hooked to it which we serviced three or more times a week. They also had an ongoing well drilling program from a floating drill ship in the area of the manifold. Once a well was established, our divers would guide the wellhead lowered by the drillship, and make the connections. After the drillship moved to new location, we would run pipes from the new

Solid Brass

wellhead to the manifold. This was a fairly shallow field of one hundred to one hundred fifty foot water depth just off Point Conception.

The drillship had a hard time getting its anchors to hold because of the hard shale bottom. To combat this, the company drilled many anchor posts in the shale to secure their anchor cable. We lowered and attached the large anchor cables and buoyed them at the surface.

While running the anchor cable, I found some good abalone beds at a few of the anchor posts. There was an abalone diver by the name of Al Green, that I'd known for a few years. He used to be a boat operator for other divers. He got the bug to get into the water himself, and from time to time, they'd dress him in and let him run around on the bottom. One night at Joe's, I ran into Al after

Chuck Lindquist emerging from a 296-foot dive off Santa Barbara, California. *H. Harris photo*

135

he'd had a few horns. He came to my table carrying his drink and proceeded to tell me he'd never be able to get a boat from Barney (the processor who owned all the boats in the famed Black Fleet). He figured Barney wouldn't think of him as a diver because he'd been tending and operating boats for so many years. "Besides, I'm a Mexican," Al said. He was on a real bummer that night. I used a kind voice and little finesse to tell him he was full of shit. He'd never know if Barney had a boat coming available unless he asked.

Sometime later, he did get to split dive on a boat, but not one of Barney's Black Fleet. I had told him about one of the spots I had found out by the anchor posts, so I wasn't surprised to see him headed for the area one morning. He was all dressed in and gave me a big grin as he passed our barge. That night Woody and I had gone in and Bob Colome remained on the barge to make the last dive. Bob called me that night. Al had died on the deck of our barge. Sometime during the afternoon he came up on deck, sat down to have a smoke, and passed out. His crew took him to our barge knowing we had a decompression chamber. They cut him out of his gear, but he was dead before they could get him under pressure. I remember seeing Al's dress laying on the deck the next morning. It was so new, I figured it probably wasn't even paid for. The autopsy showed Al's heart was a half-size larger than normal (sometimes known as an athlete's heart) and it was full of bubbles. It seemed at the moment, it was too bad Al even got a boat, maybe he'd still be alive if he was just tending or running a boat for someone. The fact is, Al wanted to dive and he probably wouldn't have been satisfied until he got the chance to decide if he liked it or not. There was no mistaking that smile as he passed the barge that morning.

The barge from which we did most of our work was the Pacific Tow Boat, *Barge 6*. It had a small crew and a barge master, Carl Foley, who, just by being the person he was, did a lot to put in place some of my values and the way I think today. Carl was nicknamed Boullion. For years Carl told these stories about his gold mine in the mother load country, near Grass Valley, California. Carl was born in 1902, had a full head of white hair and a bright twinkle in his blue eyes. He chewed a little tobacco and had a colorful vocabulary, at times only fit for the barge.

Solid Brass

In all the years I knew Carl and being in some tough situations together on the barge, I never saw him lose it. "Do the best you can, that's all you can do," were some words of wisdom he used a lot.

He had these little sayings and parts of jokes he'd use at the peak of a stressful situation. For example, we'd be sitting around on a job that wasn't going well, contemplating our next move. Things could be so bad, there didn't seem to be a way out and Carl would enter and say something like, "Just remember that old saying," and we'd all listen intently, "Fuck it." Then he'd walk away and leave us to wallow in these words of wisdom. The situation wouldn't seem so bad after a laugh. You could be having a horribly bad day and he would always have some way to pick things up a notch or so.

Carl talked so much about his gold mine that we always assumed he had spent years prospecting. He told us of an old dog he had at the mine who used to chase rabbits. He'd run and run until his tongue hung out and when he finally knew he wasn't going to catch that rabbit, he'd pull back, smell a flower or two, lift his leg, take a leak and act like he really wasn't trying anyway. He also told us about the cat he had at the claim. When Carl came in at night that old cat would see him coming, jump up and pull a string that would start the generator so the lights would be on and the coffee would start brewing. Another story he told many times was about his friend that lost his false teeth, killed a bear, fashioned a set of teeth from the bear's and ate the bear with the bear's own teeth. He cheated at cards and would steal your lunch. If he saw someone coming to retrieve a piece of cake he was caught with, he'd quickly lick it all over. Every day offshore, there was something he did to bring a smile or uncontrollable laugh. Something as simple as making his own rules to an old card game. Standing behind you to reveal the hole card you just drew, he'd blurt out, "You're screwed, the last 10's gone," knowing someone else needed it.

After several years of believing in Carl's mine, I had a time coming up when I could finally spend a month or so with him there. He used to tell me things like, "When you get to the mine you can have the Bridal Suite" (the room where he kept the horse bridles) or "You know you're really living way out in the country when you can walk out and piss off the front porch on Saturday morning."

Solid Brass

I kept on Carl to make plans to go up and work the claim as we'd always talked about. He finally had to admit he'd bought the mine to do the clean up. When a mine operation is finished, the slush boxes and equipment sometimes hold enough gold to make a fair payday. Carl never actually worked the claim, but made quite a bit of money on the clean-up gold and sale of the equipment. I never did get to meet the dog or cat or piss off the porch.

Anytime Texaco asked for the barge it had to include Carl and his crew. For all those years we worked with the same people handpicked by Carl. We became very close, if someone in the crew got sick or hurt, it was more of a family thing than just some guy you worked with. Even the support people we used were always the same. Walt the welder was so good at what he did that Texaco paid for him and his equipment. His equipment sat in his truck at the dock; they let him use the welding gear on board the barge. He was so unbelievably good at his craft, I know he could have welded your wristwatch.

On the Texaco Jade Lease project, we had to make pipeline connections to a new platform. It involved putting together and sending up many different templates for Walt to use as patterns. He took each one and built precise pipe and flange spool pieces. There were bolt holes in each flange that had to line up perfectly with the corresponding flange on the ocean floor. We sent up fifty-seven templates and put down that many spools without sending one back for a change. Each one of these weighed several hundred pounds, and had to be lowered by crane which took a diver at each end to put into place.

We had a wire line crew that used to come out, Hoot Butler and his brother Billy. Billy used to think it was funny to wait until someone was sound asleep in the decompression chamber, after a long tiring dive, and take a hammer and beat on the chamber and quickly disappear. It was like being inside a ringing bell for the diver. I waited until he was in his wire line unit and in deep concentration lowering a wire into the well, which took precise skill and complete focus. He was so engrossed in what he was doing, he didn't hear me come up behind him carrying the large hammer. I bounced it off the top of his little open aired wire line unit's tin roof. He flew out of the open door and straight over the side of

Solid Brass

Light Gear spread on the deck of the *Shamrock* in Cook Inlet, Alaska.
B. Wick photo

the barge to a very cold early morning swim. We all lined the side of the barge and took turns telling him how we got paid to do the diving and had a strong union that frowned on scabs coming into our area. As he did his poor imitation of a Johnny Weismuller stroke to the dive ladder, his frantic climb up had to do with his fear of sharks we had seen in the area. He was one to tell us, on a regular basis, how crazy we were to work in an ocean full of all those critters. From that time on, any noise we heard on the outside of our chamber had nothing to do with Billy.

The sharks in this area were mostly blues and very seldom did we see them while on the bottom. When you did, you would have to wonder how many swam by while you were busy at a project.

Through the years I worked for Woody, before we partnered up, there were many times another company would call me and if Treen's was not busy, I'd go out for them. Associated Divers was one such company.

Solid Brass

Pete Brummus and Ted Benton did most of the work for Atlantic Richfield and when they needed another diver, they'd give me a call.

On one of these call-outs, I was working two-hundred fifty feet on gas doing some repair work on a collecting tent on the bottom. This was an area of natural seep, the oil company used a tent to collect some of the oil that came up in an area near their platform. We had placed it here some years before, it was set over a very large seep. The oil would rise and go through a large hose that went from this tent to a large, several thousand gallon bag on the surface. When full, a tanker would come out and pump the bag dry. In this way they had oil to sell and help keep down the size of the oil slick from the seep.

Some days the current in this area really got moving to a point that a diver could hardly work without being dragged off. I was coming off the bottom during one of these times, using both my legs and hands to hold on. As I started up, I kept the air in my suit very low to have a smaller target in the current but the hose drag was still pulling me off.

We normally used a down line from the surface to the job site on bottom, or in this case a large transfer hose that ran the full distance. This enabled you to know where you were at all times and helped to control your assent when you had decompression stops in the water. But now struggling to keep a hold on the hose, I was about to be dragged off to drift at the end of my hose in the current. I informed the surface I would hang heavy but could no longer stay on the hose. About that time they were changing me over from gas to air, a common practice as you started up, but for some reason they started to lose pressure.

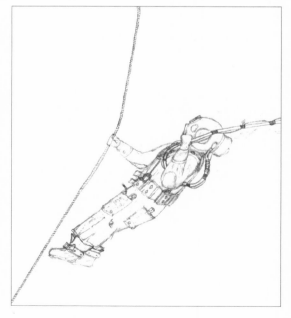

140

Solid Brass

I informed them of this. They were full out trying to find the problem, but by now I had only the air in my suit left to breathe. All the air coming down my hose had stopped. I shut off my exhaust to keep what air I had. You have five to ten minutes of good air in your dress. On a gas dive, the ascent time is so critical that we use stopwatches to get you from one decompression stop to another. You can't just be pulled straight to the surface. Air dives are a little more forgiving, you have a small window of time that allows you to get back under pressure in the chamber after getting on deck. With gas dives, you might not make it up the ladder before getting a bubble.

The time finally came when I'd used and reused all the good breathing in my dress and I was starting to see stars. I had to get myself ready in case I passed out. I had to open my exhaust and just crack my air valve. If, while unconscious, they got air to me and the valves weren't set right, I would blow to the surface. I was still alert enough to go through these procedures, but losing it fast. Just before my lights went out, I heard a sound,

The Author off the coast of California between dives. *B. Wick photo*

141

way off in the distance—a hissing—and with it, the sweet smell of the small amount of air starting down my hose. How good that felt, and timely too.

Anytime we worked in water one hundred feet or better, we had a decompression chamber and a stand-by diver. A stand-by diver is fully dressed in, only needing to put on his weight belt and helmet to be ready to go over the side. This is normally routine, the stand-by makes the next

Diver descending in full Navy Mark V gear. *E. Treen photo*

dive when the working diver's bottom time is up. On occasion he would have to help the diver out of a situation.

One stand-by diver incident happened off the California coast on a particularly large natural oil seep clean up. We were setting a large, several thousand pound, tent on the ocean floor, over the seep. The oil and gases would accumulate, balloon the tent and continue up a hose to a catch float on the surface. When full, a small tanker ship would dock alongside, pump the oil out and take it to the refinery. The tent was rolled up and lowered over the side of the barge by crane. A diver would follow it two hundred fifty feet to the bottom, cut the ties, unroll it and attach it to a steel frame that we had already put in place on the ocean floor.

Ted was the diver to go down with the load. I was his stand-by on a scheduled rotation of divers. After one diver ran out of bottom time, the stand-by diver would be ready to make the next dive and another diver would then dress-in to stand-by, and so on, until the project was completed. Divers at this depth could only put in twenty minutes on air or forty minutes on a mixture of oxygen/helium gas. In either case, they would have many hours of decompression for this short bottom time because of the depth. Some of the decompression would be done in the water while ascending and then an additional ninety minutes on oxygen in the decompression chamber on deck.

As Ted started down with the load, all was going well until the crane malfunctioned-something happened to the braking system. I looked up at the crane operator who was now frantically trying to stop the cable. I watched the boom of the crane actually let go and bend itself over the stern of the barge. The weight of the mangled boom slamming against the deck acted as a brake preventing the release of any more cable. While I watched this chaos unfold, my tender Willy, immediately prepared my gear while I got ready to go over the side.

Ted had been riding the load down, giving instructions to his tender over the phones, "coming down easy," when the load started falling. He was caught off balance and the load turned him upside down. He had to hold on and ride it down to about one hundred feet off the bottom before it jerked to a halt. It all happened in just seconds.

Solid Brass

Ted was being tended by his brother, Bob. While on the phones with Ted, he explained the situation to me as he helped Willy put on my helmet. Ted was having a problem hanging on because he was blown-up and upside down. Even more urgent, was another bit of a problem—his helmet was leaking and water was seeping in. We had to get to him fast.

Bob and Ted were very close, and I had a special fondness for Ted since he had always been one of my mentors. He was one of the old staid and true deep-sea divers that I admired when I first entered the commercial diving business. So this, to me, was like going in to help Superman! Needless to say, my helmet went on wasting no further time to conversation and, now as I look back, I believe I was *pushed* over the side.

The worst position a heavy-gear diver could get in, is upside down. The reason the Navy uses heavy lead diving shoes and commercial divers use heavy lead ankle weights. Ted was able to hang on but I didn't know how long. Bob would repeat to me what Ted was telling him. There is no diver-to-diver communication, so I relied on Bob relaying Ted's conversation.

The oncoming air had nowhere to go but up to his feet. It had no way to get out because the only exhaust is on the helmet, and in this position, the wrong end. If Ted was able to turn off his air intake valve, he would have been able to reduce the air in his suit and turn himself upright. This was impossible because his entire suit blew up like a balloon, leaving his arms extended, unable to bend. The danger being that the air will fill the feet, legs, and arms of the diving dress, balloon it to the point of blowing the diver to the surface and somewhere along the way—explode! As he leaves the pressure below, the more he ascends, the more air volume in his suit...the pressure around him lessens and the air in his dress expands, eventually causing the suit to burst. If this happens, buoyancy is lost and all his lead weights will take him to the bottom. With this fall back to pressure the diver would be crushed, or as we call it, "squeezed."

There are stories of early deep-sea divers being buried in their helmets. Situations like Ted's and more commonly, a burst or severed airhose would cause the air in the diver's helmet and dress to be sucked up the hose leaving his body exposed to the depth pressure. The sudden loss of equalizing air causes the outside pressure to actually pulverize the body and bones to a pulp. Since the dress is flexible and the helmet solid and fairly large, that pulp is sucked or "squeezed" up into the helmet. All that is salvageable is the helmet containing the remains of the diver. (Our helmets today are fitted with non-return valves which close when triggered by the rush of escaping air back up a damaged hose.)

As I headed down Ted's hose, I used as little air as possible to allow me to drop as fast as possible. Less air in your suit equals less buoyancy. Bob was throwing my hose after me so I didn't have to wait for slack.

I got to Ted in record time, there he was, upside down, feet straight up, holding on with one hand, looking somewhat like the Pillsbury

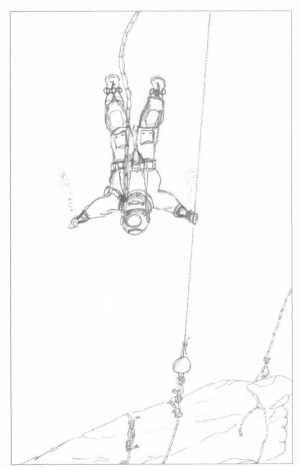

Dough Boy. I had never seen a diving dress blown out to such proportion. Ted was a large man to begin with, and now there was all this extra girth and bulk to deal with.

On my descent, Ted had assured Bob, that the seep, so far, was not a problem. I was happy to hear that, it was one less thing to worry about. I could only hope he could hold on long enough to get him into a more diver-friendly position.

I turned off his air intake and opened his exhaust all the way. I got up to the end of his feet, dumped as much air as I could to get as heavy as I could, grabbed a leg under each arm and leaned.

Solid Brass

I used his legs as leverage and my weight against them to get his buoyant body to start turning. It seemed like an eternity for his legs to start moving, ever so slowly, and another eternity for them to break over center. Once we were there, I knew I had it, and now I would not have to execute my other option of stabbing a hole in his dress. Not the option I wanted to use, but I wasn't going to let him blow to the surface.

Finally we were both upright. Still holding him down, I walked my hands up his suit, past his weight belt, past his breastplate and as my helmet leveled with his, there, looking back at me was his smiling face. I hadn't spoken a word to the crew until then, I told Bob, "mission accomplished, we're back in business." He informed me that Ted had already assured him of that and also about this handsome devil looking in at him. Bob's somewhat relaxed response was "If you guys are through screwing around down there, get your smiling asses up here and start your decompression so we can get on with cleaning up this mess you made!"

This job was becoming one exciting event after another. Just the day before, while hanging at my one hundred-foot decompression stop, I noticed something off in the distance—something very large—coming my way. The water had been exceptionally clear at this depth with excellent visibility, enabling one to observe what generally is in the shadows. As the dark figure got closer and very much recognizable, I said to my tender, "You wouldn't believe what I'm looking at!" Judging by the tone of my voice, he said, "Shark."

Solid Brass

It was massive, the largest shark I had ever seen and it was swimming right at me, coming in slow and deliberate. After confirming Bob's presumption with a simple "yes" my next answer was a simple "no" to his call to pull me up to get in the chamber. I wanted to stay right there where I could keep a cautious eye on that curious eye of my very large friend. He got so close before turning that his tail wash actually moved me around like a buoy in a boat wake. I got a good look at his eye as it met mine while he slowly oozed by, as if to show me his entirety. Holding my breath in anticipation of his next move, I kept both of my eyes on his huge mouth, fully expecting to get a close up and personal glimpse of his pearly whites. He completed his turn and left in the same direction he came, never changing his course or speed, disappearing in the distance. I spent the rest of my decompression looking over my shoulder and back again. I must have looked like I was watching a ten-

nis match. I have been in the water with a lot of sharks, but none had such presence and authority as this |creature. This was one big shark—and he looked me right in the eye.

As you get closer to the surface, decompression stops are longer, sometimes as long as one hour. Many times the tender will lower a perch so you could sit, tie yourself off and get some sleep. I have to wonder how many times one of these visitors happened by while I was taking a little nap.

I was doing one of these long hang-offs after a particularly long, hard dive off the California coast. I was tied off and in a deep sleep. My dress contained just the right amount of air, stretching my arms out in a comfortable position. All of a sudden I felt a tug on my arm...a tug that could only be made by something that could swallow me whole.

Immediately wide awake, I first checked to see if my arm was still there and intact and there, pulling on a string hanging from my frayed cotton gloves was a "small" calico bass. I knew, from the look on his face, this little fish knew, by the look on my face, that his wake-up call may have caused me to have to change my shorts.

SEVEN

Cook Inlet, Alaska

Our inlet dive boat, the *Active Diver*, sure didn't look like much. It had very little free board because the house was big for the rest of the boat. Our chamber didn't have heat, except for the hot water bottles our tenders put in the outer lock just before we left bottom. Sometimes it would be so cold, we'd stick one under each arm and between our legs, as close to the crotch as possible, and cover up with as many blankets as we could pile on.

The house was fairly comfortable for the nine men on board. There was always someone in the bunk when we weren't working, so there was plenty of room. The control, wheel, radio equipment, diesel stove, and table were all in the cabin (wheel house). There were also a couple of bunks in the wheel house. The rest of the bunks were in the bow, straight down a couple of steps from the wheel house. Although not beautiful, she was built hell for stout, and had two good diesel engines. That combination probably saved our lives more than once. And for those of us that worked on her year after year, there will always be good memories of the old girl.

One year when the water was just a degree from freezing and the outside air the same, the time of year you would lose all feeling after being in the water for a few minutes without survival gear. We had no survival gear on board. We'd just finished a diving job and were heading home. If we had any idea how bad the weather was building in front of us coming out of the arm, we'd never have left. Instead, we would have put her

Solid Brass

on the beach and let the tide go out "inlet" style, and wait it out. But, instead, we got to a point of no return, of sorts, when the weather hit full force.

The weather had been building all along so we had everything put away and battened down. Normally there's no swell in Cook Inlet, no long rolling swell like on the Pacific Coast. We have the second highest tide in the world and it happens in six hours from low to high. The tide moves six to eight knots. This day, it wasn't flat, we had twenty-foot seas doing eight knots and wind gusting over a hundred. It took us seven hours to travel a distance that normally would take forty-five minutes.

The sea was having its way with us. We'd be heading in one direction and get tossed and be headed 180° in the other direction without turning the rudder. A few guys were down in their bunks and the rest in the wheel house holding on. Karl was extremely seasick and Roger, who was in his bunk in the wheel house, was close to getting that way. We had Dutch doors in the back of the cabin. Karl was leaning on the bottom half, while the top was latched open. He was leaning hard, trying to barf on the outside. We seemingly fell off a twenty-foot swell and the concussion threw Karl and the door hard to the back deck. He went surfing clear to the stern. We all ran to get him back before the decks went awash again and tossed him over the side. Now Karl was on his elbows and knees, where the door used to be, still barfing. The smell of it all oozed up to where Roger was hanging on to his bunk. He bolted out, yelling, "It's got me! It's got me!" Now we had two in the doorway, head down and ass up, barfing with all the energy they could muster. What completed this picture, was they were both naked as newborn babes.

We now had so little control of the boat, it seemed crazy that Ted was still at the wheel doing what he could. I was standing next to Ted trying to see out, but we were under the water more than on it. All of a sudden the windows had all they could take and in they came with several hundred gallons of silty inlet water. One particularly ugly piece of glass missed cutting Ted's throat by only a few inches.

For the last few hours, it had been all we could do to stay upright and not be tossed around the cabin. And now we had freezing water pounding on us.

Solid Brass

The ship-to-shores were attached to the overhead, so they were the last to get wet, but were soon sparking. We knew we were about to lose them, so I tried "May-day, may-day, this is the *Active Diver*, we're several miles southwest of Fire Island, calling Coast Guard Anchorage or any boat in the area!" We continued calling, giving as close a bearing as we thought, without the aid of sophisticated navigational equipment. The entire time the radios were smoking and shooting out more sparks. We just wanted someone to hear us and make note of our location. Finally, the Coast Guard came back. They were getting ready to come out, but it would be at least thirty minutes before they could leave the dock. I told them thanks but we were taking on more water than we could pump out and if we didn't make it to Fire Island, they wouldn't be there in time.

We had already thrown everything that wasn't welded down over the side; large spools of cable, boxes of large nuts and bolts, etc. We had lines tied to us while we did all of this because of the huge chance of getting washed overboard. The sea would come over the stern and it would seem forever while we held on for our lives before we could finally get a short gulp of air. We couldn't dwell on how serious a situation we were in because we were too damn busy trying to stay afloat. Once your body temperature dropped below numb, you didn't think about it a lot.

Our only hope now was that we were approaching Fire Island, and, if we could make it, we'd run the old girl right up on the beach. Just before we did, a very large helicopter came over us. It was from Elemondorf Air Force Base. They monitor the Coast Guard channel, heard our mayday and dispatched this big beautiful bird. They got underway as soon as the wind allowed. They were flying in minimums now. When they dropped the horse collar down, we told Karl to get in, figuring he must be horribly weak, but after the windows went, his adrenaline (like everyone else's) started pumping and he felt great. Also, the fact that we were getting into a lee made all our spirits explode. We thanked the Air Force very much for the big warm glow they caused, but no one on board was hurt and we would now be able to save the boat. We later made a more formal thank you. Their fast action would have saved our lives had we lost the boat.

Solid Brass

We asked for all the horsepower the engine had and drove her as high on the beach as possible. She settled to one side. When the engines were shut down there was a silence more than just the lack of engine noise. It was a few seconds that each man had for himself, and then came loud cheers and handshakes that led a huge outburst of laughter that hadn't been available for the last few hours. All of this had come to a sudden halt. Everyone on board was soaked to the bone. The windows were out, the door was gone, the only stove heater on board was full of water and the temperature was twenty below with a wind that made a hell of a chill factor.

Willie and I kept our bags in the same place, which had watertight integrity. We had the only dry clothes on board, so everyone stripped down to their blue-pink-red bodies. "Nothing to brag about here boys," was our next attempt at humor. What dry clothes we had were passed around. We then took our very heavy, water-soaked mattresses up on deck and stuck them in and about our windows, in an attempt to keep the wind out. We tied lines and laid weight belts on them to keep the damn wind from blowing them away.

We bailed water out of the diesel stove, put up a makeshift stack and eventually got it going. Now we could look around and laugh at the uniform of the day. Some of us had Levi's that fit somewhere between the calf and the knee. Some of us had wool diving pants. Now we were starting to feel our feet and fingers. But the pain that came with that didn't matter. Sometime in the night the wind blew out, the sea laid down, our boat refloated, and we limped the short distance to Anchorage. Some days later, Scotty Holen presented us all with handmade stocking hats that she had knitted. They were given to us as our survivor's hats. After all the years gone by, I still know exactly where to find mine.

In the Inlet with such short tides and black water, time is very precious. There's a few times in the Cook Inlet, Alaska, when standby diver rescues didn't come off this fast. The days were getting shorter and there were signs of freeze-up, small ponds of ice were now forming in the Inlet indicating that this would be the last diving job of the season. This should have been just a routine dive. The crane operator lowered a pallet load of cement bags to the ocean floor. The diver would go to the bottom, spot the pallet under the pipeline near the leg of the drilling platform and unhook the slings on one side. The crane would then come up to dump the bags in the washed-out crater, stabilizing the pipeline.

The diver had gone down one hundred fifty feet to the crater, guiding the crane by instructions to his tender over the diver's phones. Except for my helmet, I was fully dressed in as stand-by diver. I was standing in for Jack Coglin, a very good diver and veteran of the Inlet. I used a pile of cement bags to lean on to absorb some of the weight of my breastplate and tried to get comfortable and stay warm. One thing most us heavy gear divers had in common was a breastplate bump. The large, shoulder level, vertebre that became calcified and enlarged by the constant rubbing of the breastplate. The same deformity as many surfers developed on their knees from kneeling on their boards in the 50s and 60s. I was rubbing my gloved hands together when I noticed Ted, Jack's tender, getting kind of anxious and uneasy while communicating with Jack. I walked over to find out what was wrong. I wasn't able to hear the phones (or anything, for that matter, with the level of noise from crane and deck gear). Ted told me he could not get Jack to answer. I could see that the crane was still coming up after losing communication so we immediately signaled to have it stopped.

We were not able to get a response from Jack on the phones, nor through emergency hose signals. Three pulls from the surface tells the diver to prepare to come off the bottom, four pulls, emergency. Jack was not responding. We also knew, by the feel of his hose, that there was something dangerously wrong.

Without any time lost to further conversation, my helmet was on and I was over the side, starting down Jack's hose. Dropping as fast as my tender could throw my hose over the side, I kept my body gripped to Jack's lifeline. It was the only way to get to him in the Inlet's zero visibility. I suddenly slammed on top of a snarled mess of hose, wires, metal and wood, all tangled with Jack's hose. All the wires and hoses were twisted around the crane's headache ball and pallet.

I felt my way around this mess and continued down, discovering the break in the phone line, still attached to Jack's hose, but severed at this point.

Solid Brass

I followed the hose further to find out if it was damaged. What I felt told me what had happened—but had we stopped the crane in time?

The crane had pulled so hard that the air hose was stretched to about half its original diameter and the phone wire was ripped off of it for about twenty feet. Finding all this destruction only increased my fears of what I might find when I did finally reach Jack.

Not knowing just where he was or how much further I would have to go, I continued down. It was obvious that Jack's hose, and possibly Jack, was pinned. No sooner did I get moving, not far from the whole mess, there he was, my leg hit his helmet. My first concern was if he was still getting air through that stretched out hose. I reached up to feel his exhaust and felt bubbles, he was getting air. Then his hand met mine assuring me that he was all right.

The feeling of relief and gratification to have found Jack unscathed, only lasted for that brief moment. I knew I had to get Jack's hose free and get us out of that tangled mess. I told the crew that Jack seemed all right, he was getting air and I was going to follow his hose down to see where it was fouled. Not that this wasn't enough to deal with, they knew they had to remind me that the tide had turned and was starting to rip. Having a difficult time keeping my lead-weighted feet under me, I was already well aware of this situation.

We all knew that we were moving into the tide change when I went over the side. We can only dive in the Cook Inlet during the slack water, between low and high tides. Once the tide starts to move the other way, the diver has to come up. In a very short time the water would be moving six to eight knots. Heavy debris runs in a thirty-foot tide, including logs, telephone poles, etc. We once had to steer clear of a whole cabin going out with the rushing tide. Hypothermia would also be a big problem in these near freezing waters. Whatever the situation on the bottom, I knew the tide was going to interfere with my progress. Having factored all of this into my next move, I was already working fast.

I followed Jack's hose all the way to the bottom, where I found it hung up under a piece of angle sticking out from the platform leg. A tune could have been played on that hose, it was pulled so tight. It felt like a rigid pipe. Hard to believe it withstood the strain and that Jack's air flow wasn't cut off.

I had the crane come down a little so I could pull the hose out from under and start coiling it as I headed up. I coiled it up around my shoulder, fighting its bulk as well as the running tide. The surface could not help me with Jack's slack because of the big tangle above him, but they could pull up on me as I was piling the hose to keep it from fouling again.

It was getting harder to get me up because of the tide pulling against me and the weight and drag of all the damn hose I was piling up. I finally got back to Jack; he had positioned himself around the pallet and headache ball in a sitting position. With my last adrenaline rush, I managed to sit on his lap and pile all the hose around us. I told topside to come up on the crane and both our hoses, all at the same time.

As we broke the surface we immediately took on the full weight of all our gear and the tangled hose. We had no way of knowing if we took on more than we could handle in the near weightless environment of the water. Holding on took every bit of last strength we had left and now the tide was pulling on the hose left hanging in the water, adding even more weight.

As the crane continued to lift us to deck level, it took the entire barge crew to haul in all the hoses and line left dangling. When they had deck under us, the crane set us down in one big bird's nest of hose, pallet, headache ball, and two divers in the tangle. It wasn't a pretty sight. The only difference between this unruly ball of salvage and any other was the two hard hats in the middle. As cold as it was, when the crew got us untangled and our tenders were finally able to sit us up and remove our helmets, we were ringing wet with sweat.

Jack did not mind that it was necessary to stuff him into the decompression chamber with a soft mattress, pillow, blankets and a hot cup of coffee!

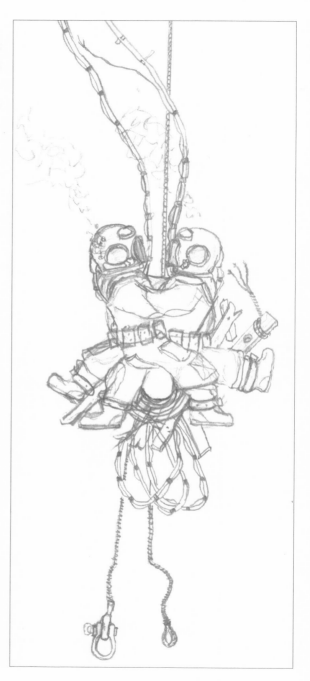

Solid Brass

Such comfort after the reality of what happened and what could have happened! Afterward, sitting in our wools in the galley, it was time to reflect on this. If the crane would have come up just a few more feet, it would have pulled Jack's hose apart and he would have fallen back to the bottom. With the current running, as it was, we would have had to depend on one of Jack's nine lives or my good luck to locate him. I would not have had his hose to follow. As it turned out, we didn't have to deal with the "what could have happened" on this "just another routine dive," and the last job of the season.

Some years before this, while one of the platforms was being erected in the Inlet, Jack got himself into a similar situation. I was on another job so I must just tell this as part of the Inlet folklore. Jack was on his way up, somewhere between the bottom and the surface, when his hose became fouled on the bottom. He could no longer go up and the current was running so hard by now, he couldn't get back down to clear himself. Of course, the stand-by diver would not be able to help either. Jack still had communication this time, someone had the idea to lower the steel basket by the crane to Jack's level and let the current push it into him. With a topnotch crew, and the edge of luck, it worked. Jack climbed in the basket. Now what! His hose was still hung up on the bottom. Jack told topside, when they could no longer communicate with him to pull the basket to the surface. He was going to cut himself loose. With a firm grip, making sure not to drop the knife halfway through, he first cut his air supply, then his phone wire. That's when they pulled him from the Inlet and on board the barge. No one could be sure it worked until they saw him in the basket, breathing the last few precious minutes in his dress.

Roger Jacobson and I went back a long way, spanning to our close friendship in the Frogs. I was the first dinner guest at his house after his marriage. We were very competitive, constantly joking and blaming each other for problems that occurred on a dive. We did a lot of work together on the bottom in the Cook Inlet, with zero visibility. Being able to second guess each other was our big asset in that situation. On some dives involving decompression, we would tell our individual tenders to give us a couple of seconds warning so we could leave our last stop, beat

the other to the ladder, and go up first. Of course, as soon as we felt each other leave we would blow ourselves to the surface, which would result in a big fight at the bottom of the ladder. To the point of the first one on the ladder stepping on the hat of the other and kicking him off. All of this in front of the customer, most of whom were used to our shenanigans. They were confident in the fact that we knew our stuff and appreciated the injection of some humor on a hard job. We always supplied the banter and jokes on our jobs together.

One incident that used up everything I had and was left to depend on our deck machinery, happened while we were working a pipeline in the Inlet. Roger was on the bottom trying to finish up. The tide had changed, the water was moving and getting past workable. As soon as Roger let go of the pipe to come up, he and his hose were swept off by the heavy current. He found the current faster than he'd expected, but he managed to scramble back to a leg hold on the pipe.

Unfortunately, the tide was running, in the direction to take his hose under, instead of clear of the barge. Even though the current had him, we would have been able to reel him in after he hit the surface. The way the hose was bent under the barge, the crew could not pull him up. They tried all different angles trying to pull the hose away from the hull. The current had it nailed to the bottom and no amount of maneuvering would free it. He now was lying partly under the pipe holding on with his legs and arms.

I was still dressed in, having just come up before Roger. Already having decided what had to be done, in no time my helmet was back on and I was over the side starting down his hose with a cable from a deck winch. The water was running so hard I could barely stay on his hose, especially where it was pressed against the bottom of the barge. It was so flat against the hull, there was nothing to hold on to.

Sheer determination got me through and I continued pulling my way down his hose. Even though I loaded my ankles with all the extra lead we had on deck, my legs were still lifted straight out in the tide. There was nothing anyone could do to help; just throw hose, let out on the winch, and hope the current didn't take it all before I got to Roger. I had a hell of a time holding on to the winch cable; the current was really pulling and jerking it around. We were going to need it to pull us both out. I couldn't let it get away, it was our lifeline.

Finally getting to where Roger was glued to the pipe, I took the end of the cable, ran it through both our belts and nylon chaffing gear straps. I then shackled the steel cable back into itself and gave the command to start up on the winch. Once we both let go of the pipe, there was nothing we could do but hold on to each other and go for the ride. We now had to depend entirely on the machinery and the crew on deck.

Both our minds were on our two hoses burning under the bottom of the barge in the same area as the moving cable. If the hoses got under the cable they would be severed and our air supply would be gone, leaving us with only the cable to pull us up and not enough air to get us up from under the barge in all the confusion. Once we got to the surface it would take some time for the crew to get us out of the current and back up from under the barge. With all the weight we had on and just enough air in our suits to breathe, we were still straight out in the tide, like a fall leaf in the wind.

At times we bumped the bottom of the barge as we neared the surface. The crew was hauling ass trying to win the struggle. Since we were sucked together with the cable threaded through our belts and in an intense embrace, we had to work together, kicking ourselves away from pounding against the steel hull.

At these times you always say to yourself, you'll leave a little earlier next time, you will never allow yourself to get in this situation again. While busting your hump on a dive, you'll save enough energy to get to the surface, but the next dive you do the same damn thing. Wait until the last minute and come up so beat that you have trouble climbing the ladder.

But this time, we barely had enough strength to climb the ladder. By now, we were being dragged at a tough angle under the barge. This made it almost impossible to climb, especially with all the extra lead I had put on to be able to get down. With our last bit of strength we managed to grasp a rung of the ladder and with as many of the crew that could reach out and

Solid Brass

grab any part of us, we were jerked up on deck.

As soon as our heads were exposed from under our helmets, we looked at each other, knowing one of us had to say something derogatory. Roger said, through his sweat-soaked beard, "I stayed a little too long." Through my heavy breathing, all I could reply was "Don't ever do that again."

We sat down on our boxes so our tenders could start taking off our gear. We both could see how totally washed out the other was. Steam rising from our heads as the cold air met our overheated bodies inside our dress and wools. It was quite a funny sight, it being the first thing we saw after the whole episode in zero visibility. We broke out in a contagious laugh that the whole crew caught before it was over. That's what it took to break the unmistakable tension that was still evident, even as we all staggered to the galley for a hot cup of coffee.

I recall that dive, as we were dragged through the ripping tide, our helmets banging against the bottom of the barge, and wrapped around each other in a loving embrace. What an image it must have been. But there we were, back aboard, in good repair, and finding the humor after such a predicament.

Solid Brass

This had been a bad couple of days for this crew. Just the day before, Roger and I were working on the bottom in the same place, when one of our new divers, Bill Morterud, was headed down guiding some crane wires to us when he passed out and had to be hauled back and dragged up the ladder by the crew. We found out later, his diving gear had malfunctioned, but this being his first "proving myself" dive, he tried to get to the bottom anyway and damn near bought it.

Bill is now one of the "old timers" of the Inlet and we're still working together today. What he didn't know that day, and in fact, just recently found out was that Roger and I had made a bet. Bill and another friend, fresh from UDT, had just shown up in Alaska seeking diving work and got hired by Roger. Because they were from our old alma mater, and young, with the "Hoo Ya" attitude, Roger and I placed a small wager on which one would prove up to be the Super Frog. My choice was Bill. Roger thought he won after Bill's incident and was ready to run him off that night. He hadn't yet heard about Bill's gear malfunctioning. Of course, I promptly filled him in and the bet was still on. Turns out, three days later Roger's pick packed it in and headed for the Philippines.

One dive Roger and I did together under a platform also involved adding some humor to the pain. We were pulling old anode cables and sleds to be replaced with new. I was working near the leg burning off a flange. Roger was working further under the platform, trying to get a sling under the anode sled. I had just finished when the torch blew up. It had such a flashback that the fire took a good layer of skin off the back of my hand as it blew off my glove. About that time my tender informed me Roger needed help with the sling. I told my tender the torch blew up and completely destroyed my glove. I'd be coming up the ladder and not to take my helmet off, just put a left-hand glove on when I stuck up my hand. Then I'd be ready go back to Roger.

At that time of year, you could not work without the special wet-suit gloves or your hands would freeze. As I stuck my hand out to the waiting glove, my tender went back to the phones to tell me I should come out of the water since my hand was looking kind of shabby. I insisted they put on the glove. It would just be a few minutes while I helped Roger and the dive would be over. Against their protests, they put the glove on and down I went.

Solid Brass

As I reached out to feel Roger's hand to know where he needed help, he reached out with his other hand and squeezed my burn. I yelled to Willie to tell him if he touched that hand again I'd put a hole in his dress. At the same time he was telling his tender something similar. It seems the hand I had a hold of had a swollen, extremely sore finger that Roger was trying to baby. We spent the rest of the dive being careful of each other, sending kind, considerate expressions of sympathy to each other through our tenders. After the dive, I was lifted to the platform by a personnel basket and flown, by helicopter, to the hospital in Anchorage to have my hand attended to. We were finished with this job anyway.

Another unscheduled helicopter flight I made was on another project off a barge anchored alongside an inlet platform. The production pipe coming out from the leg had most of its support washed out by the tide. We were putting very large blocks, several tons a piece, on either side of the leg. We would later fill the blocks with cement bags that would harden and stabilize the pipeline. For some reason one of the blocks would not fit into place, so I was down trying to find out why. I was down long enough for the tide to shift and start moving. The barge moved with it and so did the block. It smashed against the first two fingers of my right hand. I told Willie I was on my way up. After climbing the ladder and on deck, while my hat was being removed, I told Willie to take off my glove and see if anything was missing from the hand I held in the air. There wasn't even a cut in my wet suit glove. I turned my head away as he removed my glove, I was pretty sure of what he'd find. "They look all right," he said. But as I turned back to look he said, "OK, maybe this one's in trouble." My index finger was a bit shorter than it was before the dive-from the joint under my nail to the end was pinched off clean. I was getting out of my wools into my clothes and everyone was in and out with concern before I thought of looking for my finger in the glove. There was some pandemonium for a while, while the crew looked in the wrong glove before realizing their mistake and found it in the other. They put it in a baggie packed with ice.

I was standing on the deck of the tug that would take Willie and I over to the platform, when I looked up to see Karl looking very concerned.

Solid Brass

I stuck the stub in the air and said, "Karl, it's my trigger finger!" That was enough to make him look even worse than I felt.

As Willie and I were flying in the chopper, my finger safely tucked away in Willie's coat pocket, I said, "If I pass out or anything, don't let them take my knuckle off." I didn't feel a bit sick, I think standing around the deck in twenty below helped detract from the thought. I wasn't sure how your system was supposed to handle all this. The stubby finger didn't hurt at all, it was the one next to it that was doing all the complaining. It had been smashed and hurt like any smashed finger hurts.

We landed at the helipad right at the emergency room in Anchorage. We had called ahead and got the best surgeon in the state. As he looked things over, he told me the end of my finger had been smashed too severely to replace. There were infection and nerve ending complications involved that weren't worth the effort. He would have to chip away a bit of the bone to gain enough skin and flesh to pull over and stitch. This, he thought, would build a tough fingertip protecting the nerve endings.

About that time there was a call for him so he had me soak my hand in some sort of solution until he returned. He finally came back and asked, "How are you doing? Good. Well, there's been a bad car accident and they could use my help." So, I sat there and just about the time he'd be coming back to work on me, a gurney came crashing through the door. They sat it just beside me. The guy in it had a hole in his head. He'd been shot. They rushed in and ran him off to another room. My doc came running in—"I'm fine," I said before he asked, "I can see you're going to be busy again." After seeing that guy, I didn't feel there was an urgency to deal with me.

A nurse came in to check on me and I asked if I had come in during their rush hour. She explained that it wasn't always like this, I just showed up at a bad time. She said I'd be spending the night, so I asked to be put in with Del, another one of the diving crew who got hurt earlier in the day. He had busted his knee. He was in a different section of the hospital and the nurse said she'd see what she could do. She didn't need to, because when I finally got my turn I told the doctor how great I felt, so why couldn't I just go home after the stitches? He agreed, and that's just what I did.

It's tough to deal with a missing body part, but it helped to realize that with the weight of that block, it could have crushed a leg or an arm or any other part of my body. Or it could easily have been my air hose. Cedar, our crane operator at the time of the accident, was one of the best in the business and a very good friend. To this day, when I see him, he still wants to make sure I know he didn't move anything. He's always felt bad about something he had no control over.

Again, talking about your air hose getting cut off in black water, the problem being not so much the loss of air as it is for the stand-by diver to find you. One such incident was avoided while diving on the Chesapeake Bay Bridge job in Maryland. At the time, we were putting down the largest can to be placed on this project. It was awesome in size and it would take several divers to spot it on location. There were many mats full of piling which this can had to fit over without punching a hole in her and allow the cement to leak out. We were within just a few inches of setting the can in place when I had them hold everything, meaning all the cranes came to a halt. This is one of those few times in your life when something happens that you can't explain. I wasn't sure why I stopped the load, but I wanted a look around, actually to feel around, there was no visibility. I started moving around the can to my left. I hadn't gone too far before I came across Sid Jerick's hose laying right where we would have set her down. It took several cranes to lower this can, it was so heavy. We had all been moving back and forth, checking on the progress and making sure everything was coming into place. A bit of Sid's hose was laying in the guillotine, so to speak, and it must have felt OK to his tender when he pulled in his slack. That's the stuff that shortens your chances of becoming an old diver.

The zero visibility that I've talked about here is usually just something to slow the job down as well as make you watch out for your fingers. It's the Cook Inlet, Alaska. It's more than just a body of silty water with no visibility. The Inlet moves at six to eight knots, or more at times. A thirty-foot tide is usual and the tide goes from low to high in six hours, so it's really hauling ass to complete its cycle in this timeframe.

Solid Brass

Stinger and pipe-laying barges high and dry in the incredible thirty-foot tides off the Cook Inlet, Alaska. *B. Wick photo*

No diver has ever been trapped through a full tide, so we're not sure if he or his equipment could hold up under such a pounding. Thank God we've never had to find out. We've spent many a year trying and learning how to deal with the Inlet. The early days were spent learning through trial and error. We made mistakes, but it was all part of the learning process. The early drill ships even had to learn how to anchor up in this place. The four-point mooring systems we used in California didn't work here. Sixteen-point did.

When we dove the moon pool, which is a hole midship through the hull, used for drilling, it was harder to tell what the tide was doing. Also, you couldn't see the bore tides coming or the large trees that might be on their way to tangle in your hose. Probably the worst thing on a drill ship to happen to me personally was during this kind of dive.

While lowering a riser pipe, it took so much time to get it ready and near the bottom, that the tide had turned. One of the drillers asked if I could make the dive even though the tide had changed. We had people on

all the anchor winches to move the barge to enable me to stab the riser in place. The riser had to be in place before they could start to drill. I agreed to give it a shot. I knew, as I was going down, that the tide was really starting to move and picking up fast. I worked for a long period trying to stab the riser, until it was obvious, even topside, what was happening. The current had the large mass of pipe pulled way out of alignment. Even moving the barge didn't help with the pipe at this angle.

As I started up, I found I had been in a little bit of a lee on the bottom behind the large riser. Now, out of it, I could feel a current like I'd never been up against. They inched up some on my hose and attempted to get me to the surface, but there was a bit of my hose behind the riser. It was hung up on one of the bolts holding the large sections together. I was being crushed against the riser now with the force of the oncoming tide.

I could hear the despair in Bill McWilliams voice, when he told me they didn't know what to do. I'd already told them not to send Bill down, my stand-by diver. He wouldn't be able to get through the moon pool at this point.

Solid Brass

Everyone on board was so concerned about me, they hadn't thought about the riser having to be pulled back up. It can't be left unattached through the six-hour tide. I suggested they get started and I'll just ride her out. "But this is going to take too long," was the reply. "I'll wait," was mine. Each section had to be unbolted, picked out, and placed on deck before starting to pull on the next section. I was on the last section that would come out of the water. One of the roughnecks from the drilling crew, Black Bart, who helps pull the diver's hose during a dive, got so anxious when my hose would no longer come up. He was so worried about me being fouled, he ran over and picked up the stand-by helmet and put it on Bill—backwards! He was big enough to cross-thread the hat and breastplate, but they got it away from him before he got the chance. Bill McWilliams talked to me all through the long hours to come, filling me in on the progress. It seems this was Bill's calling in the business. He had the nerve-wracking job of comforting a trapped diver over the phones.

Another nerve-wracking time on the phones took place while we were diving on a new platform installation in the Inlet. The platform jacket had been floated to the location with tow legs and a large flotation tank holding it up. The other two legs were in the air above the floaters. There were two diving jobs going on at this point with two diving companies involved, a little unusual. Our company was burning out some plates inside the legs that piling would eventually go through. The other company was burning off safety gussets that were welded to the flotation tank. The gussets were only needed during transportation. After they were removed, and the platform could be tilted into position, the flotation tank would unhook itself from the platform. That was the way it was planned, anyway.

I finished cutting out the last plate completing our portion of the job. I headed up the ladder where Willie took off my helmet and clipped on my dog leash. It was a bit of a high wire act to get back to the barge. As we moved up the platform leg, he cut all the lines holding our burning gear and airhose. The line Willie cut also freed the hoses of the other two divers, Owen Boyle and Jack O'Brien. They would be finished cutting off the gussets in a couple of hours. Owen and Jack were working with Associated Divers.

Solid Brass

I had taken a shower, walked past the barge poker game, and climbed into my bunk. As I just started to dose off, I heard the terrible noise of ripping steel and the cannon-like sound of two-inch steel cable parting. This gigantic barge surged and moved around like a cork. I leaped from my bunk and put my pants on in the same motion as I headed out on deck. Before the gussets were burned through, they broke and split the rest of the way, releasing the flotation can and allowing the platform to sink at one end, without the usual control. The two divers working, one on each side, went down with the platform. The two-inch cables holding the platform tight against the barge had popped like worn-out shoe-strings. When the barge surged, one of the huge Burger Blocks that held the anchor cable, was torn out of the deck, leaving a large jagged hole. Owen and Jack's hoses went from a volume tank on the barge to the plat-form jacket, where they were trapped. The first thing to do was to rese-cure the platform to the barge.

It was decided for me to dress in heavy gear and get to the divers and for Pete Blommers to use light gear to swim the surface area as needed. Again, the tide had turned so we had that to deal with as well. We also had a bunch of pile buck welders to fish out of the rushing tide. They were working on the platform when it sank.

While we were collecting welders, Jack O'Brian surfaced. His weight belt was actually torn away and he was blown to the surface. What a turn in our favor. It turned out the lashings Willie had cut after my dive was a piece of good luck. Jack wouldn't have been able to reach the surface and it would have taken more time for me to cut the lashings.

Owen Boyle had also blown out, but was still hung up somewhere below the surface. They pushed a make-shift log raft over to where he was floating just under the surface. With Pete in the water and the ten-ders on the raft, they managed to get him up. The raft was so unstable, they cut Owen out of his gear just to be safe. The time it took for this turn of events was about the time it took to get me dressed in. I had a good adrenaline rush without having to do anything.

Through all of this chaos, Mac kept his comforting conversation going over the phones with Owen and Jack. Mac was one of the best

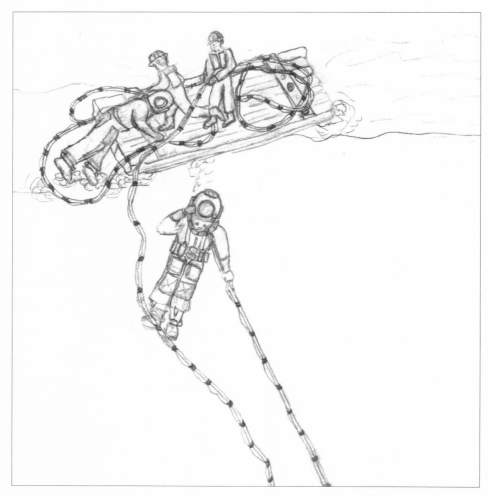

people working with us in those early days, but it wasn't too long after this incident he decided a career change was in order, a change which would put him onshore. He has since spent many successful years with his construction company in Soldotna, Alaska.

Unbelievably, with the tons of iron changing position, pieces of broken cable flying through the air, two trapped divers, and a dozen welders dumped into the now rushing inlet, all the injuries were minor. Owen split his lip and Ed Snyder, one of the tenders, had a perfect razor cut ear, no pieces missing, caused by a piece of flying cable.

Solid Brass

We found early on, you can't tell what the tide is doing by how it appears on the surface or by the direction of the driftwood. It could be coming in on the surface and already have turned and going out on the bottom. This situation accounted for many of our diving problems. Getting in before the surface water stops gives the diver a little edge on time in most cases. It also means the drift had to be poked away from the diver's hose with long pike poles. The extreme high tides would pull even more logs and other debris off the beach, including trees with their complete root systems. Once we saw a log cabin, perfectly intact, coming down the Inlet. We were waiting for the resident to wave us over for a drink, but he never appeared in the doorway.

One of the many times I stayed too long trying to finish a job, I had to climb a tree to get on the barge. It was a very large tree, over sixty feet. It had moved in and jammed itself under the bow of the barge, totally engulfing the ladder. Luckily, this tree had lots of limbs, which I

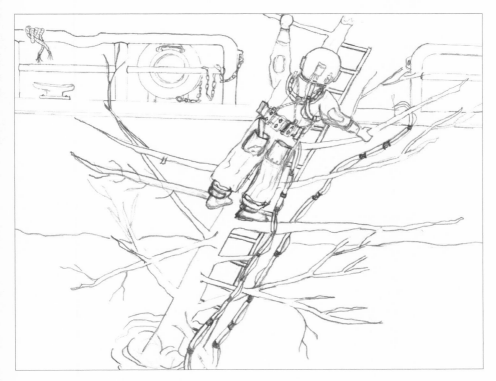

climbed to get on board. No easy feat in heavy gear. In the winter months, this problem is compounded by large ice pans. We are usually finished in the Inlet when the ice starts up, but not always, and some seasons start before the ice is gone.

There have been several boats lost to the Inlet ice. While tied alongside a platform in a tide change, ice pans start to build up against your hull and can actually push your bottom out from under you. The pressure from the rushing tide keeps building until it rolls you over. Some very large boats have gone down to ice. Smaller boats have been trapped alongside the platforms just by the fast moving water itself. In a few cases, the structure of the platform allowed the crew to just step off before their boat sank. Once the entire crew of a dive boat stepped off as the boat got trapped under the platform and was taking water across the deck. When the tide turned around, instead of rolling over, it popped out and drifted off. It was later recovered by another boat.

I recall another tricky situation involving the unpredictable ice pans. This one started out as a routine dive (as routine as a dive in the Arctic with icebergs floating by can be). The diver, who will remain anonymous, was down to rig up a very large anchor chain partially buried in the mud. His movement locating and dragging the large slings around, killed what visibility he might have had. The crew had been watching the ever-moving icebergs and large ice pans, when one huge iceberg started moving in the direction of the diver's hose at an uncomfortable rate. The crew told the diver he had to get out and finish the job after the ice passed. The diver was clearing himself to come off the bottom when he discovered his hose was trapped in the rigging. With zero visibility, he had inadvertently put the large sling around his hose. His first words over the phones were, "Ah, shit, I didn't do that!" Now things were getting anxious as the berg was closing and the diver was in irons. He was working as fast as he could and the guys on deck were helpless. Anxious minutes that felt like hours until he got his hose free. By the time they got him up the ladder and on deck, the iceberg was where his hose used to be.

Early or late in the season, we kept a close eye on the ice. We went as far as designating someone whose job was just to keep the ice away,

Solid Brass

again, with the long pike poles. It was already late in the season when we started a job for Marathon, putting twenty-five eight-ton anodes under a platform. After the anodes were in place, we had to finish the underwater portion of the installation of a special ice breaker that protected the anode cables. The anode cables would normally be encased within the leg with the other cables, but in this case, there was no room for them. We had used all the available tubes that were built into the platform. All this had to be finished before hard winter set in. The ice was building fast. Dealing with the Inlet tide is always crucial but the ice adds a new degree of hazard. We routinely make a dive every six hours during the slack water, which is normally about half an hour. Once the tide starts to run we have to either anchor out or tie up to a preset buoy and wait the six hours until the next slack.

Solid Brass

Attempting to salvage the *Deborah D*, east of Homer, Alaska.
P. Cook photo

Each time we came back to the platform to work, Captain Buoy would pace back and forth on his bridge, worrying about the ice, even though he had one of the largest boats in the Inlet. The divers were having their own ice problems; this was before air dryers when the moisture in your breathing air would freeze. Little ice crystals would move down the hose until there were enough to plug the air valve. We had some warning as you could hear and feel the small pieces of ice. Some would go through the valve and bite your face. Up we'd come, put our helmet in front of a Herman Nelson kerosene heater until the ice melted and then back down we'd go.

The last dive of the last day of the job was spent like a yo-yo. This caused us to stay late and the tide started moving, bringing in more large pans of ice.

Solid Brass

I was the last one out of the water that year. When I came on deck there was Capt. Buoy standing on the bridge watching his crew continue the struggle to keep the ice floes back, waving his arms declaring he would not bring the boat in again this year. As my tender took my helmet off, I grinned and yelled back, "We're finished! Why the hell are we still hanging around here?"

The following spring we started the season at this platform on our small dive boat, the *Active Diver*. We waited until the tide slowed enough to pull alongside the leg, throw a buoy into the tide and let both

Ice flows letting us know that our dive season is officially over in the Cook Inlet. *B. Wick photo*

175

it and the attached lines, be carried around the leg. We would fish the line out on the other side and tie ourselves off. The first diver was ready to go over the side. We always jumped a little early, just before slack, to get more dive time. The moving tide also enabled the first diver down to maintain contact with the leg by pushing him up against it. He'd tie off a line from the bottom of the leg to the boat. This down line is used to guide the divers to the leg in the zero visibility. We'd hand it off to the platform each time we left.

I had to go over the top of some pipelines, through a very congested area of cables and junk and under a diagonal. It took a while to get under the platform. My air started to get a burnt oil smell and was starting to burn my eyes. I reported this as I went about my business. It got worse before I was told to come up. I argued the tide wasn't bad where I was and it took too long to get here. Then I received a very loud reply of "Get out right now" in a very worried voice, so I started the trek back through all the debris. I wasn't out of the woods when my air started to get a little tight. Turning my valve didn't bring the extra air I needed. Now I knew without anyone telling me, not to dally and hope to hell I didn't get fouled. As I cleared the bottom and started up, there wasn't enough air to help lift me off the bottom, so they pulled and I climbed until my helmet hit the bottom of the ladder. I still had a small hiss of air coming in as I made it over the side. About the same time I got under the platform, the crew heard a type of explosion in the engine room, where the diving compressor also lived. Somehow, there was build-up in the lines from a faulty pop-off relief valve and the system blew up. The air I was breathing was the air left in the volume tank and the check valve kept it from escaping from the damaged plumbing.

Another time that sticks out in my memory of having a hard time keeping enough air to breathe, happened while we were installing a jacket in the Inlet. We had to jet two or three feet of mud off some knockout plates that were jammed. To get to the job I had to ride a stage down the inside of the leg to the water, get off the stage, drop down through a small manhole to another level, walk across a distance to another manhole. I did this while passing through some hose-grabbing obstacles. There were busted hydraulic hoses, used during the flooding operation, that

Solid Brass

were hanging everywhere. Being the first diver down I also had to take the jetting hose and burning gear through all this debris. After I came up, the second diver would just follow the hose to the job. Not having any visibility made this a long haul.

I had to weave my way down to the bottom with all the gear. My air started to drop so I told topside. They came back with "Get back to the stage." Up through the first manhole, passing by all the spaghetti again to get to the next manhole. I was getting less and less air and remember thinking, let's see, was there another level, another manhole? I didn't remember walking by this junk—Bang!—my helmet hit the stage. By the time they got me to the surface, I had used all the air in my dress.

While the crew worked with the compressor, I waited on deck. When they were reasonably sure the problem was solved, down I went again, through the manhole, across through the spaghetti, down the next manhole, finally getting to the job. Paul Pettingill called on the phones telling me to get back to the stage. Man, here we go again. By now I've got a pretty clear picture of the route. This time on deck I waited while they made sure they had the problem fixed and a stand-by compressor in line.

Because several cranes were working on the makeshift wood deck and there were all kinds of machinery running, the crew couldn't hear our own compressor. There was not enough room nor did we have an ideal situation for our gear on deck. The volume tank was too far away to see the gauge, the reason why I had to tell them about the loss of air the first time. By the time I knew about it, it was already too late to come up comfortably.

Being a little short on air is one thing, but running totally out of air is a bit more exciting and in some cases, completely stupid, which holds true here. On the Jade Lease job off of Gaviota, we had *Barge 6* moored over the manifold while we were putting in a spool piece that went from the subsea well head to the manifold. While two divers were down tying in, Woody thought we could go out, in our scuba gear, to the other end of the pipe and do the small jobs that didn't require the crane. We had to take off blank flanges, rig snatch blocks, etc. We boarded our tug, the *Case Ace*, and traveled about twenty minutes to the end of the pipe. We had just enough bottles to do the job, no spares.

Solid Brass

As so often happens, we worked harder and longer then had been planned. When our regulators started to draw hard, we made the signal to get the hell up. Woody ran out as we left the bottom. I gave him my mouthpiece. As he pulled the last breath from my bottle, we wasted no time and headed to the surface as fast as our fins would allow. We looked at our Mickey Mouse, which at the time, were the first underwater decompression meters. We did need to decompress, which wasn't an option since our bottles were empty. As we broke the surface to take our first breath, Willie was going to step on our fingers so we couldn't climb the ladder. "You have to go back and decompress, damn it." Only after we explained our situation, not one breath left in the bottle, did he help get us on board. But not without a few sarcastic comments aimed at our stupidity.

Frog, the skipper, put the old *Case Ace* in the smoke hole trying to get us to the barge, and to the decompression chamber. She was a real slow rig, even at full throttle. Even knowing we were about to get the shit bent out of us, we laid on the deck and joked at the fact that we did it again— just one more crank of the wrench. Willie wasn't laughing, he just paced the deck, shaking his head.

We were beginning to unquestionably feel the bubbles shaping up and finding places to go that really hurt. Frog brought us both a cup of coffee and assured us he had the engine doing things it hadn't been asked to do since it was new. It was thousands of hours from being new.

By the time we got to the barge and in the chamber, we weren't joking anymore. I can't remember how long we had to stay in the chamber, but I know Willie added more time to a long table. He yelled things into the speaker like, "You had to get just one more bolt, did'ya. I hope it hurts, you stupid shits!" All a nervous reaction that didn't start until he was pretty sure we'd be all right. He didn't have any humor to offer while helping us get in the chamber. We couldn't get in by ourselves, we were so bent. The chamber was a safe place to hide while Willie calmed down.

On another occasion, Woody and I were going to make a quick inspection dive on a platform in the Inlet, in the middle of a twenty below zero dive. The wind was blowing at forty knots, which made the wind

Solid Brass

chill factor awesome, in a wet suit anyway. The crew was outside rigging up the spider on the leg we'd be diving. Woody and I stayed in a warm-up room until just before the dive. When everything was set up, we ran out, put on our gear and got on the spider, were lowered to the waterline, where we got off, made our inspection, finished, got back on the spider, and headed up. Just in time because the tide had started and brought the large ice pans back in and they were now below our rising stage. We suddenly stopped about halfway up. We found to our disbelief, the air tugger above had frozen. Just that quick and we were starting to do the same. Everyone was running to get something to put a quick thaw on the air tugger. I knew if I had hit my wet suit it would have shattered. We were dancing now, just trying to keep from freezing. We now had our hooded masks off because they froze and we couldn't breathe through them. We decided we'd be better off jumping back in the water to hold on to an ice pan rather than stand here and freeze to death. The tide was really starting to move, but the water would be much warmer than the air. Just before we had to make that decision, the tugger started to jerk and in a few more minutes, which seemed like hours, we were on our way up. The crew had found a torch and thawed out the tugger. As soon as we cleared the rail, we started for the hot showers. We couldn't feel our feet on the frozen steel deck. We were hardly able to move in our frozen wet suits, our hair looked like a shiny hat, solid ice.

Our wet suits would not come off until they thawed. I had an underwater torch blow up in my hand bad enough to send me to the hospital and that didn't hurt near as much as the thawing out we did in the shower that night. Thawing out was another great test of your pain threshold. If you've ever submerged icy cold fingers into hot water in an effort to warm them, then you have a small idea of how our warming process felt to our entire body.

If we had to jump back in the water, no telling how long we'd have been there. The tide was already moving in an absolutely black night. We couldn't use lights under water in that silty inlet, so we wouldn't have them to show our location. There were no boats out at night in the ice. We came to the platform by helicopter, which dropped us off and returned to its home base. The possibilities of what might have happened that night have been subject matter in many bull sessions throughout the years.

Another time jumping was the only option was, this time, off the California coast. Again working on a new platform jacket. We were working inside a leg in two hundred feet of water. This was a mixed-gas dive using heavy gear. We had to be lowered a long way to the water. We'd get off the stage, do the job, get back on the stage and ride it to the top where we'd hurry across some wood timbers to the chamber for the needed decompression. On a gas dive it's extremely important to get to the chamber without any loss of time. Each time, we felt as though we'd just made it as we'd close the hatch to blow down.

On one of these runs, I was up the leg about halfway, when the stage stopped. "We've got a problem with the tugger, Bob, we're working on it." Some time passes, "How ya doing, Bob? We're still working on it." A little more time passes, "How ya feeling?" By then, the way I felt is only known to someone that has had the bends. All the pre-bubble symptoms were there. I was just about to jump back in the water, which was a long way down, when the stage started moving. They were using another tugger to pull slack from the broken one. This was just a bit slower, but it got me up and I went on a very long decompression table. What's normal chamber time? What's long? I once spent forty-eight hours with a serious case of the bends, which is long. The bubbles you get in the joints or a skin bend, come with the territory, but with a central nervous system (CNS) hit, you're treated not so lightly. In over thirty-five years of diving, I've only had one and it almost got me.

We were flown out by helicopter to within a few miles of San Miguel Island, where the drillship sat at anchor in more than four hundred feet. Today, these dives are made from a bell and not considered a super deep dive. Back then, we were using heavy gear and gas and four hundred feet was a record for the West Coast. It probably still is for a working dive. We weren't there to break records; we were there because all the guide wires going to the bottom had been busted. They needed at least one connected to the bottom to get out of the problem this storm was causing. We knew the way our chopper had been bouncing around on the long trip out, that we'd have no picnic this outing.

Solid Brass

After landing on the pitching deck, we could see we were in every bit of a twenty-foot sea. I'd be tended by Don Stratton, Willie would be running the gas rack as the divers would be on helium and oxygen because of the depth. After getting our gear set up, Willie told me they would not put me in the water in this swell because I couldn't get proper decompression. We'd just have to wait until it laid down. He was right, but I argued the fact that this was the beginning of a very long storm and the drill ship needed to get off the hole. They needed one wire attached to release and retrieve their equipment so they could get out of there. I tried to convince Willie I'd hurry. He came unglued, but reluctantly put me in the water.

I barely got the wire on before my time was up. I had just a small stub sticking out of the bottom in which to secure my new line. Almost impossible. Using cable clips took more time than if I could have just shackled in.

As I was making my ascent very slowly to my first decompression stop, somewhere in the one-hundred foot area, I could feel my ears clearing while hanging there, indicating that I was in a pressure change. Instead of being in one depth, as I was suppose to be, I had at least a twenty-foot depth change as the seas rolled under the floating drill barge. Willie was pacing the deck, triggering the phone from time to time to tell me how stupid this whole goat rope was. "I should never have let you talk me into this," etc.

On gas, your last stop in the water is at forty feet, then up and into the chamber as fast as possible. This time, as I left forty feet to the surface, I started to get hit. I'd never before felt the bends come on while under pressure. By the time I started up the ladder, my left side was going numb. I made it to the top of what seemed to be an incredibly long ladder and Don removed my hat to get me to the chamber while I could still function. I told him to hurry, I'd lost feeling in my left arm and was starting to lose it in my right. He came in to dress me out and we blew down to fifty feet. Once under pressure, I got my feeling back. Don sat and drank coffee for a time, checking on me. When I assured him I was fine, he locked himself out. I then went through a long decompression.

181

Solid Brass

I was sitting by the hatch at the end of this long decompression, waiting for the last few pounds of pressure to drop so the door would open, when all of a sudden my head started spinning. I remember reaching out to hit the air valve handle to allow air to rush in and start me back to bottom pressure. Luckily, it was an on or off position valve and not one of the turn forever type. The next thing I remember I was looking at the gauge at one hundred sixty feet, thinking to myself...you're all right now. I glanced at the porthole and saw Niggy Pratt's big eyes that filled the whole back port. Everyone on deck was trying to stop my descent, they thought I'd gone whippy. Don Stratton was in the outer lock trying to blow himself down to catch me. Willie was trying to raise me on the phones. Lucky for me no one thought to go to the upper deck and shut the valve on the volume tank. They didn't know I'd been hit again and with the severity of the bends I had, any stop of my descent would have been disastrous. I shut off the valve to stop my descent and when Don got to my depth, I told him what had happened at lesser pressure. I got so hot I had to take off all my wools, I got violently sick and must have passed out. After I finally woke up at pressure, I was freezing cold and had to put my wools back on. My system was totally out of kilter. I told Don he'd better get back to the surface before he got bent from being at pressure so long himself. At one hundred sixty feet, he was deeper than most tenders ever get. After he was assured I was all right for the moment, he blew himself back out. Willie told me over the phones, they were going to fly Dr. Rutten out. I told him not to do that, we didn't need Doc, I was fine now and we didn't need to have him fly all the way out in the middle of the night to tell us I was bent. We already knew that.

The next thing I knew, Dr. Rutten was blowing himself down to give me a visit. Willie didn't listen to one word I had said this time. Doc was an expert on submarine medicine and never charged us for any of his visits or medications. He was interested in submarine medicine, plus he was one hell of a person. He always sent the information about each case to the Navy for documentation.

I told him I was sorry he had to fly all the way out here in this lousy weather. He ignored all the "I told them not to call" stuff and started his very thorough investigation. Doc looked into both eyes with his instrument very carefully explaining he could see no problems there but when he checked my blood pressure he exclaimed "Wow, you won't believe this," which didn't make me feel any better. I mentioned something about his bedside manner. "I've never seen blood pressure so erratic," he explained. He told me to come to his office the minute I got back to town. After some shots and medical attention, Doc blew himself out, but stayed around for several hours watching me come to several stops. He set up a schedule with the crew outside and then caught the chopper back to town.

After forty-eight hours in the tank, I finally got to the surface. Willie looked in and suggested I lay there for a few minutes, "until we know you're out of the woods." "No sir, boy, I want out right now to let that fifty-knot wind blow through my hair and stand at the rail, like any good sailor, and piss over the side." First I had to get help getting out of the small chamber door. Then, I found I had to have help to stand. I had one guy on each side holding me up while I exercised every seaman's God given right. Everything functioned all right but my legs would not hold my weight. "If anyone is interested in kicking my ass, now's the time," I laughed and gave in to Willie's insistence that I lay down in the chamber until enough time passed that we knew there would be no recurrence.

As I lay down, I yelled out, "Leave the hatch open, I'll be right out." When I finally did come out, we found our way to some bunks to lay our heads down. I normally am an eight-hour person, but this time I slept for fourteen hours without waking. Still unbelievably weak, but able to walk on my own, I made it to Doc Rutten's office where he explained the weakness came from the terrible jolt my system had gone through. It was three more days before my blood pressure got back to normal.

This had been my one and only central nervous system (CNS) hit in all my diving years. I'd met Tom, a tender on the East Coast, who'd been a diver but gave it up after having CNS bends twelve times. Gas diving did keep you from getting nitrogen narcosis, also called "Rapture of the Deep." Gas works out of your system faster but also gets into places air doesn't, so a gas bubble is much more severe than an air bubble, in my opinion.

Doc Rutten was asked to be a guest speaker at a diver's gathering in Santa Barbara. There was some big time insurance guy that arranged this

Solid Brass

meeting with aspirations of signing up all the divers in the world. Doc talked on the subject of submarine medicine, explaining his thoughts that as divers grow older they may pay the price of having been bent. He thought some pain would show up as we tended to our turnip patch. Each time we bent over, some shooting pain would remind you of a distinct time spent in the chamber with a bubble. This led to someone recalling a time when Bill Billers got hit, which led to another story of someone else's bubble. We'd laugh at one story and hear another "OK, remember when" and on and on through the crowd, as if rehearsed.

A glance at the insurance guy showed him ringing his hands as he listened to the endless stories that seemed to include everyone in the room. After a long night of sea stories, you could see he wished he could just disappear. I don't remember just how he did get out of there gracefully, but I do remember he didn't sign anyone up before leaving and we never heard from him again. Probably the story that sent him packing was the one where we bent Doc Rutten. He spent so much time in the chamber, he actually got a bubble of his own. It happened to be a time when he'd rather not have spent so much time in the chamber. The abalone diver that was being treated had a bubble somewhere that gave him diarrhea; I mean big time diarrhea. And in real close quarters, in the small chamber. Willie tried to keep fresh air circulating. After each fresh air purge, Doc would say, "Thanks Will, thanks Will."

While on that subject, the question has come up through the years, "What happens during a dive when you have to answer the call of nature?" I am happy to say that the following case is not the answer to the question. We had a diver, (who shall remain nameless) who, after his dive, flew up the ladder and over the side, down the inside of the boat and to some timbers in the middle of our large dive boat. The entire time he was frantically tugging at the zipper of his wet suit jacket, which had to come off before he could get to the bottoms. He didn't make it. A disgusting seepage took the place of the sea water coming from where his booty sealed against his leg. Soon he was standing in a pool of crap. He moved over as if it would go away only to create another puddle. He kept moving around nervously. We knew at this point, as everyone cleared the area, we'd have to get him settled into one spot.

Solid Brass

He was tracking raw sewage over the entire boat. In the pressure of getting his wet suit off, he'd done in five minutes what a hundred seagulls couldn't have accomplished over the weekend. All work on board had come to a stop while everyone turned this into some kind of comedy routine. Finally getting him aimed to the ladder, up and over the side to continue getting out of his dress and into the water. Someone tossed him a bottle of Joy soap to finish the job. That was certainly the worst case of the two-step I'd ever witnessed. A circumstance one would wish could be a private matter. Instead, crapping his pants turned out to be a spectator event and forever part of the diver's folklore.

Nasty Ed had to go to court because some lady turned him in for standing on the rail of his small dive boat relieving himself. When the judge found out through a series of questions to the complainee, that Ed's boat was some distance offshore and she had used binoculars to see him, he threw the case out. Another judge further up the coast wasn't so forgiving. One morning, Ed had just been released from the Newport Jail for something he'd, no doubt, done the night before. He strolled down the walk and over to the corner stone of the very building he'd spent the night in, unzipped his pants and, as Ed put it, sort of expressed himself. He went back inside at the insistence of the two officers on either side of him.

When the subject comes up on dangerous situations a diver might encounter, it seems sharks always take the limelight. This is simply not true. The stories I can tell about sharks happened over thirty-five years of being in the water. If you walk down a street and pat every dog you see on the head, one is going to bite you. I feel this could also be the case with sharks. They are dangerous to man and should be shown respect and caution, but every time you see one on a dive, it's not the last day of your life.

There were an astounding number of sharks where we worked at Wake Island, attracted by all the coral blasting we did. While working on the bottom, we could look up and see groups of sharks circling. We always had one eye on the job and one watching the circling sharks. All of a sudden one would leave the pack and swim at you as fast as he could, get within a few feet, make a fast turn next to you, and swim away.

Solid Brass

I feel certain if any one of us in our aqua-lung swim gear would have panicked and made an attempt to swim away, he might have lost a cheek of his ass or worse. The sharks were with us for a month, with no incident, but some years later, we heard of and saw pictures of a Scripps Biologist who lost his tricep muscle on one arm to the sharks. We later found the reason for the attack was his cornering the shark in the wreck of a ship, taking pictures. The diver was in the shark's only exit. He took his muscle on the way out. We were setting tons of underwater explosives at the time and that was the primary danger, not the sharks.

Your compressor quitting, getting your hose hopelessly fouled, or any number of gear malfunctions are way out in front on the danger scale to a shark encounter. Such as a time when Bud Swain was diving on a cement operation and guiding tons of gravel to the bottom. The water was clouded up, so he could no longer see and his hose was graveled over with a good layer of cement to boot. The stand-by diver had to bring down a new hose, take off his old hose, and screw on the new.

Solid Brass

Huey Hobbs was using a very large air lift on a mud digging job, when it got up over his head and settled down on his shoulders. The immediate danger wasn't being crushed under the weight but from the air in his suit getting sucked out of his exhaust and straight to the surface up the airlift. He couldn't tell his tender because the air was now being sucked out of his lungs so he couldn't talk. His tender, sensing something was wrong, stopped the airlift, saving his diver from a most horrible death. Given a choice, he'd rather have faced a shark.

On a two-hundred-foot dive, some masking tape came from somewhere in Huey's helmet and stopped in his exhaust, which in turn stopped his air from escaping. It blew his suit up so fast, he couldn't bend his arms to shut off his air. Before he knew it, he was on his way to the surface out of control. He was communicating with his crew on the way up. They kept up with his slack, got him to the ladder and up into the chamber. Blowing up from that depth as fast as he did, the bends were certain unless they could get him back to depth in record time. Only a seasoned

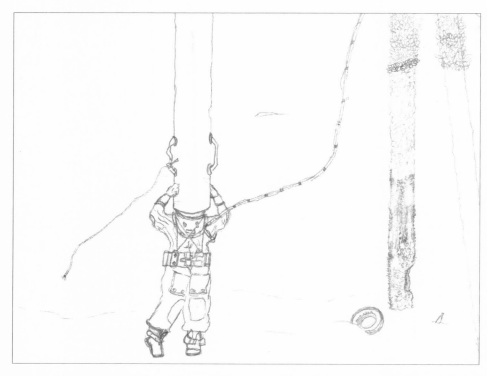

crew, as he fortunately had, could and did pull it off. While they were blowing themselves down, his tender made the sign of the cross, and being a good Catholic himself, Huey said it wasn't necessary because he'd already talked to God on the way up. Again a shark wouldn't have been near as exciting.

We were removing a platform off Point Conception one year and Huey had another close call. To get him out required almost all luck, because the crew couldn't help. Huey had to just luck out and we hoped he'd make the right move. We were removing some legs that weighed one hundred tons. We had to dig around them with a large clamshell worked from a crane off the barge. We went down and crawled under the leg by the freshly dug hole. The leg was nailed to the ocean floor by several H beam pilings that had been driven through the leg and cemented in, which made up a good part of the one hundred tons. We were setting explosives to blow them, the problem being the Fish and Game

Solid Brass

Department would only allow us to blow five pounds at a time. That wasn't enough to do the job, so we had to make two shots. We feared, when we went in to do the second half, that the already damaged half wouldn't hold the weight and would fall while we were under the leg. On the very last leg, Huey was setting the second charge when we heard him yell, "Oh, shit, oh shit!" The leg didn't come to the surface, so we couldn't see that it had fallen over. Being in the hole, he knew it was going, but there was no horizon to use as a reference, so he had no idea which way to go to keep from being crushed. This was where he needed the luck. His instincts were right, he went the right way. To have his hose get out of the way of the falling leg was also good fortune.

Something equal to encountering a shark happened to me while investigating a hydraulic leak in the deep, cold California thermo. I had been bragging for several weeks about my new wet suit being custom made for me by Bill Johnson, who at the time, made wet suits for the UDT/SEALS in San Diego. It fit like a glove, just like I bragged it would.

Before its maiden dive, I strutted around deck, proudly pointing out its fine features and quality construction. After jumping in, hitting bottom, and becoming engrossed in my project, I got a stunning shot of cold water in the crotch, "Whoa...what the hell," followed by another down my back, then up my leg and under each arm. Each time felt like a shock of electricity, which caused involuntary body part spasms. I looked down to witness my seams opening up as if they were being unzipped. As my suit came apart, it started to float to the surface and I followed. As I headed up, I gathered detached parts along the way. By the time I reached the surface and climbed the ladder, I was ball-ass naked with my worthy wet suit under my arm. I stood humiliated, shivering, and turning various shades of blue, while everyone on deck laughed their warm asses off. I didn't have to say much when I phoned Bill. As soon as he heard my voice, he apologized for the bad batch of glue and informed me my new wet suit was already in the mail.

Jack Fonner, one of my closest and dear friends, had one accident before I knew him well. He was working on the bottom on a unibolt. The crew was told all the pressure was off the line, so when it wouldn't

189

Solid Brass

come apart, they rechecked and were assured all the pressure was off. Therefore, Jack got real tough with it until it finally started to come apart. One last blow with the hammer separated the flanges, releasing a tremendous pressure. So much for the theory that they can't come apart with pressure on them. The explosion rattled Jack's head around inside his hat and knocking him unconscious. After getting him to the surface, it was hard to tell what needed the most attention—his head was bleeding profusely, and he had bit off the end of his tongue while unconscious.

Solid Brass

First they had to get him in the chamber under pressure or he'd die for sure. They brought Jack around, got him stitched up, but he had to learn to talk all over again. He wasn't able to go back to work for over a year from all the damage done on that one dive.

Jack and Lill Fonner had a son who seemed to always be where trouble was in those days. I didn't think he'd make it to voting age, especially considering the crowd he traveled with. He's always been family to me and somehow he jerked himself around and today, young Jack is one of the best divers in the business. One of the few left who likes to get into heavy gear once in awhile.

Young Jack has had some of his own adventures throughout his career and he has a lot of diving years behind him now. I call him Young Jack, but that doesn't apply anymore and even though he's now over six feet, he's still Young Jack to this old one that knew his dad so well.

Just a few years back, Young Jack was on a dam job up in Northern California. There was a leak the crew was to locate and repair. Jack's dive was over and Don Thompson went down. During his dive, Don's leg got caught in the flow of the leak and he was unable to pull it out. Bob Rogers, the stand-by diver went down to try to pull him out and his arm promptly got sucked in. Now there were two divers stuck. Woody got the call and called me at the ranch, it was Sunday. I grabbed my personal gear and drove to Santa Barbara to meet Woody. We planned to fly up to the dam site in his plane and land on the highway since the nearest airport was too far from the site. The CHP would take us up to the dam in a black and white. I hit Route 101 doing 100 mph. Normally the drive to Santa Barbara takes forty-five minutes. I tried to cut that in half, figuring at that speed I'd pick up a Highway Patrol on the way and have an escort after an explanation. I had all that driving time to think of how cold the water had to be at the dam, not sure just how long they had been in. Hypothermia could play a role, so I was sure in my mind they would have a spare compressor being that far from the shop and by now there were extra people to help. And, of course, how the hell to get them out. Hundreds of thoughts crossed my mind along with some muddle because of the lack of information before I ran out the door. Getting as much out of this new Jimmy as possible as well as being very careful, knowing I couldn't have a problem on the way to a rescue mission. As it has so many times before in this business, time has become extremely important. Luckily, there wasn't much traffic on the Coast Highway, therefore, no highway patrol to chase me.

As I pulled into the shop, I was greeted by Woody's smiling face. They're out and they won't need us. Even though Jack Fonner had made

Solid Brass

the first dive early that morning as well as his decompression, he went back to the bottom. He pulled Roger out then tied a line to Don's leg and used a small crane on the back of the old truck to pull him free. Don didn't come easy and there was a possibility they might pull him apart in the process. Don told us later, the thought of leaving part of this leg there didn't seem that big of a deal after being trapped for those several hours.

The pressure that pulled his leg in the dam also pulled the boot and part of the leg right off of his dry dress. Bob's hand looked a little hamburgerish for a few days but was OK. Don sustained some permanent nerve and muscle damage but doesn't have a noticeable limp any longer. And Jack got by with one hell of a decompression.

Many years before, Bob Benton and I were doing a job in Lake Piru. The water was right at one hundred feet. There was a grizzly or grating that was used to catch debris when lake water was released to run downriver. There was too much silt build up and sunken driftwood over the grizzly. An extension was made for us to put in place after removing most of the debris. The engineer in charge of this job had been there prior to us. He was running a TV survey, and used this very large cumbersome underwater camera case. It got jammed in the grizzly and in the process of getting it out, bent and broke some bars.

I was using heavy gear to make an inspection of what had to be removed before we could put the new extension in place. The engineer had built some long hydraulic cutters for us to cut the large limbs that were in the grizzly area. The dam keeper told us the flow was cut down to just a small trickle. Well, his small trickle sucked me right through the grizzly only to stop because my arms were outstretched which caught me at my armpits. The strain on my shoulders cut off circulation to my arms at once. Bob got everything he could on my hose, as I tried to squirm up just a little to get the flow of blood back to my shoulders. Normally, your body wouldn't fit through these gratings but the camera had made a hole big enough and no one had told me about it. I couldn't have hit the hole more dead center if I had planned it that way. They sent the skiff in to notify the dam keeper to cut off all the flow and to get new batteries for his calculator. I felt that keeping the circulation in my shoulders was the most important thing now, because if I lost feeling there I might slip

Solid Brass

through without even knowing it had happened until it was too late. Then I suppose they would have to pick me up in a river bed somewhere. It's customary to have radio communication with people like a dam keeper, I don't remember what the problem was that day, but it took one hell of a long time. Finally, I could feel the flow slowing down, and I worked

my way out of the structure. Not nearly as exciting as Don's entrapment, but it had its moments.

We were very careful when working on oil platforms to make sure all their intakes were off before making a dive, but just recently, we had another set of wools that needed changing after a dive. I was working as a diving consultant for Marathon Oil in the Cook Inlet. The diving crew and I lived on and worked off the *Shamrock*, Martech's dive boat at the time. The *Shamrock* was built many years before by my good friend, Gene Cleary, exclusively for diving the Inlet. Gene is another one of the old divers that spent most of his diving career in the Cook Inlet. The skipper of the *Shamrock* was another old friend who was one of the saltiest sea captains around. I'm sure he helped decide how much beam Noah needed in the Ark. Nick was consistently more accurate than the weatherman, and in the North Country, that's most important. Every day we'd learn just a little more from Nick about weather conditions, tides, currents, wind, and sea conditions, all in a day's conversation.

On this particular dive, Leif Simcox, a seasoned Inlet diver and a friend with a very quick mind, was following out an anode cable we had just set the tide before. We had reason to believe there might be a problem with the way it laid on the bottom. Normally, when we come into a platform to make a dive, we call ahead to make sure all the sea suctions are turned off on that leg. On this dive, we had them shut off the suction on the leg on which Leif would be working. He would be going down the buoy cable to the anode, which was away from the platform. As he followed the cable, it started to leave the bottom and before we realized, he was at the leg next to the one that was shut off. We heard one of those noises you let out involuntarily, like when surprised in a dark room, followed by, "Get up on my slack!" We knew Leif was not easily excitable, so the crew was in high gear hauling him out. He was mumbling that something had him and now he was taking on water somewhere around the crotch area. We knew before we got him up that he got into an intake on the platform leg that had all its suction. After getting on deck, sure enough, there was a hole in the front of his dress you could put your fist in. It came dangerously close to changing his voice to a higher pitch.

Solid Brass

It's a good time to talk about the old *Shamrock*. She's sixty-five feet stem to stern, has a stern cabin with a second level wheel house, and one Captain quarters bunk. Instead of a large wheel, there is a small hydraulic lever to steer by, added by a Woody Freeman auto pilot. To the left a twenty-mile radar and fathometer, overhead, a couple of ship-to-shores. Down on the main deck there are several airtuggers and winches, and a very large A-frame that works over the bow. When put in place, we've placed eight-ton anodes with it many times. That's pretty close to all you want to handle. The deck is covered with war-torn, four-inch thick timbers. Walk back on the starboard side and there's a hatch that goes into the house deck level. You're now in the galley, rec room, lounge, and decompression station. The forward bulkhead has a long countertop running side to side, used for everything. On the port side of that is a deep sink used for dishes, as well as the stove and oven (which also provides the cabin heat). Walking around to the back of the house, there is the decompression tank that runs from port to starboard with just enough room to get into the hatch. In that same corner hangs all the rain gear and coveralls. Above the chamber there's a series of shelves storing crackers, cereals, bread, a checkerboard, and anything else there's no room for elsewhere. There's a very old couch sitting in front of the chamber. That's the main part of the lounge. In the center of the galley is an old, very large, cable spool table, built around a support beam and escape ladder going to the wheel house. At the end of the ladder, is a hatch that opens into the captain's quarters and is used mostly to pass food up to Nick while we're underway. There are several chairs sitting around the table where we eat or patch our suits, repair our gear, play cards, and all the things you normally do on deck if it wasn't snowing, raining, or just plain miserable to be out there.

On the days when the sun is out and we're finished with our work and waiting for the next tide, all the chairs are on deck and transformed into patio furniture in which to sunbathe. In the front of the house there's a hatch going down to the inside of the hull below main deck. At the bottom of the ladder there are two large freezers with supplies of frozen meat and fresh caught salmon. There are spools of rope and other spare parts and diving gear, a portable bilge pump, a hatch going into the engine room and a hatch going into the shower area. Next to the showers, there are shelves of bed linen and towels, and a place to put dirty linen and towels. On the forward bulkhead there's a small sink with a crack in it and a mirror that's pretty dog-eared and a door that goes into the bunkrooms. There are three rooms on the starboard and three on the port that hold two to three bunks each. The central passageway goes back to a very small shop and chain locker, which is also the escape route in case of an emergency. The bunk rooms are just big enough for the bunks and storing sea bags—that's it—and that's why so much time is spent in the galley. I've written a good portion of this book in that galley. While the crew slept, I'd sit on the couch, bare feet up on a chair with nothing but the hum of the generator and engine. Unless it was a sunny day, then I'd write while sitting in the sun, as long as my eyes could stay open, that is.

I described the *Shamrock* because it's the Inlet boat we live on and work from if not working off a barge. We've had over ten guys on board and sometimes, weather permitting, we lived aboard for thirty days, just going in for fuel, water, and supplies. A big day off might be going in to get groceries. So needless to say, the crew was handpicked and very close. Big Ed usually planned most of the meals, but everyone fixed their specialty at sometime or another. Everyone took turns at galley chores, like cleaning up and doing dishes. The boat was always clean, just cluttered. We had all the gear we needed to live and work but just a limited place to store it.

There was usually one guitar, sometimes two, and we had a VCR used for underwater photography, which doubled as our entertainment center. There was nothing that John Wayne did that we didn't know about. Usually, movies were shown at meals or when tied to the dock taking on fuel or groceries. If we were working the tide, we'd be up getting ready a few hours ahead and putting gear away after, so we'd have to get sleep in between. When the boat was sitting in the mud, or anchored, waiting out some bad weather somewhere, is when we'd get some time to ourselves. That happens quite often in the Inlet. It seems everyday someone else had a crack at being the recipient of all the bullshit, the pranks, the jokes, etc. And everyday we could depend on Leif and Bill

Solid Brass

Bill Morterud and Leif Simcox on the bow of the *Shamrock* in the Cook Inlet. *B. Wick photo*

to argue about anything and call each other every name in the book. If you didn't know them, you'd think they had great contempt or even hatred for one another. There's hardly a time they're both awake that this is not going on. You can bet one of them will get home with an extra five pounds of junk steel in their gear bag or the zipper glued shut, for example.

Ed would bring his reloading equipment out, John his black powder gun, someone would bring a bear gun, lots of pistols, and while anchored up in Trading Bay, we'd do some shooting. We always had fresh salmon during the season and kept a smoker on board. Some days when we knew we'd have the whole day before the weather laid down, Bill and I would go to work his gold claim or just do some prospecting. Most of the crew flew from Anchorage to Kenai to catch the boat, but a few made the four-hour drive to have transportation at the dock. Walking distance from where we tied up at Arness Dock, there's the small town of Nikiski; one bar, one grocery store, one auto parts and hardware store, one restaurant, and one phone booth. The town still looks like it did twenty-five years ago. The bar is still a meeting place for many of the same locals from that many years ago. Thirty minutes down North Road, Kenai, and Soldotna have made some big changes, large markets and plentiful shopping centers, the Golden Arches, and all the other signs of a big city.

In most of the world, high-tech equipment is being used in the diving industry; there are ROVs, (remotely operated vehicles), state of the art underwater TV, saturation diving systems, and large plush diving vessels. The Inlet, with its silt-filled zero visibility, fast moving water, and thirty-foot tides, thumbs its nose at most of this and much of the diving and tending is still done by the same people that pioneered this type of diving. Although we do have some high-tech equipment that works in the Inlet, not much has changed in this region in thirty years. Ninety percent of the diving gear is the lighter gear now, but the tides are the same; Nikiski is the same; the place we let the tide go out and sit the boat in the mud to wait out the weather is the same; the rivers still swell up with spawning salmon, and there's no change in the number of bear and moose walk through town. The other night in town, a fight broke out in the bar and a fisherman got his ear bitten off, that's the same too.

Which reminds me of another bar story that took place out there. Very late one night, a whole station wagon full of divers and tenders (who will remain anonymous) pulled away from an all night watering hole. The good news was that they were driving down a gravel and dirt road with no other traffic. The bad news was that they left without their designated driver.

"Just keep an eye out for moose and bear," as this was North Road on the Kenai Peninsula, Alaska. The designated driver must have fallen in love sometime earlier, so everyone was helping drive. "Head a little to the starboard...quick, back to the port!" This is how they progressed up the road for many miles. Somehow they moved a little too far to the port, the wheel caught a berm on the shoulder and they rolled over into a ditch.

Solid Brass

"What the hell happened? Are we alright?" "You're laying on my leg, you shit!" "I can get out the window." Pretty soon everyone was standing up outside the company's station wagon.

"So how are we going to explain this?" This question prompted one of the divers to crawl back inside the wagon. When he reappeared, he had a .45 pistol in hand. After getting to his feet, dusting himself off of dirt and broken glass, he unloaded the gun into one tire, and looked up claiming, "Some blow-out wouldn't you say?"

A tough day at the office for this company car. *J. Jackson photo*

EIGHT

Hunting up North

This morning's like any other morning, right? The snow-capped mountain turned fire red again at first light. The horizon is full of large volcanic mountains, every canyon filled with glaciers and large ice fields. There's a small ribbon of trees that divide this from the Cook Inlet. The rivers are full of spawning salmon, and therefore, we have beluga whales around us every day to get their share of the salmon. Some days there are so many of these little white whales, it looks like whitecaps at first sight. On the Alaska Peninsula side of the Inlet, where our diving boat sits at anchor, the salmon have to get through the belugas and bald eagles, as well as the bears further up the streams. It's not uncommon to see ten-foot bears in this area.

The Alaska Peninsula is home of some of the largest bears, moose, and caribou in the world. There are also world-class trout in the lakes and streams. Very early this morning, in the light from yesterday's sun, I saw many ducks and geese flying overhead. I watched clouds being born, coming off the ice-capped mountains, rising like smoke to gain in size and as dictated by the wind, eventually take their place among the others. On one mountain the sun shines on a high meadow, full of berries and a splattering of new wild flowers. Just a few miles away there are sheets of rain falling from a gray clouded area. Yes, just another day beginning in Alaska.

My mind started wandering to a time several years ago. My close friend and hunting partner, Karl Engelke and I were hunting on the peninsula in the Cinder River area, just southwest of here. We both had assistant guide licenses and would fly in with Lee Holen to his camp to help guide his clients. When they got what they came for, we would then hunt for ourselves. We didn't get paid for guiding and didn't pay to be there. It was a perfect set up for a couple of guys that would rather hunt than most anything. Karl's biggest problem on this trip was that he told Marlyss, his wife,we would be back in about a week—this was not to be. The trip from Anchorage to King Salmon was perfect. Going through Lake Clark Pass, Lee gave me the wheel. I was a fledgling pilot then, and my friends that flew would give me air time whenever possible. The Pass can be a nasty place to fly at times, but not this day. The air was still and we could see forever. After landing in King Salmon, we picked up a few things, then off to main camp at Cinder River. Right in the middle of the alder and willow bush there would be a volcanic cinder strip. In the middle of another big strip sits the main camp. There were other tents and small buildings in the area used for sleep and storage.

We unloaded the 206, which had full sheets of plywood cut in half to make them fit easily in the cargo door. We also unloaded many 2x4s, nails, a john, and a fiberglass shower. This, along with guns, all kinds of bags of personal equipment and four people were unpacked from the plane. A typical load to be flown into the bush. There were some royalty-type clients coming later in the season, so we spent some time building indoor plumbing. We built the septic system from fifty-gallon drums and used a Browning 12-gauge "drill" to put holes where needed in the drums and walls of the lodge.

Finally time to hunt, we went to Moose Camp from the main lodge by a tracked vehicle. I drove. Karl and I used the same vehicle at Lee's Wrangle Mt. Lodge. You could fly into most of the camps in the Wrangles. There was no flying into these camps, the bush is too dense and there is no place to set down. By the track rig, the trail though would take most of the day. Along the way, when we made rest stops, the clients were told to take their guns if they left the trail to drop their pants. The small bear here are seven feet. The camps are typical wall tents, one used to cook in and the other used to sleep in. Karl and I set a small two-man mountain tent up behind the others. There were a lot of moose and brown bear in this area. Every night a very large sow would bring her twin cubs through camp, knocking equipment over, but never bothering the tents.

The moose hadn't started rut, so at times we could see several bulls in one herd. An example of this happened when we had some hunters from Minnesota with us that were doing some unguided hunts. Ernie had not taken a bull yet, and tomorrow would be the last day of moose season. I told him I would take him out first thing in the morning.

I got up at first light, located a really big bull in a herd that boasted three world-class bulls, went back and held revile and hiked Ernie off to get his bull. When we got back to the area, we had to pass by many cows to get to the bulls. The alder bush is extremely thick so it was tough going. Ernie came unglued when he saw the first bull, I had to hold him back. It was a very good bull, but the one we wanted was still a good distance away. Just when I thought the stalk was going our way, we came to a clearing. Charging across the clearing and headed right for us, was a young bull with one horn. He had a fairly good-sized board on one side and just a gnarly looking growth on the other. Something must have happened to it while it was still in velvet. Whatever the case, right now, he was charging us. I moved a round in the chamber, Ernie standing behind me now asking if I was going to shoot. "I don't want to shoot him, but if he keeps coming, I will have no choice." He stopped a few yards short of us and stood pawing the ground. I don't know if the other moose had been laughing at him or what, but for some reason, he was pissed. He turned and walked to the other side of the clearing, stopped and pawed the ground some more, put his head down and charged again. Again, he stopped short, short of running over the top of us this time. After some very anxious moments and having to put the cross hairs on him several times, he turned and with one last grunt, showed us his derriere and left through the alders. For the next week we saw him somewhere everyday, but this was the only time we saw him act like this. With all this commotion, you would think everything for miles would have fled. The cows seemed to be just getting up and milling around, but by the time we got to the big bull in the back of the herd, he was standing up in a small clearing looking right at us. Ernie was on my left as we moved up to some small alders for a better view. I said in a low voice, meant for only Ernie to hear, "Bust him, bust him, Ernie." I quickly looked his way to see him jumping up and down trying to see over the alders. Ernie was fairly short and about a head short of seeing over the alders. I motioned to him to come over to my viewpoint. He took aim and unloaded his semi-auto 30.06 on the bull. I could see all the shots were in the right area, but when Ernie lowered his gun the bull was still standing. He yelled, "I missed him," as the bull wandered off into the brush. Ernie was frantically loading and running toward the clearing. I pulled him back to wait a few minutes and assured him I had seen hair fly with each shot and his bull wasn't going anywhere.

After a given time, we went in and started working on his bull. Ernie could give meat to all his friends and still have enough meat for several years. His rack was sixty-five inches plus, with nice, wide boards. His first thought was to tie the horns to his packboard to take pictures. I told him that was not a good idea with us standing in willow

The conclusion of a good moose hunt. We were asking a lot of this SnowTrack loaded with tons of meat. That is Ernie, our satisfied customer, and my hunting partner, Karl Engelke. *B. Wick photo*

Solid Brass

with just horns sticking above, we could become the hunted. We did it, but in a hurry.

The weather in Alaska changes very fast. The day we dressed Ernie's bull, we had to proceed as fast as possible with this sixteen-hundred pound animal and get the meat into the shade. A week later there would be snow on the ground. This latter part of the season is responsible for other changes in Ernie's herd. There were several bulls in the herd, paying no attention to each other. A week later they would be spar-

Ernie had to hurry to get this picture taken because there were other hunters in the area. *B. Wick photo*

ing, fighting each other for their right to the ladies. I was walking the trail a few days later when I heard two giants crashing their horns together. I moved around to a vantage point to watch this spectacular event of nature. Both of these bulls would have gone into the record book, their horns were massive. They would back off, lower their heads, than charge together with a tremendous force. Then dig in and push. I watched this for a long time. Then I had to get the moose hunters back to main camp and bring in the bear hunters.

Bear season was only two days away. On this same hunt was a hunter from Chicago. A young man running his family business. He was president of the Safari Club, and several other similar organizations. A big guy with a little baby fat and seemingly a bit spoiled. We thought this guy would have to be dragged around. As first impressions aren't always right, he was over eager to do his share. While skinning his moose, he

205

jumped right in and in the process, stabbed his thigh and drove his knife up to the hilt.

He was hunting with Super Guide, who got him back to camp (Super Guide was nicknamed by other guides in the business for his "super" ego). We cut his pants open to expose the wound. He did a good job; it was wide and deep. I held the wound shut to stop the bleeding, he had already lost a lot of blood. I was trying to think of what to do next and said we have to get this thing closed. The patient said that he had a needle and thread in his toothbrush kit, if someone would get it he would stitch it up. Someone got it, threaded the needle and while I held the cut together, he threw in some needlework. I looked at him through different eyes from that day on.

We got him back to main camp to a doctor and his wife. They were there to hunt but luckily, he brought his little black bag. We later used the doc again for a whitesox antidote. Everyone got some whitesox bites which are kind of like a mosquito, but a different kind of pain. One of the Minnesota hunter's face swelled up so bad it looked like his skin was going to split. His head got grotesque and every part of him that wasn't covered was swollen. He couldn't bend his fingers, they were so fat. The shot the Doc gave him finally made the swelling go down. This guy loved to hunt Alaska and had this to look forward to each time. It had happened to him before.

It was late by the time we got the moose hunters back to main camp. We would leave early in the morning to take the bear hunters in. We hung most of the moose meat on the meat rack, some distance from the camp. We had one pack board with a hind quarter tied on ready to take on the rack. It was leaning against one of the tents and resting on the cot inside the tent. Joyce, who had a kidney infection waiting to be airlifted when the weather cleared, slept on that cot that night. During the night, a very large brown bear sow with a cub at her side, came in, picked up the hindquarter and pack board, in her mouth and walked off, leaving no skid marks. At this point the bears muzzle was only inches from Joyce's head. This pack board and hindquarter took all you had to get under and lift it. The sow picked it up and walked a long distance from camp, across a creek, and through the alders before finding a place of seclusion

Solid Brass

where she and her cub proceeded to dine. I found the pack board some days later while hunting ptarmigan.

The next day we were on our way back to the camp we had used for moose. There were a number of spots along the way where the carnivores could dine. At that time in Alaska you could leave the neck and rib cage, the gut pile and head after cleaning your moose. I was driving the snow track, in the back were several hunters and Super Guide. The snow track had a nifty little push-up hatch in the roof. Kind of like a sunroof that you could stand up and look out. We had traveled about half the distance to camp when I saw something move way off in the distance near a gut pile. I stopped the rig, and stood up with my binoculars to get a better look. Just coming out of one of the only stand of trees in the area was the largest bear I'd ever seen. After studying it for a minute, I realized it could be the largest bear anyone had ever seen. Nine and ten foot are record-class bear. This bear was more like twelve to fourteen feet, not even adding something to make a better story. I watched him put his paw

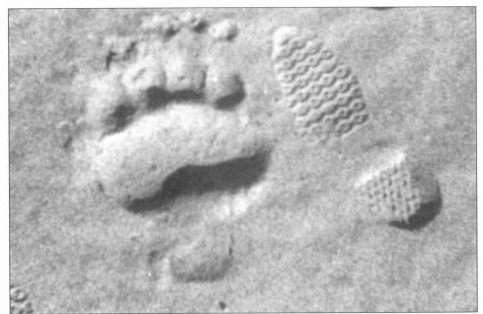

A grizzly track dwarfs a human boot print in Susitna Valley, Alaska. *B. Wick photo*

on the ribcage, pull a large piece of meat off and swallow it by pulling it in much like you do with a single strand of spaghetti. With the adrenaline pumping, I left my seat, headed out the back grabbed my gun and day pack and went by everyone as if they weren't there. While I was outside adjusting everything, Super Guide came out to see what the hell was going on. Everyone figured by the way I exploded through the back hatch without saying a word, I must have had a nasty case of the Aztec two-step. I pointed out the bear. Super Guide, who had been on many, many bear hunts, agreed this was one hell of a bear and probably the largest he'd ever seen. "That bear is a long way off," he pointed out as the lecture began. "He's in one of the only clearings for miles," (the only way I was able to spot him) "and you'll never find him once he starts to move. The fact is that the season doesn't open until tomorrow and if you do get him, how are you going to hide a 1200-pound bear when the Fish Cops fly over. Not to mention," he continued, "we have a whole bunch of hunters that traveled hundreds of miles and spent thousands of dollars to hunt that bear." Well, what the hell, I had to take a leak anyway. I called everyone out for a rest stop, like a thoughtful guide. I zipped up my pants and got back into the cab to feel sorry for myself. I hope the bear is alive and doing well, nobody took him that year.

After getting back to main camp, we had to wait several days for the ground fog to lift so we could head back to Anchorage. We were late, but more important, Joyce was forced to wait even longer with her bad kidneys. On the way back to Anchorage, I had my sixty-seven-inch horns (my perk from this trip), but I'd never see the meat that was to come out of camp later. After everyone got what they came for, Karl and I took our hunt. The day after we left, a 90 mile per hour wind came and blew the meat and meat rack to raven and fox food. A doctor and his wife had dropped into main camp to say hello the day before the blow, to have their Super Cub totally destroyed alongside the meat.

I was coming back from Anchorage with Karl and Marlyss, from a salmon fishing trip on the Kenai River. We passed some large mountains on our left and halfway up we spotted what looked like wolves stalking something. We stopped and glassed the area for a few minutes. There was one big black wolf who kept reappearing. I decided to go up to take

Solid Brass

a closer look, maybe get some pictures. I took an old beat up 7-mm magnum that Karl kept behind the seat in his pickup. I took the gun for all the reasons we carry guns in Alaska. After going through the bogs, devil's club, and heavy alder, climbing the mountain would be a snap.

I'd climbed a little knoll and sat at the edge taking a break to decide where to go next. Just below me was a large grassy meadow and standing off to one side was a tall dead, limbless tree. The meadow was surrounded by large spruce trees and I could hear a stream running on the other side. I don't know how long I'd sat there when I heard a heavy splash in the stream. It was something big. A couple of minutes later, a young black bear came into the meadow. He wasn't very old but still weighed a couple hundred pounds and looked like he'd never missed a meal. All of a sudden he took off running through the grass, tucked his head, and rolled ass over his head in a type of somersault. He got to his feet and did it again. I was having a hell of a time keeping the laughter muffled, it was a funny sight.

This went on so long I was starting to hurt laughing so hard. Then he got up and ran straight at the dead tree and fired up it like a cat. Then his whole mood changed and he started to back down real slow. When he got to the bottom, he walked slowly to the edge of the grass where I could no longer see him. All of a sudden, off to the edge of my knoll, there he was—looking right at me. He must have winded me at the top of the tree, which would explain the mood change.

He started coming toward me making a bawling sound, which I'd heard on other bear encounters. There was no more humor in this picture as I jacked a shell in the chamber. I decided to shoot a round over his head to turn him around. I aimed, pulled the trigger, and nothing happened. He was still coming, moving his head side to side and making louder noises. Not typical of a bear bluff, he wasn't stomping nor popping his jaws, just kept coming forward. I frantically moved the safety back and forth and tried again, with the same result—nothing. I hit the butt on the ground in hopes of loosening some of the dirt or rust or whatever. He was now so close I could have thrown the gun and hit him. I grabbed the bolt and ejected the old round and put a new one in its place, aimed, and pulled the trigger. This time it fired. He jumped up and around in the same motion and starting walking away. Not running, just walking. At the end of the meadow, he turned and took one last look back at me. I knew if he came back I wouldn't be shooting over his head and that would be a shame after the entertainment he'd provided me. I kept my eye on him until he disappeared over the edge. There was no need to climb the mountain now. I was rather anxious to go back to the truck and thank Karl for the use of his gun.

The Author with another large bull moose taken on the Alaska Peninsula. *B. Wick photo*

NINE

Kivalina

Enjoying the view from my room at the Hotel Captain Cook, I was thinking about the job we had just finished in the Inlet and also about going outside again. Every time I leave Alaska, even knowing I'll be back, I have some emotional adjusting to do.

The phone rang, it was my old friend, Super Guide. "You haven't seen the Arctic yet...have you?"

"No," was my curious reply.

"Well, Phil Driver is going up to set up a grizzly bear camp and could use your help. When I heard you were going south, thought maybe you'd rather go north."

Phil had already left for Kotzebue when I called, so I arranged to meet his wife at the Anchorage Airport the next morning. She gave me a ticket and several hundred pounds of salt to carry as excess baggage. I was sorry to have missed Phil, I knew he had flown up in his bush-plane. Although, flying commercial on the mail runs in Alaska is an adventure in itself, I'd still rather be stopping for coffee and fueling up in the bush with Phil in his Super Cub.

By now, I'd made my living as a commercial diver in the Cook's Inlet for several years. All my free time was spent hunting and packing back into the bush, so I got to know many of the guides and bush people. I felt fortunate to guide for them in exchange for camp and equipment when there was no diving going on. I had many outstanding experiences but I had never hunted the Arctic before. There was certainly no way for me to know what an important and inspiring episode in my life was about to unfold on this memorable first trip.

I arrived in Kotzebue early in the day and right beside the landing strip was an enormous pile of recognizable camp gear. As we taxied by I could see a long boat, tents, stacked plywood, 2x4s, and cases of food. There were just a few locals and myself on this flight, so no time was wasted. A couple of minutes after the door was lowered I was standing with my old friend, Phil. There was a light mist falling and I could see that there was still some ice along the beaches. We walked over to the Village Hotel-Bar-Restaurant, sat down and talked about the coming events.

All the equipment on the runway had been flown in by a Hurc from Anchorage but we had to wait for the weather to break so we could use a Twin Otter (a twin-engine bush plane) to move it all up river. Phil had a couple of guys there to help, besides the local help. They had been sleeping in a makeshift tent under part of the pile on the runway because each day was supposed to bring better weather.

With no break in the weather in sight after I had been there for several days, I offered to run some supplies up to the new camp location by boat, plus we'd have one less load to fly in. Phil liked the idea—at least we'd be getting something moving. I asked some more questions about the location and waters. His brief answer was, "You can't see the point very well right now because of the weather, but when you get to it, you take a right up the coast and then you'll come to Kivalina. That's all there is to it."

Several of us carried the boat to the water. We had two large cans of outboard mix ready to hook up, two large wall tents, cooking utensils, stove, lantern, two cans of Blazo, two cans of Super Cub fuel (80/87), a case of outboard motor oil, a side of bacon, several sacks of potatoes and onions and all the other essential camp goodies. I was also taking along Charlie, a friend of Phil's who had come to help build the camp but had never been in the bush before. Phil thought he might be of some help on the trip.

I was just finishing tying everything down and making sure that the 375HH magnum was secure, when an Eskimo from the village walked up to the boat. It seemed he, like many others, had been watching for

Solid Brass

some time and wanted to know where we were going. I told him we were going to the point, taking a right, and following the coast up to Kivalina. Now the worried look he had when he approached got even grimmer. "First place," he said in his broken English "it is very tricky getting to the point because several miles out there are sand bars and it is easy to go aground, even in a flat bottomed riverboat like you have. And second, when you pass the point and head up the coast, you will then be in the Chukchi Sea. It gets very mean."

We talked for some time. He knew I was listening and because of my knowledge of the sea, my replies to his questions comforted him. But I'm sure he had reservations about anyone that would take a flat-bottomed riverboat loaded with gear and a green Hand into the Chukchi Sea. Once we were finally ready, he and others helped us push off. He waved good-bye and said something in his Eskimo tongue. I hoped it was "have a safe trip" and not his views on how bright we were.

As predicted, a few miles out we were pushing the boat with the oars (with the outboard up) and for the next hour or so we didn't get to use the outboard very often. With the point now in sight, we finally hit deeper water and caught our last glimpse of the not so very visible Kotzebue.

"Watch out when you round the point" the Eskimo had said "the sea builds very fast in the Chukchi." Again as he predicted, when I rounded the point the sea changed dramatically. All the things he had told me came to mind; the ground swell was very big, the wind was blowing stiff and my boat was too damn small. One glance told me my deck hand would rather be back under the pile on the runway.

Now it was decision time, so I weighed the options. The gravel beach laid in front of us as far as I could see without the usual breaks in the horizon of trees and rocky peaks. Nothing but a strip of beach and low hanging cloud cover. Although the ground swell offshore was humungous, there was hardly any shore break. I decided to pull in closer to the beach and follow it to Kivalina. If we had outboard trouble or any other problems we could pull up on the beach. We had plenty of supplies.

As we progressed up the coast, the wind freshened and the swell kept building. Then it seemed to stabilize to about medium-nasty.

Solid Brass

Ahead I could see a large lump on the beach. It stuck out because it was the first anything I had seen. As we got closer, I could see that it was a dead walrus. I headed in and ran the boat on the beach, not without a struggle, but I wanted to check for tusks. I asked Charlie to hold her straight ahead with the engine going forward while I checked the carcass. He was somewhat uneasy with his new command but it was the first time he didn't have his butt in the air and his head over the side since we left. I hurried only to find that someone else had taken the head. There were snow machine tracks coming and going. I didn't think they had come from Kivalina because I had gone through one tank of fuel and there still was no village in sight. The tracks led straight back from the beach, not to the north. I knew when I plugged in the second gas can that that would be it, there wouldn't be any rowing in this weather. We would have to pull into the beach and make camp if the tank got close to low. Finally, with less than half a tank, off in the distance, we could see the village.

Phil's flight path to the village must have been quite different than the Chukchi route, I thought, or he would have never told me that "just a little way around the point—off in the distance—we'd see Kivalina. We had been underway for most of a long day and we still had to get to the village with less than half of a tank.

I was told to go to a large lagoon behind the village. Now offshore of the village we had the most white water I had seen on the entire trip. To the right of the village, which looked to be the only place there was a break in the coastline, were several lines of large breakers. The water in front of the village seemed calm enough, so I ran the boat up on the beach (to the amusement of several of the villagers). While we were circling, looking for a place to get in, we drew a crowd. They all came down to see who came out of the weather and why we were out in it. They helped pull the boat in to shore. I asked one man how to get to the lagoon and he pointed to the large line of breakers. (I knew he was going to tell me that.) With a push from the crowd, we pulled back offshore. I took a check, making sure all the gear was tied down and told ol' first mate Charlie to hold on. He pulled himself further down in the boat and white-knuckled the gunnel. He knew in his mind that this was all a bad dream and he'd wake up before we hit the breakers.

214

Solid Brass

I laid back for a minute to study the breaking pattern. There was no break at all, so away we went.

As I got in the curl of a good size wave, I chuckled as I flashed back many years to another, almost identical situation. My tender and I were coming back into the harbor off Mission Bay, San Diego, because of bad weather. We had been picking abalone. As we headed down the breakwater, we got into the curl of a very large ground swell and my tender, an ardent surfer, wasn't concerned about the possibility of not getting out of the curl and either broaching or crashing into the rocks. Instead, his only thought was that we were in the curl and being a good surfer, he ran the length of the boat, hung ten on the very point of the bow, dropped his shorts and mooned everyone on the beach who had come to watch the large swells running down the breakwater.

Not quite the same thought pattern this time for ol' Charlie—his moon was somewhere in the bottom of the boat and it didn't see daylight until I yelled at him to stick his head out and take a look at this some kind of paradise. It was as if we had dropped into another time and place. We came crashing out of the waves into this beautiful lagoon. As we cruised along the shore, we saw *oomiaks* (handmade Eskimo seal or walrus skin boats) leaning against pole frames to dry, a small cluster of little houses, dog teams tied up behind several of them and racks of ugruk seal hanging, being dried to a type of jerky. I remember smoke coming up in several places along the bank, probably to smoke the seal or fish. I don't remember where it was coming from, just that it added to this unforgettable scene. I pulled the boat in where the most people were standing. They quickly pulled our boat up above the high waterline. The kids especially were full of questions and laughter. I asked if they could take me to Arthur Swan. Two or three of them went running off to try to locate him. Meanwhile someone took us to the native store where the proprietor showed us to a room in the back with its own entrance, where we could get into some dry clothes and also spend the night. As we were finding places to hang our wet clothes to dry, Charlie confided in me that he thought when the Eskimo told us to go through the breakers to get to the lagoon, it was a trick. He figured that it was a place they send their enemies to die. Charlie was young and apparently watched a lot of TV.

Solid Brass

The seams on the bottom of this Oogruk Umiak shows the width of the hides used. Oogruk (seal) skins are smaller than a walrus's, so it takes six or seven hides to cover an umiak, where it only takes two female walrus hides. *B. Wick photo*

Soon Arthur Swan came to the door. Art was to be my guide up the Wulik River. The Wulik ran into the lagoon, which it created over time. It exits to the sea at two locations, one where we surfed in and the other several miles to the north. So in reality, Kivalina is an island.

We would be going quite a distance to the headwaters through miles of willow brush and the many tributaries joining the Wulik. It would be easy to make a wrong turn and get lost in those areas with no landmarks.

Art took me to get more fuel and he made sure we had plenty of mosquito dope. We got things ready for the trip and then walked through the village, meeting the people Art thought I should meet and I got to see the old and the new Kivalina. I felt very fortunate to have come to this village when I did. The state was building a few plywood homes to bring up the village standards. So when I was there half of the village was

Solid Brass

plywood and the other half was still sod houses in the ground, the way all the people of this village lived in the past. Some of the sod houses had long whalebone tunnels leading into them and all had electricity. They all had oil heat from their cooking stoves. A barge from Seattle would come once a year bringing oil for heat, gas for the snowmobiles and supplies for the various villages along the Arctic coast. A mail plane came in once or twice a month, weather permitting, with special catalog orders, and sometimes a new movie in addition to the regular mail.

They also had a ham radio in the building where school was taught. It was used in case of an emergency, like when the wind changed and pushed the ice pack out to sea with hunters on it making them unable to get back to shore. Two of many things the hunters had to watch out for were losing sight of land (compasses do not work well in the north) and watching for the dreaded east wind, which would push the ice pack off shore. They also had a generator that supplied the village with electricity. Art was also the maintenance man for this.

One of the Kivalina's sod houses with a whalebone entrance. *B. Wick photo*

Solid Brass

As a child, Art spent a lot of time in Seattle. He was born with a bent spine and a Native Association had sent him to Seattle for surgery. He had to make this trip several times in his adult life. While there, he enrolled in different classes, taking courses such as welding and diesel mechanics. Therefore, he did many of the fix-it jobs in the village.

At one of the last wooden houses in the village, walking north, we met Amos Holly. He invited us in for coffee. In a short time his wife brought soup for everyone, a very delicious fish soup. Amos told some great stories while we ate. He was the old Kahuna of the village—the old hunter whom the young men learn from.

Most of the houses consisted of one large room, with beds along the wall and a kitchen at one end. The john was a little phone booth-sized room containing a thunder mug with a lid and a curtain for a door. The permafrost doesn't allow for septic tanks, so each day one of the kids took the mug down to the dumping area some distance from the village. Amos had a couple of curtain walls in his home that divided the bedrooms. In one of the rooms his youngest boy was sick and barfing with a lot of voice. I could see Charlie getting a little uneasy as he was eating his soup.

After some really good stories from Amos, we went to meet Reverend and Mrs. Swan, Arthur's family. Art's father had been made a reverend by the missionaries and I suppose he presided over Sunday services, although I did not witness this. Mrs. Swan was a very beautiful lady, with whom I spent much time talking and got to know quite well, as I also did the Holly family. In the evening a few of the village kids came over. We were a new source of entertainment. They knew a lot of card games and we played them all. Also, they taught me some of the dialect and how to count in Eskimo. In return, I taught them how to count to 10 in my best high school Spanish. They kept track of the time because the kids in the village had a curfew and if they weren't in by ten o'clock the Curfew Marshall would get them.

As we finally got into our sleeping bags that night on the floor, in the little room in the back of the native store, I gave a lot of thought to the day and evening we had just experienced. These were some of the happiest people I had ever met. The kids had such honest intelligent questions and their sense of humor was so easy to reach. Even Charlie had a good time. That evening with the kids seemed to make him forget the worst day of his life, the life that he thought he was going to lose earlier in the day.

The next morning, I jumped up early. I thought I'd walk down the beach, wash up, and do all the things that morning brings. Charlie had already told me as he crawled into his sleeping bag that he wasn't getting up early. As I started through the village, it became apparent that there were no early risers in Kivalina. We would be spending the day and night here because Arthur had something to finish up before we left. I found some small pieces of baleen and a dead spotted seal on my trip up the beach. I skinned the seal because it was fairly fresh and I brought the skin back. Amos saw me coming and asked me in for coffee. I gave him the hide.

Walking from Amos's, the Swan's asked me in for coffee, I really didn't need more coffee, but I certainly didn't want to seem ungrateful and I enjoyed their company and hospitality. Everyone made little rolls for breakfast. They were kind of like those rolls you get on the road at a fried chicken place. Mrs. Swan put raisins in hers. They were eaten with butter and pickle relish (the kind with mustard in it). You have to wonder how that got started. In later days, I looked forward to having my rolls in the morning, traveling from house to house (although I never quite acquired a taste for the pickle relish).

Mrs. Swan cooked on a little cast iron oil stove. The smell was welcoming. The first thing you generally smelled in all the houses was the Lysol that was kept in the thunder mugs.

I pulled the gear from my boat after my last coffee stop. The sun wasn't out but the wind was blowing so I thought I'd air dry everything. After Art was finished with his project, he came down to give me a hand and we loaded his bags in the boat for the trip. We were all ready to leave. The only thing I had to bring in the morning was the gun I took out to clean. I was buzzing all day, not because of all the coffee but just the thought of going to the headwaters of the Wulik River had me anxious.

Solid Brass

I didn't mention loading Charlie's gear. He wouldn't come near the boat, he wanted to wait until the planes could fly. The kids stayed a little longer that night. The curfew marshal was on the trail somewhere. I also said my good-byes to Charlie that night because we would be leaving at first light.

Day broke and it was beautiful. I saw blue sky for the first time since I arrived in the Arctic. The sky was dotted with large, full clouds, very flyable, not even a slight breeze. Arthur, who would guide us around snags and other obstacles up the river, was sitting in front of the boat with his hood pulled up. The morning was still crisp once we got under way.

The river was running gentle and clear. It was easy to see most of the snags and get around them. We wound around shallow shoals and points of land for several hours. Then as we rounded a hairpin bend there stood this magnificent granite wall. It towered above my right shoulder and loomed overhead while we made the turn at its feet. This wall seemed to be there so that the river had a place to bounce off of to make its turn. It grew from the river to rise to its massive towering height. It made such an impression because it was so out of place compared to the rest of the terrain we had witnessed so far. In fact, the mood of the river changed at this place. The calm we'd enjoyed was interrupted when we reached this wall. It squelched any Tom Sawyer type feelings of just rafting along by making me wonder if this was what to expect from here on or perhaps it was just an isolated incident. This place was full of surprises.

We were down to our last half tank of fuel and were deep in concentration at a slower speed. The river was full of snags and small gravel bars at this point. It also seemed to be full of damn big fish. Several times I'd seen shadows or the streak of something large. We both turned our heads downriver to the sound of a Super Cub off in the distance. Phil finally got off the ground.

At first it looked like he was going to land in the boat but he chose a nice gravel bar in front of us to set down the Cub. We got to the bar about the time he got the Cub turned around and settled down.

Phil got out apologizing for the long delay and the horrible trip we had coming up the coast-he had already talked with Charlie.

Solid Brass

He was surprised at my reply that I was having a hell of a time. I had enjoyed every minute at the village and there couldn't be a better choice for a guide than Arthur. I then mentioned (with a grin) that we were about out of gas for the second time on this trip. He laughed about his calculations of the distance from Kotzebue to Kivalina. Now Arthur took over the boat so I could fly upriver with Phil to see our destination. After landing on the biggest gravel bar on the river, Phil pointed up a small bank to a level area where we would cut out the willow and put up our two tents. We walked down to the edge of the gravel bar where we had to place small flags in soft areas for the Otter pilot to see and stay away from when he returned. Phil would be flying out and coming back up with the Otter pilot as his guide. They would bring the Twin Otter up empty, just to get a feel for it. This would be bush flying at it best.

I was almost finished setting out the flags when I saw the boat limping in. I had left Arthur in the worst snag area of the river. Without a pointman on board he hit a good one. It took off one blade of a three-bladed prop. We pulled the boat up and started unloading.

I pulled out the chainsaw, climbed the bank, picked a flattened area and started cutting bush willow. There was not a tree in sight but willow everywhere. There was no way a plane could land anywhere in miles, except on the bars. Which made a big decision for me later in the days to come.

About an hour before Phil came, I saw what appeared to be a giant woven basket sitting back from the riverbank. Art told me that was exactly what it was. His people built these before he was born. This river has a large Arctic Char run. Nets were set in the river and the catch was put in the baskets until the fishing ended. Then the fish were taken to the village's underground freezers, which were cut though the permafrost and sealed with large walk-in doors on the side of the bank. They were shared by the entire village.

While flying in with Phil, he assured me that this spot, this camp that we would be building, would also become a world-class fishing camp. With that in mind, after he took off and after Art and I had the area cleared, the tents up, and everything put away, we took some fishing gear and headed to the river. The Otter wouldn't be in until morning. Art didn't feel like fishing, but he came along to keep me company.

Solid Brass

I found a little spot at the far end of the bar where a small creek came into the river. We caught some nice grayling right there with a Meps spinner. Then I put on a treble daredevil lure and tossed it out in the center of the river. Several casts later I caught my first Arctic Char. The first one was a keeper because I wasn't sure how plentiful they were, plus he was big. The second was a keeper because he was a monster. We caught several more but released them. I will admit that in those days I didn't know that much about Char, and wasn't even sure how big "big" was.

We got back to camp and decided that it would be a shame to fry this beautiful fish over a Coleman stove. I told Arthur I'd cook it in the ground like we cook pigs. I added onions, lemon, butter and some spices and wrapped that large Char in foil, then rolled it in a wet gunnysack. Art was a quiet man, he was really quiet as he watched every move I made. We picked dead willow limbs from the live plants and used the ones we had just cut on the hill. Art showed me the Eskimo way to harvest the live bush and keep your firewood plant alive by just picking its dead wood.

I dug a hole in the ground, built the fire, put more gravel on the coals, laid the fish in and then covered it all with gravel and built another fire. Art never said a word but I'm sure he thought this was a waste of a fine fish. We also put the grayling in the same pit. I had no idea how long to leave that fish in. Somehow I got lucky, for when I opened the foil, it was cooked to perfection and the meat just slid off the bones.

The sun had set by now to a beautiful quiet evening. We kept the fire going, which made just enough light and kept the mosquitoes away. With the rivers quiet roar, the fire popping and flaring up, Arthur and I truly enjoyed that meal we had prepared there on the banks of the Wulik. All of our senses had been filled and satisfied, making that evening the most memorable I had ever spent in the bush.

Another memory of that night, which I will never forget, happened when we went to the tent to turn in. Arthur pulled his sleeping bag from the bag he had it stored in and it smelled like one of the fish baskets on the bank (or a brown bear during salmon season). When Eskimo hunters hunt seals on the ice or fish the river, after the gutting and skinning is finished, it's time to sleep and they just crawl in their bags. No telling how long this bag had been around collecting seal oil and fish slime.

Solid Brass

My guess was a very long time. It certainly isn't a popular item to have in the tent in bear country.

Each morning before going outside, you must spray your hands and each other's face with mosquito dope. The Arctic Mosquito will take a hind seat to no mosquito. They are big and there are a zillion of them.

They must have gotten the Otter off the ground fairly early. We had finished cleaning up and just started fishing when we could hear their engine coming up river. There was a little wind coming downriver, which helped them set her down on the first run. Phil and the pilot got out before turning back for take off. We showed the pilot how messy it was on the other side of the flags. He felt good about setting down with a load, so they boarded, turned around, taxied down to the flags, started a wide turn and went through the flags and sank the nose gear into the gravel, clear up to the fuselage. Now this was no little bush plane, this was a big bush plane—twin engine and could carry fifteen to twenty people when the seats were in.

We tried everything to get the wheel up but now, halfway through the day, the weather was closing in. We finally took anything with weight and stuck it in the tail of the plane. We took the wooden boxes from the Blazo, several fuel tanks, and a lot of willow and got it ready to put under the nose gear. We showed Arthur where to place it because he was the lightest while the rest of us got into the very tail and started rocking. It worked and Arthur was able to cram enough stuff into the wheel cavity to hold up the nose gear.

Phil and I were up at the camp looking for more things to stabilize the ground when he noticed the skeleton from the char we had eaten. He asked me what I had used to catch it and then went on to tell me that we shouldn't have eaten it. It may have been the record judging by the size of the skeleton. Imagine that, he said, "You may have had the world record for dinner last night." He was still mumbling as we walked back to the plane.

We packed the ground around the wheel as good as it was going to get. They got in, taxied very lady-like until they were out of the flagged area, turned her into the wind and beat the weather by about thirty minutes.

Solid Brass

Later that evening, still in the light, Art and I were talking by the fire. I was facing Art when a movement over by the fish basket caught my eye. I took a sip of coffee and moved a little to my right to see past Art. Standing approximately six-hundred feet beyond Arthur was a good-sized Grizzly. I looked at Art and said "How would you like a bear hide for your house?" He started to answer when he realized that I was talking very softly and looking off. He kept looking at my eyes, "He's over there." I nodded my head. Arthur turned slowly. We watched for a while until that bear finally winded us. He stood up, took a better look and smell and then left through the scrub willow. What a long-distance grizzly caller those baskets were. The ground around them is saturated with fish oil—kind of like Arthur's sleeping bag.

We couldn't enjoy much more of our coffee because it started to pour. Not just a drizzle, the skies opened up. Within an hour it was blowing gale force. We put the tents up to withstand the weather and we were sheltered a bit being above the bank among the willows but you had to wonder if anything could stand up to this pounding. It didn't let up at all, all through the night. By morning the wind had let up some but the rain kept coming. We went out several times, once to bring food supplies from the storage tent and once to pull the boat up higher after first bailing it out. I looked at what had been the quiet clear river. It took on a new look; muddy, faster and creeping up on the bar. Already there were snags and drifts coming down. Like last night, it rained and blew all day.

I kept an eye on the river most of the day and before dark we went down to move the boat. Our flagged area was now underwater. I had to yell so Arthur could hear me, this was not good. We bailed the boat once more and moved it clear up to the bank. I then took the bowline up and tied it to a willow on top. It was all we could do to walk against the wind. Those gusts must have been blowing 100 miles per hour by then. At least we didn't need mosquito dope.

Morning came after a long night of weather. I quickly got on my rain gear and headed for the bank. The wind was still stiff, but with no big gusts and the rain no longer hurt when it hit my face. My worst fears were recognized; the boat was barely afloat with all the rainwater that was in it. There was three feet of water under her, the gravel bar was history.

Solid Brass

I went back to the tent to tell Arthur about our problem. There was no longer any way for the plane to come in and get us. There was not even a place to land a Super Cub. And even if there was, we had no idea when they would be able to fly. We knew we were going to have to get out on our own. I gave that some thought; our outboard had one blade missing, we didn't have any gas, the boat wasn't supposed to go anywhere and the supplies, like extra props and gas, were coming in on the returning Otter. We did have a case of outboard motor oil, so we could put Super Cub fuel and Blazo in the outboard cans and mix it with the oil and give it a shot. You might think we could put the boat in and keep it straight and let the river rush us all the way home.

Well the river was five times bigger than when we came up and many times as fast. I knew we'd need power to get around that granite wall because the river would be pushing us right at it. Art agreed and we mixed our fuel, bailed the boat once more and tied down the gear. After loading our riverboat, which now seemed much smaller than on the trip upriver, we spent some important time tying everything in. Chances of us ending upside down were much better than 50/50. We went about our work with a few glances and hand gestures. The roar of the river and the wind-driven rain pounded on our rain gear made it impossible to hear each other speak. We were moving very fast now, as if we had to keep up with our surroundings, being driven by the wind like the rain.

The time came for us to push off with no ceremony. Every move we made took so much effort that entering the boiling white water, we didn't even have time to reflect on all the possibilities. Maybe just as well, being most of them were out of favor. Arthur held the side while I jumped in and pulled the rope, which finally fired the engine on our super mix. He pushed off and jumped in and I headed her out to the middle of the river.

We looked like we'd practiced these moves many times, which was good. We started out well, traveling around twenty knots. I had control of the boat but no control of how fast we were going. Art had his back pressed against the bow, facing me, as he scooted down out of the weather. I motioned to him to cover up. He sure didn't have to look for snags and I didn't need a guide, the river was running right over all those little turns

Solid Brass

and bends and points of land. When the water in the boat rose to his crotch then he'd come out and bail. The now ice-cold rain was being driven into my face making it difficult to see. I wondered how my face could be so cold and numb and still feel the pebble-like rain pelting it? The boat wanted to skate and wander at times, but I couldn't allow that to happen. With just a few inches of free load, it would be disastrous to get broad side for just a moment. The engine had less vibration at higher speeds but at times I thought the poor girl would rattle apart. She took our super mix with no problem.

As busy as I was, my mind had to deal with that big granite wall. I didn't have to think about what would happen if we didn't pull out of the turn. I envisioned what we had to do to make sure we didn't end up as a smudge at the bottom of the wall's face and then my time to think about it had expired; all of a sudden it appeared downriver. Nothing looked the same from this height coming out of the mountain canyons. It appeared that the entire river slammed at the base of the wall to be churned and sent in the air before it continued downriver. The river that was wide enough to bring a steamship through started to neck down very fast. The boat was now obtaining a speed hydroplanes aren't designed to handle. It must be a bad dream; why else would I have our boat coming down a bobsled run? We picked up the main funnel that was going to hurl us down the shoot at the granite. I had been planning this moment all the way downriver. I'm sure at this point I quit thinking and all of my movements were reactions from the excessive flow of adrenaline. I started to turn the bow into the white water away from the wall. I gave it all I had until I couldn't get any more on the rudder and the engine. My efforts seemed insignificant matched against the power of that river and the defenseless encounter with that wall. As I braced myself and pulled my body back from the closeness of the granite engulfing us, a large wash came back off the wall and pushed us away, launching us downriver. We shot right by that big sucker as I let out a couple of celebratory hollers. Still moving at the speed of sound, we were now guided by the river's swell and rush, straight toward the Chukchi.

A very short time later the river fanned out to the flat land below and calmed down enough that I knew we could get home now without the

226

engine if need be. Art came out with a big smile; he knew that we had just slayed the dragon.

Arthur's smile stayed bright as Kivalina was now in sight. At this slower speed the rain wasn't beating at us. In fact, the closer we got to the coast, the less rain fell. As we approached we could see everyone lining the bank. They knew that one of their people had been in danger and now he was coming home. We could see the kids jumping up and down and with that, my smile was as big as Arthur's! All of a sudden, I wasn't cold anymore.

There was a lot of hugging and kissing going on and Art tried to stay humble through it all which was his way. Amos came up and put his large hand on my shoulder and said, "Get your bags and come to my house. You will get dry and we will eat some soup." A better idea hadn't been suggested on this entire trip. On the way to his house Amos told me that I would be staying with his family while I was in Kivalina, and that was that. There was a long picnic type bench along the wall at the dinner table where I was sitting. As we ate our soup and drank coffee, there was a knock at the door. On command from Amos, someone came in and sat at the table. After a greeting, he didn't say anything, just sat there and watched and listened in on our conversation. Then another knock at the door, another person entered, came to the table and sat down in the same fashion. Each time, Mrs. Holly would bring soup and coffee. This kept up until all the seats were filled. In all of this time, I never heard Mrs. Holly say a word. She always had a pleasant look on her face and seemed to take everything in stride. With all of these guys coming to watch Amos and me talk, it seemed there were more people interested in the newcomer than just the kids. That night I found a comfortable corner, rolled out my bag and slept like a baby.

I got up early and made my trip up the beach. The weather was still above minimums for flying, but the rain had subsided. I personally hoped it would be a long time before they flew in to get me. It was an adventure of a lifetime to be here and I had so much more to find out about this village and the people that I had grown so fond of. I knew Phil would be really concerned. He didn't know we had gotten down the river safely. The radio in Kivalina was not working for some reason. I tried to call out several times to put Phil's mind at ease.

Solid Brass

After our morning coffee, rolls, and pickle relish, Amos and I wandered around the village. First, he showed me his famous dog team, which was tied beside the house. Every year Amos and his dogs would travel the 100 mile distance to Point Hope, rest a few days, win the sled dog sled race, then come back to Kivalina.

Not too far from Amos lived a lady by the name of Millie. Millie was in her seventies with beautiful long gray hair and a beautifully weathered face. She wore a typical Eskimo dress with long wool boot socks and suede chukka boots. Millie had, drying outside, the only ugruk (seal) hide I'd seen in the village. After cleaning and fleshing the hide and slipping the hair, they would lay a long lodge pole on the ground, lay the hide lengthwise across the pole and drive pegs in the slits they'd made along the edge of the hide. It would then be left out to dry and bleach in the sun. The hide of the ugruk is used to make skin boats called Umiaks as well as soles for their mukluks (boots).

Millie did not speak a word of English but she made me feel very welcome. I asked her, through Amos, what she would be doing with the hide. She said it would be going to the native store. Millie, like many of the villagers, never had money in her life, only points or credit at the store. I asked what the equivalence in dollars would be for what points she got at the store. Amos said ten dollars would be more than enough. This was a very large hide and I wanted to buy it, especially when I knew it would be sold anyway. I wanted to give her more than she could get at the store but when I showed an interest, she wanted to give it to me as a present. After my firm insistence, Millie took the money. She seemed very pleased. She inspected the money, much like one would a rare coin. She rolled the hide and tied it with several pieces of sinew (string made from animal tendons).

Today you wouldn't be able to buy that hide for any price. Since the adoption of the mammal laws, the white man cannot own raw ivory, raw hides, baleen, etc., that hasn't been scrimshawed or carved by natives. It turns out that Amos, also in his 70s, has only dealt with money three times in his life. Once, Eskimos who wanted to make some

Solid Brass

money were taken to work in the cannery and one other time he was hired to fight a forest fire somewhere.

The people of Kivalina are primarily whalebone carvers, and carve very little ivory. When they brought their works-of-art to the store, they were given either points or credit. When they went to pick up supplies they either went into the red for points they owed or paid with points they had on the books. Sometimes a person would sit down and do a carving just to clear the books.

At the edge of the village there was an old Quonset hut. I never found out if it was left from the war or a government issue. Tonight it was to be the local theater. Everyone in the village goes. It must have been put on by the native store because it cost one dollar to get in. People without money must give up points. That night when I handed the boy my dollar, he waved it off and said that Millie had already paid my way. When I spotted Millie she gave me an ear-to-ear grin.

In a theater the floor usually rises from ground level to a height in the back, which allows everyone to see over the heads of the people in front of them. In the Quonset hut, the floor was obviously paved level, so to compensate, some sat on the floor in front, then short stools in the next row then each row grew taller stools until benches, similar to bleachers filled the rear. It was a funny sight to see when I first walked in. Some people were yelling and waving from nine-foot stools. The movie was an old Audie Murphy war movie. Everyone cheered for the good guys, giggled, and yelled. It reminded me of the Saturday Matinee when I was a kid. This was a real entertaining evening for me.

Everyday brought something new and exciting to learn about the Eskimo way of life (the way it was at the time anyway). One day while talking to Mrs. Swan, she told me it would be hard to go back to the old ways; they used to pick willow bush, soak it in seal oil and burn it for heat and cooking. It would fill the house with smoke and stink. She didn't think all the changes were for the better any more than Amos did. He said at one time the kids were even forgetting their native language. The teachers were told not to let this happen and a big effort was made to keep their native tongue from being forgotten. Some of the old ways are taught by people like Amos. While seal hunting he would show the

Solid Brass

young hunters how to build an icehouse, an emergency shelter to get out of the freezing arctic wind. They are also taught how to walk on the rotten ice. Many centuries of knowledge are handed down this way to ensure the village's survival. A few minutes in this type of a harsh environment with limited survival knowledge could mean the difference between life or death.

I had one experience falling through the ice. A time that can show the importance of quick action in sub-zero weather. I was hunting near the Denali Highway. At one time this gravel road was the only road going into Mt. McKinley Park. It was late in the day and a friend and I were headed for Cantwell where we would be hunting for caribou. The road was solid ice, so I was driving very slowly. The temperature outside was dropping fast as the sun was almost used up and being replaced with lots of snow clouds. The last time we checked it was twenty below. Although we were headed to a destination where we would hunt tomorrow, I'd always keep my eyes open and searching. Up on a ridge to my left I spotted what appeared to be a very large bull caribou. I pulled over to study it through my binoculars. There was one bull with a couple of cows and he was just what we traveled all this distance for, world-class with double shovels. This one bull would be meat enough for the entire winter. In those days you could take three caribou in one day in this area. With moose and sheep also available, caribou was not the most sought after due to its flavor, so it was used a lot in sausage. Being so plentiful, it was also used to feed many dog teams throughout the winter.

When the main herd would cross the Denali Highway, some people could shoot their caribou a very short distance from where they parked their pickups. In fact, I remember some roads having blood, guts, and hides for several miles lying in the snow, just a few feet from the tire tracks.

I grabbed my rifle and skinning gear and headed off through the snow. I didn't take my snowshoes, it didn't seem that deep—mistake number one. I was moving as fast as you can in snow from calf high to crotch high. The bull and cows were moving slowly at times digging for food, not knowing I was there. I got into some shrub alders and stepped

230

out without paying enough attention to the little snow clearing and broke through the ice. I sank to my armpits. I must have had my hands on some of the alder, because by the time the water hit my crotch I was pulling on the alder in attempt to slingshot out. With gun and skinning gear in hand, I was making it back to my pickup as fast as possible. This little dip in freezing water had robbed my body of all its heat and most of it's feeling. My hunting partner had watched me go out of sight and because I was running back and there was no bear chasing me, he guessed what might have happened. He was pulling the bag of dry clothes from the back of the pickup by the time I got there. I stood in the middle of the highway, next to the truck and I took off my clothes. There were no other people in sight as I stood there with my pink and blue body totally exposed, but I wouldn't have cared if there were. I carried some sheepskin-lined moccasins behind my front seat, they went on first. The outside air was a hell of a lot colder than the water I just got out of. In the time it took to drop my wet clothes to the road, pull the dry clothes out of the bag and put them on and bend over to collect the wet ones— they were frozen solid. I was probably less than a quarter of a mile from dry clothes and still had to hustle to keep from getting some degree of frostbite in that sub-zero weather.

This made Amos' lessons on how to read the ice, how to use the pole to test what he called "rotten ice," really sink in. Cold is cold. It doesn't matter if you are in the Arctic or on the Denali Highway. The difference of being a quarter of a mile from your pickup or several miles offshore on the pack ice, out of sight of land with a sudden shift in the wind or an open lead in the ice that could cut you off from your planned route back is unmeasurable. The knowledge of these old Eskimos, if learned, will provide the extra edge needed to survive a mistake made in a most unforgiving environment.

Amos and I talked about hunting for many, many hours. He also told me the story that had been handed down for generations of how Kivalina had come to be. He taught me how to walk on rotten ice and invited me to come back and hunt with him on the ice. Arthur and Reverend Swan both told me what a great honor that was. Amos had never asked a white man to accompany him on the ice. I was honored and grateful to have met and mingled with this unique and gentle man in my lifetime. I will always regret not having had the opportunity to return to Kivalina and hunt with him.

One night, toward the end of my stay, I was sitting at the table eating a piece of dried ugruk, which I'd grown to like a lot. I thought everyone was asleep, when Mrs. Swan came in and sat next to me. She was carrying her sewing basket and was sewing a wolverine ruff on someone's summer parka. She took a piece of sinew and cut it with a very small oolu. I let out a small chuckle and smiled at her. I had never seen such a small oolu. She smiled back, seeming to know what had struck me funny. A few more minutes of silence, then she said without looking up, "You will hunt with Amos on the ice next spring." This was the first time I had heard her voice in these many days. I was beginning to think she did not speak English. I told her how I was looking forward to the hunt. She asked if I had knee-high mukluks. I told her that mine were calf high. "I will make you a pair for the hunt." She drew an outline of my foot and told me of the things I should have for the hunt. The mukluks would have caribou hair inside because caribou have hollow hair good for insulation. She told me to wear woolen socks with them. My first night of conversation with Mrs. Holly turned into more survival training. For several hours she explained to me, not only what Amos takes on his hunts, but why. We talked for hours that evening.

The next day I was at the native store with Reverend Swan. This store was like any trading post in the far north, with the exception of a brass cannon and harpoon darts used on whales. There was fur and cloth for making clothes, canned goods, rope made from seal hide, etc. Reverend Swan showed me some pieces he had made. A whalebone carving caught my eye, a walrus with big ivory tusks, laying on an ice floe. When I picked it up, Reverend Swan said he wished he had known that I liked it, he wouldn't have brought it to the store. All the things we were looking at were to be shipped to Anchorage to be sold.

Later that day, the weather to the north started to clear for the first time in weeks and before long we heard a plane in the distance. It was coming from the wrong direction to be Phil. We went to the strip and out of the Cub stepped Butch King, another guide and old friend.

Solid Brass

Butch guided with Lee Holen, later to become his partner. He had received a call at Point Hope that Arthur and I might still be stranded upriver. With the first break in the weather, he came to see if he could help or if we were already back, to take me to Point Hope.

It was a sad moment for me to say good-bye to my recently found friends. I walked to everyone's houses to say goodbye and talked of returning in the spring for the hunt with Amos. I had grown to love this village immeasurably. Arthur helped me carry my gear to the plane. After we loaded up and I bid a last farewell, Butch headed the Cub into the wind and we were off to Point Hope to the North.

Point Hope is the furthest point Northwest. Its people are whalers and had just celebrated their Whale Festival. As we walked from the plane, we could see evidence of the whale kill everywhere. Pits still wet from being filled with blubber, bones drying and baleen still left to be sorted and cleaned. The village cemetery was decorated with whale-bones.

Point Hope is situated perfectly along the coast for whaling. The whalers can see the whales coming up the coast before setting their boats out from the point. When the whales turn to make the point the boats have them in ambush. This is very different from Kivalina where the coast is straight and, consequently, they only take one or two whales a year.

Lee Holen had a house in the village of Point Hope that he had since the days of the big polar bear hunts. The chief back then allowed Lee to build his house in the village and that decision was still honored today. Butch showed me around for the rest of the day. I saw the largest piece of baleen I have ever seen. It was in the house of Butch's friend. It was good being with Butch and Lee. I had spent many days in their camp in the Wrangells and the Cinder River on the Alaska Peninsula, but this time our visit was all too short. The weather broke in the morning and they had to go to Kotzebue so I would go with them. It had been several weeks now since Phil and I helped dog that million dollar Otter from a gravel bar on the Wulik River and now I was back to where it all started. Like it or not, I had to get back. I had committed to work in the lower 48 and was expected to be there. I didn't want anyone else to be worrying, as Phil had these last few weeks.

Solid Brass

Before I left Kivalina, Reverend Swan asked me if I would look for a scope mount for his seal gun. His mount was broken. He only needed one end. He offered to give me money, but I refused, explaining that I wasn't sure if I'd find one. When I got to Anchorage, I found it right away and dropped it in the mail before I left for California. In early spring that following year, I received two boxes from the Anchorage Post Office that were addressed to me from Kivalina. One had a very strong odor as I opened it. It was a very beautiful pair of knee-high Mukluks with a letter enclosed: "Hope you receive this and we look forward to your return for the hunt."

In the second, smaller box, was a letter that read: "Hi Bob, Thanks for the mount you send me. Just right for my scope so I send you gift. Everything fine around, but weather is bad for two weeks now. Rain, rain, south wind. That is all for now. See you sometime again. Your friend, Rev. Clinton Swan." And wrapped in tissue paper was Reverend Swan's walrus on the ice floe carving that I had admired at the native store.

Author's Note

A lot of these stories deal with drinking, raising hell, and some of the "not to brag about" things that were done off the job. The fact is, none of us could have done our jobs if we were seriously abusing our bodies. The time to raise hell in the abalone business, for instance, was when the weather was bad and we couldn't go to sea. The parties would go on for days, but once the weather changed, everyone got back into focus went out and competed to bring in the boat with the biggest load. We all knew we needed clear thinking and a sound body to get the job done and keep an eye out for your partner. This held true with construction diving and the teams. The Frogs were a crack, by God, do-it-all type, and there was no better military group in the world. Throughout training, as well as making the teams, we worked side by side and held each other in high regard. After working together in a field which brought on certain life-threatening situations, being totally dependent on each other would only thicken the gel. Officers and enlisted men together went through the same training. When you stuck your head in the mud, the officer next to you did the same. If the officer didn't have that little something extra to get him through training, he went back to the fleet. We also got into trouble and caroused together, but there was a big separation between party-time and work-time. Perhaps partying was a way to let off steam or celebrate a job well done. After the total focus and no-room-for-error situations of the daily work day, the extreme burst of off-time merriment seemed to fit.

I have been making my living in the diving business for over forty years and feel very fortunate to have known and worked with the people about whom I've filled these pages. In an era of strong ties and comradery, lifelong friendships were born from the banter between men who staked their lives on each other and partied irresponsibly between jobs. Influence and inspiration has been a gift to me from several good friends and mentors throughout my career. Together, we were pioneers of our industry. I cannot conclude this book without paying tribute to my many comrades and dear friends I've lost over the years. Each one is a hero in my eyes.

My career also brought me to Alaska, where I lived many new adventures. One being Kivalina, finding a warmth and friendliness from a people that I grew to respect and love in a short period of time. I would be a poorer man had I not had that extraordinary experience in my life.

I wouldn't trade five minutes of a good day to erase one entire bad day. Well, perhaps I should give that last line a little more thought....

About the Author

In the early 1950s, Bob Wick and his friends were skin diving up and down the Pacific Coast, including frequent trips to the Baja. Most of their diving was in the Laguna Beach, California area. They formed the Bellflower Reef Combers Club to enter skin diving contests and succeeded in winning the first Pacific Coast Jr. Underwater Spearfishing Championship at Laguna Beach. Bob left Bellflower, California to pursue a diving career in the Navy at the age of 17. He volunteered for UDT/SEAL training, graduated Class 17, and was placed in UDT Team 12, Coronado, California by the mid-fifties. This part of UDT made a significant impact and he drew from these lessons throughout his life. The teams allowed him to go to Navy diving school to qualify in Navy deepsea heavy gear diving equipment. After his enlistment was up, he bought a diving boat and joined the abalone fleet on the California Coast. Some of the fondest memories of his career are from his years as an abalone diver. He left the abalone beds to work in the oil patch and construction diving. His 45 year diving career has taken him from coast to coast, from Mexico to Alaska and to various points throughout the world. During that time he co-owned two diving firms, which were later sold to international companies. At age 63, Bob is still diving and consulting for various companies. Bob, his wife, Theresa, and their two daughters, Kinsey and Kyler, left their Santa Ynez Valley, California horse ranch after 24 years and presently reside in Eagle River, Alaska.

Diving Books from Best Publishing Company

- Dive Like a Pro
- Essentials of Underwater Photography
- Death of an Aquanaut
- Scuba Diving Explained
- Underwater Ear & Nose Care
- Scuba Divers Sign Language Manual
- Dangerous Marine Creatures
- Beating the Bends
- Mixed Gas Diving
- Simple Guide to Snorkeling Fun
- Best of Alert Diver
- Recreational Nitrox Diving
- Cold Water Diving
- Guide for Teaching Scuba to Divers With Special Needs
- Spearfishing for Skin and Scuba Divers
- Psychological and Behavioral Aspects of Diving
- Small Boat Diving
- Marine Conservation for the 21st Century
- Expedition and Diving Operations Handbook
- Essential Guide to Live-Aboard Dive Travel
- The Practice of Oxygen Measurement for Divers
- Simple Guide to Rebreather Diving
- Diving Above Sea Level
- The Unpredictable Mistress
- Deep, Deeper, Deepest
- Diving and Dredging for Gold
- Histories and Mysteries, the Shipwrecks of Key Largo
- Technical Guide to Gas Blending
- One Man's War
- Ironsuit
- Scientific Diving Techniques
- Taking the Plunge